THE DIANE FRANCIS INSIDE GUIDE TO CANADA'S 50 BEST STOCKS

KEY PORTER BOOKS

Canadian Cataloguing in Publication Data

Francis, Diane, 1946-
 Best stocks

ISBN 1-55013-218-0

1. Stocks – Canada.   2. Stock-exchange – Canada.
3. Investments – Canada.   I. Title.

HG5152.F73 1990   332.63'22'0971   C89-095258-2

Typesetting: Computer Composition of Canada, Inc.
Printed and bound in Canada

   Printed on acid-free paper

Key Porter Books Limited
70 The Esplanade
Toronto, Ontario
Canada M5E 1R2

90 91 92 93 94 6 5 4 3 2 1

CONTENTS

AUTHOR'S NOTE

This book is not intended to give investment advice, but is merely my opinion as to worthwhile companies I would invest in myself if the timing were right. They are also companies that meet my subjective criteria as outlined in the introduction. The only advice I feel qualified to give investors is to encourage them to do their own independent homework before buying any stock. This should involve studying their financial statements as well as consulting persons who understand the companies and their sectors. That is why investors should zero in on ten or fewer companies to keep the research task manageable. I would also like to add that the vast majority of companies named here are not in my own personal portfolio. As of July 1990, I owned common shares of Tridel Enterprises Inc., Dofasco Inc., Hollinger Inc., BCE Inc., the Toronto Sun Publishing Corporation, Burlington Resources Inc., Deprenyl Research Ltd., the Toronto-Dominion Bank, the Royal Bank of Canada and Stelco Inc.

At the beginning of each company chapter is information drawn from the *Financial Post*'s data base or from company spokesmen. At the end are caveats plus some historical information about stock prices based on *Post* data. Gains and dividend calculations take into consideration stock splits over the course of one decade.

The manuscript deadline was June 1990. Any material changes in company affairs since then are not included.

FOREWORD

"Imagine being in a department store. The manager stands on a counter and with a bullhorn shouts that everything is on sale with 30 per cent off the prices. Tell me, would everyone then head for the exits? That's what happens in the stock market. After prices fall, everybody leaves. It's crazy."

> Benjamin Horwood, investment counsellor with First Montreal Capital Ltd.

On October 19, 1987, the day the stock market crashed, I was in Vancouver with mining magnate Bruce McDonald. I wanted an interview because people love to read rags-to-riches stories and McDonald was an ideal one, a hard-drinking Grade 10 drop-out who had scored big. He was on top of the world and worth $30 million in stock, after gold discoveries propelled his stock in Noramco Capital Corp. and others to stratospheric heights. Unfortunately, I waited a long time that morning. Like millions of others, McDonald was preoccupied with what was happening outside the office.

Trading floors were in chaos as computer-driven sell orders sparked one of the most dramatic stock price free falls in history. There were simply no buyers at any price for many stocks. One market-maker for Canada's Northern Telecom, assigned in New York to buy NorTel stock from anyone who wished to sell, threw his tickets in the air that afternoon and strode off his exchange floor in utter despair. He had run out of money to satisfy the sell orders that were falling in all around him. Even venerable IBM suffered a massive sell-out, without buying in return, and was forced to request a trading halt in the absence of any bids at all for its stock that morning. It eventually reopened at half the price it had traded at the Friday before. With such blue-ribbon companies in dire straits, the high-flying financial world was once again at the proverbial brink.

But McDonald was essentially unruffled. He padded out to see me, apologizing for his lateness, and suggested we meet later for lunch.

"Give me half an hour. I'm kinda tied up with my brokers. The market's falling apart and it's great. We're cherry picking. We have millions in the bank and no debt. We're in terrific shape to pick up bargains today."

He arrived at 12:30 P.M. Vancouver time, half an hour before New York's closing time. Half an hour later, an associate slipped him the closing prices for his stocks. I asked him how heavy his personal losses were. "About $25 million on paper. No problem. Who's for another Scotch?" he asked.

Most of us would have headed for a ledge. But this was not McDonald's first market crash. He had ridden the stock market roller-coaster for decades and all afternoon he swapped war stories with brokers and bankers who came and went. Around 4 P.M., he invited everyone in the place to his wife's birthday party. On the way to the party, I asked him if he wasn't secretly worried about what might happen the next day.

He wasn't. McDonald may be a wild and crazy gambler, but he's not stupid. He never went for broke. Even when he wagered $100,000 on that year's Super Bowl game (and won), he only did it with money he knew he could afford to lose. He said he had virtually no debts, savings stashed away in trust for his family and a mortgage-free home. Secure from ruin, he proceeded to host a lavish party as if to celebrate the loss of a king's ransom.

Spending Black Monday with Bruce McDonald certainly taught me a great deal about the stock market and about the difference between the amateurs and the professional players. Unlike the rest of us, pros are not emotional. Pros consider crashes to be corrections, points in time when fear overtakes greed and there's money to be made. Some pros cynically refer to corrections as economic justice or "when money returns to its rightful owners" and small investors are shaken out of the market.

That's exactly what happened on October 19 to those millions of small investors who had been lured into the market following the highly publicized, five-year rise in prices. The greediest borrowed to the hilt to capitalize on the boom and the naive expected it to never end. As always happens with overheated stock markets – auctions driven by the law of supply and demand – the new buyers snapped up stocks at inflated prices until the pros put a stop to it.

By midday, the general public got wind of the capitalist carnage, alerted by broadcasts comparing events to 1929. Evening newscasters amplified the situation, thus guaranteeing another price disaster the next day. Sure enough, the next day on Black Tuesday, two New York Stock Exchange market-maker brokerage firms went bust. Days later, many were in ruins. One investor leaped to his death from a tall building, and another shot his broker in Florida because phone lines were jammed and he couldn't bail out in time.

Meanwhile, Bruce McDonald fearlessly bought and bought and bought. As things turned out, that was exactly the right strategy because now, three years later, most indices have regained losses. McDonald has not been quite so lucky, mostly because he speculates in high-risk gold stocks. He has yet to recoup the $25 million lost, but he has made a few million just the same.

Unfortunately, few others can say the same. Many fled, never to return. Others still lick their financial wounds. Market volumes are half what they were as small investors avoid buying individual stocks, preferring instead to invest hard-earned savings in mutual funds, low-interest bank accounts, or risky propositions such as buying heavily mortgaged Toronto condos at inflated prices.

The fact is, the extreme backlash against the market is as foolish as the extreme love affair many had with it while the bull market was roaring ahead. Right now, Canadian markets are in poor shape. We are near a recession if not in one already as profits and prospects collapse due to high interest rates. The high rates, in turn, prop up the Canadian dollar which is hurting exporters. Smart investors like Andrew Sarlos of Sarlos & Associates in Toronto estimate the stock market will perform poorly until the end of 1991. Now is the time to buy fundamentally sound companies. But be cautious. Keep your hard-earned savings in cash, or interest-bearing instruments such as T-bills or Canada Savings Bonds until you make up your mind. Study individual stocks (and the sectors and commodity cycles that affect their prices) then invest, as McDonald did, when the time is right. Timing and patience are the secrets of stock market success. Biding your time until fundamentally sound companies' stocks are at or on their way up from the bottom of a cycle means bargains.

Peter "Mr. Magic" Lynch, formerly with Boston's high-perform-ance Fidelity Magellan mutual funds, is a contrarian who believes the time to buy is when everyone else is uninterested, such as now. He picks companies with good products and good managements and plans to hang onto them for at least five years. He retired early in 1990 after posting record gains for his funds. In an interview, he suggested that investors should establish what he calls his "farm teams," or small initial stakes in companies they like (buying only when the cycles are right). As the stock begins to move upward, they should consider buying more and turning these into what he calls his "ten-baggers," or superstar big hitters. He also said that people who become nervous when markets are as lousy as they are now, should avoid stock market investments because they are likely to panic, thus unnecessarily taking losses on stocks or prematurely selling.

Canada's most successful portfolio manager, Stephen Jarislowsky of Jarislowsky & Fraser in Montreal (which manages $16-billion worth of pension and individual savings) also suggests only long-term investing. He says individuals should invest in companies that sell brand name products or those in counter-cyclical businesses that cater to an aging population or future trend. He advises investors to avoid cyclical stocks unless they can tie their money up for years and can watch the market like a hawk. Dividend entities should also be spurned. "Going for income means you are paying taxes twice [first, on the capital invested in a stock and second, on the dividend income]. Dividend income is only tax free to pension fund [or RRSP] accounts," he says. Of course, dividend income is partly tax free while interest income is not and the first $100,000 of capital gain per person is tax free.

Market guru Sir John Templeton, whose Templeton mutual funds manage some $16 billion of other people's money, says the secret to investment wealth is to hold stocks at least during one, if not two, market cycles as well as to spot bargains worldwide. Every ten years, he says, there are two bull and two bear markets. Sometimes a bear market lasts a matter of weeks, as was the case in October 1987. He forecasts that the Dow Jones will hit 5000 in the next bull market after this one and that "the chances are better than even that by the year 2000 the Dow Jones will have reached 6000."

Stock markets outperform other investment vehicles, according to a 1989 study done by the *Canadian Investment Review*, published jointly by institutional investors and a handful of brokerage firms.

The *Review* computes that the Toronto Stock Exchange 300 Index since 1973 has yielded higher returns than have treasury bills, residential mortgages, bonds or real estate. The 300 Index averaged 8.3 per cent compounded annually between 1977 and 1987; treasury bills yielded 4.2 per cent; residential mortgages, 4.5 per cent; real estate, 5.5 per cent; and mid-term bonds, 3.2 per cent. Only small capitalization or international stocks outperformed the 300 Index, earning 8.6 per cent and 16.7 per cent respectively.

Of course, such figures can be somewhat misleading. Anyone who invested in Toronto real estate between 1987 and 1989 would have made a killing. But that is not the case elsewhere in Canada, much less over the long haul. Besides, real estate is an expensive and inconvenient proposition. Troublesome tenants, rent controls, red tape and interest payments on large mortgages add significantly to the cost of the property. For instance, a $100,000 house with a large mortgage may end up costing another $300,000 in interest payments over 25 years depending upon rates. That means the house price in 25 years must surpass $400,000 plus the rate of inflation compounded just to break even.

Although the stock market is the best bet, getting going is a daunting and tricky task. There are 5,000 stocks listed on Canadian exchanges to choose from and tens of thousands more in the United States. With so many horses to bet on, successful participants must do their homework carefully, check track records and racing forms, avoid rigged racetracks and stick with proven horses and jockeys.

This book is nothing more than an extensive racing form, written by someone who's been paid for years to hang around the track. I know the jockeys, the horses and their track records. I have covered the business beat, hanging around touts and owners of horseflesh. I hope the information and insights I have picked up over the years – whether learned over lunch at Winston's or cocktails with McDonald – will prove to be both illuminating and profitable. So based on shamelessly subjective sources and criteria, I have chosen what I feel are Canada's 50 best stocks.

INTRODUCTION

This is my third book and a logical extension of the first two. *Controlling Interest: Who Owns Canada?*, published in 1986, documented the dramatic degree of economic concentration of power in Canada and profiled the country's 32 most successful families. *Contrepreneurs*, published in 1988, was about stock fraud and money laundering and the scandalous way business is conducted on the Vancouver and Alberta Stock Exchanges. Now this book, *50 Best*, simply draws upon my knowledge of Canada's good guys and its bad guys in order to provide a subjective, journalistic exploration of worthy companies.

This is not a book for beginners, and I am not an expert. I have merely tried to pick companies that are good bets in the long-term, based on my best guess as to what the future holds for Canada and for these enterprises. Some are small and some monolithic, some cyclical and some defensive stocks, some dividend-paying monopolies, some speculative, and still others are growth stocks.

Caveats which summarize most of the major risks attached to each company follow each entry. For instance, Noranda Inc.'s stock price has been declining with the price of forestry and mining commodities. These are dropping in price because economic growth is slowing. Noranda is also heavily in debt, and high interest rates are going to erode profits. So those investors interested in Noranda or other cyclicals listed in this guide should keep their money in T-bills and bide their time until commodity prices begin to increase along with economic growth and interest rates go down. Similarly, banks or real estate outfits should be avoided until interest rates begin to fall. Conversely, however, oil and natural gas prices have already bottomed and conventional wisdom is that the only way is up. That is why now might be the time to buy the best finders in that business, providing they are not dragged down through special circumstances or large debts. It is also the time to buy special situation stocks which are virtually counter-cyclical such as medical labs, food and beverage outfits, broadcasters, funeral home operators, bill collectors, utilities, school bus or waste management companies and some publishers.

I also want this book to bury once and for all accusations that I am anti-business. It's true that I'm often critical of certain practices, but my commentaries are intended to be a broom, not an axe. I am an unapologetic capitalist who believes that the system must be protected from those who would destroy it through their greed. The price of free enterprise is eternal vigilance in our stock markets. A system that tramples shareholder rights loses both the public's confidence as well as its capital. And a society without an efficient system of capital formation is doomed to one of two fates. It either becomes a branch-plant economy, bankrolled mostly by foreign capital, or it becomes one bankrolled mostly by government hand-outs. Unfortunately, Canada has too much foreign and too much government investment due to inefficient capital markets and insufficient shareholder protection.

This book is intended to be a guide to Canadians who are interested in helping build this country with their savings. I believe the entrepreneurs and professional managers interviewed in these pages are building worthwhile enterprises and are trying to create real wealth. When they succeed, they make the pie grow larger and, as such, deserve the support and partnership of Canadian investors. In my opinion, these 50 have demonstrably good track records, good management, good prospects, enlightened controlling shareholders, ethical mindsets and solid products or services. But judge for yourself.

I began my task by turning to the *Financial Post* data base, which includes some 420 blue-chip companies, as well as institutional investors such as pension and mutual funds. The hunt began with print-outs of those companies that met two criteria – returns on equity of 15 per cent or better for ten years; and stock price increases that beat the TSE 300's performance over ten years of 309 per cent (based on dividend reinvestment). I also included companies that had been around for less than a decade but had also met those two performance criteria. That narrowed down the field to about 120 companies.

I soon learned that you cannot look strictly at a track record. The top performer using those two criteria was the financial basketcase, Campeau Corporation, the real-estate giant that was run into the ground by high flyer Robert Campeau. Now the biggest embarrassment in Canadian business history, Campeau blew his corporation's brains out when he bought two U.S. retailers for borrowed billions. It was easy to cross Campeau off the list, but most eliminations were judgment calls on my part. Rogers Communications Inc. was another high flyer in the past decade, but I dropped it from my list because Rogers is overwhelmingly a cable company. Investment and cable profits will decline in the 1990s as Ottawa's regulator, the Canadian Radio-Television and Telecommunications Commission, reins them in and competition erodes their market. Another reason I excluded Rogers is because of its intention to enter the telecommunications fray by taking on the gigantic phone companies over the lucrative long-distance market. I wish Rogers well, but I would not back an entrepreneur in a potentially cut-throat competitive business when his company's past success is mostly due to its ability to manage a monopoly.

Another case in point was high flyer Noma Industries Limited, a manufacturer of lawn mowers and Christmas tree and ornamental lawn lights. Product innovations catapulted its stock during the 1980s, but there is very little that Noma can do for an encore. Besides, it has entered the competitive U.S. market and has been dogged by the typical start-up problems. Furthermore, Noma chairman Thomas Beck is getting on in years. In short, Noma faces tough sledding in the 1990s and Beck will probably sell control in the near future. I wish Beck and Noma well, but in a cut-throat marketplace I would not back an aging entrepreneur whose past success is mostly due to a few innovative products that others are now imitating.

I also excluded Hees International Bancorp Inc. and all but two of the dozens of companies that form part of the Hees-Edper-Brascan-Trilon empire of Peter Bronfman. This group represents the largest concentration of economic power in Canada with a combined market capitalization equivalent to 15 per cent of the entire TSE 300. But the group has done this by weaving a complicated, interlocking corporate quilt, often indulging in corporate cut-and-paste through byzantine restructurings. I simply find their structure unfathomable.

I also worry about the group's dealings one with another. True, there are checks and balances, the most important of which is the group's practice of paying officers with stock options. This means each one has a vested interest in preventing his or her company from being taken advantage of. The other check is that companies have ethics committees on their boards made up of independent directors. These people are there to ensure that transactions are fair and square. However, I believe that if these people are worried about potential conflicts, then so am I.

For these and other reasons, my two Bronfman corporate choices are Noranda Inc. and Trizec Corporation Ltd. I admire them both because they are outstanding operating entities with independent managements, great track records and good prospects. Most importantly, however, in both cases control is shared with arm's-length partners.

Once my list was narrowed down to 100, I began interviewing top financial analysts and investment counsellors. I also reviewed the research of many more. Among those consulted or studied were Stephen Jarislowsky, Tom Caldwell, Richard Lafferty, Bill Allen, Marty Kaufman, William Foote, Stuart Hensman, Terry Ortslan, Derrick Leach, Harold Wolkin, Frank Mayer, Alison Ironside-Smith, Hugh Brown, Patrick Mars, Jack Puusepp, Peter Lynch, Sir John Templeton, John Pepperell, Avner Mandelman, Richard Osler, Gino Blink, Jim Doak, Wilf Gobert, Albert Thompson, John Lydall, Luc Bertrandt, Murray Pollitt, among others. The result of those interviews was the pruning of a few dozen and the addition of others.

To help cut back choices even more, I used the "refrigerator school of investment" technique. I literally opened my fridge to see what my family was eating and who was making it. I also examined all of our lifestyle and consumer habits as a means of finding investor opportunities. I wanted to see where our money, Mr. and Mrs. Average's, was going. For instance, we loved Kentucky Fried Chicken, Swiss Chalet, Harvey hamburgers in the 1980s, but began to become more health and weight conscious, choosing products such as Dempster's whole wheat bread and Diet Coke. We avoid red meat, because we read somewhere that it is harmful in the long run, but we smoke and we buy fancy cognacs and Scotch. We are switching away from Molson's or Labatt's beers to imports or micro-brewery specialties.

We rarely shop in large department stores unless we are in small towns but love to patronize boutiques and specialty shops in large, regional indoor malls. I buy fewer outfits but spend more on them, preferring classic designs that will last for years. My husband buys something in Canadian Tire at least twice a month. We own a VCR and rent a lot of movies even though we pay nearly $40 a month for cable television services. We also tape shows and have a zapper so we can skip over commercials; our phone bill for long distance calls and facsimile messages has tripled in as many years. We subscribe to two daily newspapers and get five more periodicals weekly. We own three cars and have a monthly gasoline tab as large as the rent for our first apartment. We all listen to the radio for hours while driving.

We spend more time these days in drugstores and health food stores and recycle as much of our garbage as we can. We try to buy biodegradable or environmentally benign products and use automatic teller machines all the time. We are members of Greenpeace and are worried about global warming, the ozone layer and pollution. We don't want Quebec to leave Confederation.

We have more money tied up in real estate than any three Americans we know and also own a second home in the country. We have undertaken enormous renovations on our home, rather than move, because there is so much value in our property. This has increased our square footage dramatically which, in turn, has increased our hydro and natural gas heating bills. Many of our friends speculate in real estate, owning condos or cottages. This is partly because real estate is the only tax-free way to earn capital gains. Another way out from under the oppressive tax burden is our huge nest egg of RRSPs. We shop around banks and trust companies for the best rates and are putting increasing amounts of money into stocks and mutual funds.

The next step was to examine the big picture. Companies do not operate in isolation and some economic sectors, or niches, have better futures than others. For instance, between 1978 and 1988 real estate companies streaked ahead with average gains of 25 per cent; gold stocks followed with 22 per cent; communications with 21 per cent; transportation with 18 per cent; consumer products, merchandising and metals with 15 per cent each; management companies and forestry firms with 14 per cent; oils with 11 per cent; pipelines with 10 per cent; financial services with 8 per cent; and industrial products and utilities, 7 per cent each. Extrapolating that result is a dangerous business. So my next step was to make some assumptions about the future and who was poised to profit. Here is my fearless forecast about the future and what I believe will be the ten most significant trends in the 1990s.

GLOBAL TRENDS

1. The Green Movement. Environmental concerns are sweeping the world and will dominate headlines in the 1990s. Extremists south of the border are booby-trapping mines and forests to stop exploitation. Some U.S. groups operate under the banner "mine free by '93" and are using litigation effectively. The most dramatic example is the halt of logging in vast portions of the U.S. northwest for months because of fear that a certain endangered species of owl will become extinct as a result of the activity. The owl has never been spotted.

These groups, many of whom effectively stopped the growth of the U.S. nuclear power industry, are targeting forestry, mining and coal activities through courts and the political process. They have a war chest of US$230 million designed to elect or defeat politicians based on their environmental platforms alone. This U.S. environmental radicalism will play into Canada's hands. It is unlikely in resource-rich Canada that the same brand of militancy or urgency will take root, any more than it did with respect to nuclear power. Canadians are significantly more dependent on the resource sector for their standard of living and they know it. Besides, this simply isn't the society that threw the tea in the harbor.

Paradoxically, such virulent environmentalism promises huge benefits for Canada's resource industries because it creates high barriers to new entrants. This could result in increased values for both fixed assets and commodities just as the anti-nuclear movement in the United States can be blamed for higher power prices. Similarly, prices in some metals will rise if barriers are erected against further exploration or exploitation and particularly if metals are also recyclable and compete against plastics that are not recyclable. Take the case of zinc, which increased dramatically in price beginning in 1986 because automakers chose zinc as an anti-corrosive coating on steel. Zinc was chosen because it is easily removed from scrap metal and can be re-used, giving the metal more value.

Klaus Zeitler, president of Metall Mining Corp., a Canadian subsidiary of West German giant Metallgesellschaft AG, paints a rosy picture for metals prices in the 1990s. He says demand will be driven up by the rapidly growing economies in the Far East and agrees that environmental concerns will make plastics less desirable compared to metals that can be recycled. "Recyclability will determine the future of a metal," he says. Metal prices will rise as supply diminishes because mining has become a currency game. "In 1985, when the U.S. dollar doubled against the deutsche mark, ancient German mines operating for social reasons produced profits to the astonishment of everyone. But fluctuations create uncertainty in decision-making."

That uncertainty, combined with the concentration of ownership that resulted will lead to consultative decisions, creating a de facto cartel in some situations. "Hasty and parallel behavior created problems in the past and won't be a repeat of the capacity race," he says. "In the U.S. Southwest, there were 12 copper producers in 1980 and now there are four major ones. There is more networking and joint ventures."

A London analyst estimated in 1989 that six corporate groups control 34 per cent of the free world's zinc and lead mining capacity, which operations also produce silver. Three of the six groupings are Canadian - Teck Corporation and its partner Cominco Ltd., Noranda Inc. and Falconbridge Limited (Noranda bought half of Falconbridge during the summer of 1989). In addition, the Teck-Cominco group is involved in a joint venture with Zeitler's Metall consortium while Noranda jointly owns Falconbridge with a Swedish mining conglomerate.

Of course, environmental concerns will also cost some of Canada's resource industries. The first sign was in 1990 when a pulp mill consortium was denied permission to build a plant on Alberta's Athabasca River until a comprehensive study by the federal government was completed. But even in that case, the action kept out the least harmful player to date, making those already there more valuable and secure from competition. The Alberta situation showed that the politics of the green movement will be played somewhat in Canada too, but, characteristically, with a lot less rhetoric and hysteria.

Recycling and the environmentalists' politics of obstruction will make existing ore bodies and facilities more valuable as the "supply" of mines, smelters, refineries and exploration lands shrinks. Meanwhile, on the demand side, more resources will be required by the fast-growing economies in the Far East and if the promise of further industrialization in the Eastern Bloc occurs.

Some exploration activity will shift to more accommodating Third

World countries, but there are constraints on their activities, too. Those borrowing from the World Bank must undertake environmental assessments before obtaining funds for resource projects. And any wholesale exploitation of the Soviet Union is unlikely since the fall of communism. Open societies mean that reckless practices can be discovered, criticized and halted.

Another bullish factor in metals and minerals prices is the fact that the mining world is more concentrated following the near-depression in 1981. Now only a handful of giants remain in the mining game, with the result that the hasty and parallel development of mines in the past that caused gluts and plummeting prices is less likely to happen.

2. *The Liberalization of Trade Worldwide.* This phenomenon should continue unimpeded but will mean more competition as the Soviet Union and Eastern Bloc join the fray. Liberalization has led to the free trade initiative in North America (which could also include Mexico by the middle of the 1990s) and the economic integration of the 12 common market countries in 1992 will result in the continuing rationalization of manufacturing and agriculture, thus diverting jobs to those regions where labor costs are lowest. That is why I favor manufacturing companies that are global in their perspective and operations. As for those operating within the domestic framework, I look for ones protected from international onslaughts by monopoly or brand-name prominence. Those with advanced technology are greatly imitated, but a brand name is the most valuable asset any corporation can have. Among resource giants, winners are those that can produce commodities at a *lower cost* than competitors.

As for the political wild card, Canada would be permanently damaged if the protectionist New Democrats or Liberals got into federal power in Canada and began restricting foreign investment or opting out of trade agreements. I think that possibility is remote because trade liberalization is a global shift.

3. *The Restructuring of the World Debt.* The rescue of Mexico by the U.S. Treasury and the conservative bookkeeping imposed on Canada's chartered banks, forced by regulators to set aside reserves for losses to Third World countries, now give our big six banks a unique competitive edge. They have put potential loan losses behind them

and enjoy better credit ratings than most other banks. Mexico's rescue also opens up the distinct possibility that Mexico is on the way back up, offering a trading opportunity that Canadian businessmen would do well to exploit. Some are poised to do so, particularly Northern Telecom Limited.

Mexico is certain to be asked to join the North American free trade initiative, in some limited capacity, during the 1990s. With an economy and population the same size as the Eastern Bloc's, Mexico presents a huge market opportunity. But it also means Mexican natural gas and oil may give Canada's oil industry a run for its money in the 1990s in an attempt to capture the thirsty U.S. market. Likewise, Canada's auto parts manufacturers and textile makers will find themselves under increasing attack from Mexico's *maquiladoras*, colloquial Spanish for factories built and owned by foreigners which use cheap Mexican labor.

4. The End of the Cold War. The triumph of capitalism over communism in Europe and the Soviet Union yields new challenges and opportunities for businessmen around the world. Companies such as Vancouver's Finning Ltd. or Toronto's Tridel Enterprises Inc., with its Aluma Systems Corp., already have a unique toehold behind the former Iron Curtain. On the other hand, those that have been dependent upon huge defence contracts may find business less than brisk.

5. The Return of the Cartel. Oil prices should jump in the 1990s again as production declines and consumption increases in the Soviet Union, Eastern and Western Europe and the United States. Production is also declining among the less disciplined members of the Organization of Petroleum Exporting Countries, notably the African members Libya, Algeria and Nigeria, who ignored quotas and helped bring about the price collapse in 1986. As their reserves deplete, and the Persian Gulf members regain their dominant position (they have one-quarter of the world's reserves), the world will once again be in the cartel's hot little hands. Increased oil prices, in turn, mean higher coal, natural gas, electricity and uranium prices, mostly good news for Canada, which is the world's fifth biggest exporter of energy of all kinds. It is, of course, bad news for the consuming nations or consuming corporations.

6. The Global Village and Golden Age of Information. Canadians own more information assets, per capita, than any other citizens on earth. Every year, Canadian media giants gobble up media assets around the world and make pots of money doing so. They are well-positioned to capitalize on this trend. So are pulp and paper makers. Contrary to popular notions, the golden age of telecommunications and computerization has not created a paperless office, home or society. It has done the opposite. The growing literacy rate worldwide and burgeoning demand for information has resulted in more paper than ever. This is bullish for Canada's forestry and media companies.

CANADIAN TRENDS

7. The Aging Population. Canada is one of the youngest countries in the OECD, demographically speaking. When combined with a low birth rate, this phenomenon will dramatically affect our economy and society in the 1990s. It is estimated that by the turn of the century, there will be three workers for every pensioner, compared with the mid-1980s average of five to one. There will be an explosion in demand for such services as medical, retraining, home renovation, health, fitness and travel. It will also result in an increase in the national savings rate as older couples reach their peak in earnings, have lower living expenses and begin to sock it away for their old age. It also means the death rate will increase. The same applies to the United States, which already has three workers per pensioner, making it, demographically, older than Canada.

Companies offering products or services with a high labor-content reliant upon entry-level low-wage earners will face tougher, more expensive times. Those who can automate will enjoy better times. (Cheap labor is a disincentive to automate: The cost of one industrial robot is equivalent to 100 wage-years at an entry level.) Significantly, McDonald's is introducing labor-saving machinery in its fast-food outlets because of this problem. It is also recruiting senior citizens to work in its outlets.

8. Government Deficits. Canada is out of step with most industrialized countries, whose deficits are being reduced more quickly in relation to their gross national products. In fact, some bond specialists have stated that there may be a worldwide shortage of government bonds in the 1990s, which would indicate a lowering of worldwide interest rates. Canada's politicians have spent like sailors and gotten away with it because our political system provides fewer checks and balances. Majorities result in near-dictatorships and automatic transfer payments to provinces are akin to giving whisky to ten drunken sailors. The result is that both levels routinely offer gold-plated social services to buy votes and politicians ignore the deficits. The aging of our society will aggravate deficits because of our open-ended medical care system.

Higher deficits mean higher taxes and higher inflation which, in turn, mean higher interest rates in Canada. More taxes mean the continuing diversion of Canada's capital into tax-free real estate speculation. The only break a Canadian taxpayer gets is that he will not pay capital gains taxes on the increasing value of his principal residence. This is why Canadians speculate in real estate by continuing to pay excessive prices for housing. Regulatory red tape and real estate speculation will help well-managed real estate companies to outperform other sectors.

Higher taxes, combined with the aging population, will also result in a higher savings rate. Ottawa's concern about looking after the elderly in a future with a declining worker base has led to a policy that increases the amount of money that can be sheltered from taxes and placed into a Registered Retirement Savings Plan. This increase, up from $7,500 now to $15,500 in 1992, is profoundly significant. Investment guru Sir John Templeton of Templeton Management Limited estimates that there will be more money in RRSPs by the end of the century than the sum total value of all stocks available in Canada. If so, it will create a hothouse effect, causing stock prices to spiral up as demand exceeds supply, and will also fill the coffers of financial intermediaries such as banks, brokers and trust companies that specialize in RRSP business.

9. *The January 1, 1993 Tax Deadline.* This looms as a problem for some of the country's richest families. Innocuously known as the "21-year deemed disposition rule," it will trigger corporate takeovers and unravel some of Canada's largest public empires as wealthy Canadians

sell assets to pay awesome tax bills. The rule specifies that on January 1, 1993, taxes will be payable on capital gains generated by assets, such as stocks and bonds or real estate, that were placed in trust before January 1, 1972, the day the first federal capital gains tax became effective in Canada. The capital gains tax was overhauled during the 1971 tax reform and gave owners of the trusts 21 years to pay the capital gains tax on the rich contents of their trusts.

Those affected are not talking about it but we have already witnessed some divestitures (that often make minority shareholders handsome profits). These transactions are more than likely tax-related: the Reichmanns' sale of GSW Inc. and Consumers' Gas Company Ltd.; the sale of Canada Packers Inc.; the sale of Cadillac Fairview Corporation Limited by Edgar and Charles Bronfman and their sisters; the cashing out of the Edper empire (Brascan, Trilon, Hees) by Edward Bronfman and his three sons in 1990; and the sale by Mike DeGroote of his control in Laidlaw Inc. Other family-owned enterprises that are on my hit list for potential sell-outs to pay taxes are Eaton-controlled Baton Broadcasting Incorporated; various parts of the late Stephen Roman's empire, which comprises Denison Mines Ltd., Lawson Mardon Group Limited, Standard Trustco Limited or Roman Corporation Limited; Reichmann-owned Gulf Canada Resources Limited and Abitibi-Price Inc.; the Sobey family's Sobeys Inc. and Empire Company Limited; J.M. Schneider Inc.; Galen Weston's George Weston Limited or Loblaw Companies Limited; Ken Thomson's The Thomson Corporation and The Bay; Hal Jackman's National Trust Company and related financial corporations; and the Belzbergs' First City Financial Corporation Ltd., to name just a few.

For investors, this can translate into profits if the sale of controlling interest leads to higher stock prices, as it usually does. Of course, many family-controlled companies sell only subordinated vote, or non-voting, stock to the public, which means that the controlling shareholder can get a nice premium for his multiple rate stock and those with one or no rates may not. That is why a "coattail" provision (a guarantee that a bid is extended to all shareholders) is important.

10. *Quebec Nationalism.* This pervasive political reality will eventually lead to separation from the rest of Canada, but only if Jacques Parizeau is around to lead the movement. He has no peer or protégé in

eloquently, and pragmatically, making separation a reality. I think Canada and Quebec are in for a long, painful divorce. To split quickly means that Quebec would have to undergo a massive drop in living standards, which would not be politically palatable.

Even though my fear is that separation is inevitable, I have chosen companies based in Quebec that could be disrupted by it, such as Repap Enterprises Inc., CAE Industries Ltd., the Royal Bank of Canada or the Seagram Company Ltd. They would probably relocate if separation occurred and moving could be an expensive and painful process. If I thought separation was inevitable within five years, I would avoid investing in any Quebec-based corporation. I think if it happens, it will occur over a longer period of time.

Another problem for Quebec corporations in an independent Quebec is that the province would have to assume one-third of Ottawa's national debt and would find its credit rating dramatically downgraded, ringing up higher costs for keeping up its infrastructure. A Quebec separation will also destabilize the rest of Canada. I believe if Quebec leaves, Canada will divide itself into five separate countries: British Columbia, the prairies, Ontario, Quebec and the Atlantic provinces. The Atlantic provinces would probably be forced to merge and join Quebec or the United States to fend off a massive decline in living standards. The other provinces are big enough, and wealthy enough, to survive independently. There would be no need, and no advantage, to politically joining the United States. With only two senators per province, there would be little incentive and Canadian voters would reject that option. My best guess is that what is now Canada would function as the Benelux countries and Denmark do beside Germany and France.

Even if separation never occurs, Quebec nationalism will continue to have a profound effect and is a reality that must be taken into consideration when making stock market selections. Canada's largest single shareholder is the nationalistic Caisse de dépôt et placements du Québec, the Quebec Pension Plan with $12 billion invested. It owns large blocks of stock in every sizeable public company with a head office in Quebec. This has given it a veto of sorts over their activities, has resulted in more shareholder protection and has also served to encourage corporate ambitions. The Caisse's deep pockets and watchful eye is why, in part, I have been drawn towards many of its companies. Quebec companies, not all of whom have Caisse support, are in fact over-represented among my 50 best. They are often more highly leveraged and therefore speculative, but they are dynamic nation-builders.

These and other "big picture" considerations led me to make more revisions to my list. For instance, Canada's changing demographics mean that investors are better off with a company that will benefit from the aging population, such as funeral home chain Arbor Capital Inc., over one that will not, such as Irwin Toy Limited. Likewise, the environmental movement led me to pick a mining-manufacturing giant, such as Alcan Aluminum Limited, with its recyclable metal as opposed to Cominco Ltd., dependent upon lead as well as zinc.

I also added a few to my list who were out of favor or misunderstood by the market, such as Tridel Enterprises Inc., tainted by scandal and considered simply a Toronto condo play. Others in this category were the tobacco and liquor companies whose businesses are declining as people smoke and drink less. These were good bets, I figured, because the market over-reacts to headlines, and bad publicity has made their stocks relatively cheap.

Eventually I was left with a short-list of 65 companies. Now began the final stage, which consisted of interviews with each company's chief executive, chief operating or chief financial officer. Only three companies did not oblige. But even where access was impossible due to timing or policy, overall co-operation was impressive. Based on these interviews, my list of the 50 best follows. As for whose stock to buy, when and in what quantities, I defer to brokers, investment counsellors and their research departments. These are the experts who can make those suggestions. I am just a storyteller who tries to pick the intellectual pockets of persons much more astute than myself. Consider this book merely a start. Happy hunting.

ALCAN ALUMINUM LIMITED

Head Office: Montreal, Quebec
Incorporated: June 3, 1902
Ownership: Widely held

Revenues in 1989: US$9,047,000,000
Net Income: US$835,000,000;
Earnings per share: US$3.58
Employees: 57,000
Year End: December 31

Canada's most tasteful head office also houses the country's most successful multinational corporation. Maison Alcan, on Montreal's fashionable Sherbrooke near the Ritz-Carlton Hotel, is the former mansion of Lord Atholstan, philanthropic founder of the now-defunct *Montreal Star*. Behind the red brick façade is an interior courtyard with a ten-storey atrium, a streetscape complete with a British pub and 19th-century street lamps. Inside, the Alcan offices are a maze of sitting rooms, with indirect lighting, flock furnishings and handsome wainscotting in muted tones. It is a five-star setting for a gem of a giant.

Alcan was an offshoot of the Aluminum Company of America (Alcoa), spun off through a sale forced in part by U.S. anti-trust authorities in 1928 amid concern about Alcoa's market dominance. Alcan was Alcoa's only asset outside the United States, so it is ironic that Alcan has now surpassed Alcoa to become the world's lowest-cost aluminum producer. This gives it a critical edge in a business based in great measure on price alone. Alcan is also Canada's most successful multinational, well-positioned in markets all over the world, including the normally impenetrable Japan. By contrast, most so-called Canadian multinationals are merely North American companies, with

15

the exception of Bombardier Inc., whose chairman Laurent Beaudoin is, not coincidentally, an Alcan director.

As important as Alcan's positioning abroad is its positioning at home. As Quebec's biggest manufacturer, Alcan enjoys important leverage when it comes to political decisions that can affect the bottom line, such as pollution-control deadlines or tax hikes. Its leverage will increase if Quebec separates from the rest of Canada. Alcan, and four other companies in Quebec, represent 12 per cent of the world's aluminum smelter capacity and nearly half of North America's. Quebec is becoming the Ruhr Valley of North America.

Although Alcan is a great company to invest in, timing is every-thing. Buying stock in a commodity-based business like Alcan re-quires two bets: Investors must pick the best player in the market; then they must evaluate the market itself. Like other commodities, aluminum prices fluctuate wildly and are cyclical, because aluminum sales track global industrial growth. For instance, aluminum sold for 78 cents a pound during most of 1989, after peaking at $1 a pound before the last recession began in 1980. It collapsed to 50 cents in 1984 before gradually climbing back, due to a glut of supply. Such a roller-coaster ride wreaks havoc on portfolios loaded with Alcan and buyers must cautiously invest in this company, picking valleys and selling at peaks. Current forecasts are for static prices through to 1991.

"Buy close to $20 a share and sell close to $40," advises Allan Hodgson, Alcan's vice president and chief financial officer. Although said in jest, the advice is near the mark and an indication of how volatile Alcan stock prices can be. The company aims to continue its policy of somewhat smoothing out fluctuations through buying back stock from the public for its treasury during troughs.

But there are some fundamental, longer-term reasons why Alcan is a buy, providing entry is carefully timed. Alcan owns two enormously undervalued assets that the market may eventually reward. Of par-ticular importance, and the reason for its cost efficiency, is its grid of hydro-electric power projects that yield up to 3,500 megawatts of electricity, enough to supply two cities, one the size of Montreal and the other of Ottawa.

Aluminum production requires huge amounts of power, typically 20 per cent of costs or roughly 14 cents per pound of aluminum produced at an average of two cents per kilowatt hour. Alcan's hydro costs are a fraction of that, giving the company an incredible competitive advantage but also giving it an underlying asset worth as much as $9 billion at current replacement costs of US$2 million per megawatt. This more than counteracts the drag on aluminum prices caused by jumps in oil and other energy prices. And as the oil cartel gets its act together by the mid-1990s, as supplies diminish, oil prices will climb, hurting aluminum prices, eliminating higher-cost producers, thus making Alcan's enormous hydro potential more valuable. Alcan may break ranks and trade at higher prices than aluminum competitors.

Alcan's only operational disadvantage is the cost of raw material, bauxite, which must be imported to Canada. But the company is well positioned here too and will profit from the environmental consciousness that should sweep the world in the 1990s. The green movement places Alcan increasingly onside, as recycling means scrap metal is used and all producers pay the same price for it. Currently, some 14 million tonnes of primary aluminum is made annually and 4 million tonnes is recycled. (Alcan will produce a total of 2.3 million tonnes in 1990.)

Recycling is going to be big business in the aluminum business; the lightweight metal can be recycled indefinitely because of its strength, as long as it is topped up with about 20 per cent new metal. "In the U.S., 54 per cent of cans are coming back. In California, 73 per cent and Sweden, 90 per cent. Canada's significantly below that but increasing," says Hodgson.

Another undervalued asset, worth another $9 a share according to some estimates, is Alcan's Japanese interests. Unsung is Alcan's enormous, and unusual, success in Japan, thanks to its former chairman, David Culver, who without fanfare in Canada received one of the highest awards available to a foreigner, the Order of the Secret Treasury Class 1.

Alcan's entry into Japan was in 1953 at the invitation of the government to help clean up the postwar mess. The results were its 50 per cent interest in Japan Foil Company, now with sales of US$500 million a year, and half of Nippon Light Metal Company Ltd., with US$4.5 billion in sales. (Alcan shares control of these two with Japan's gigantic trading houses. Nippon is part of the enormous

Japanese trading company, Daiwaichi Group, which owns Fujitsu and Kawasaki; the foil company is part of the Sumitomo trading conglomerate.)

Although Alcan originally owned 50 per cent of Nippon Light Metal, its interest was diluted to 44 per cent in the early 1980s when it wouldn't guarantee debts or subscribe to new share issues to pay down loans. Nippon has been dogged with financial problems because it overbuilt smelters and was clobbered by oil price hikes earlier in the 1980s. Even so, it trades at 40 times its earnings and turned the corner in 1988, when it broke even. Alcan got its first dividend in 14 years during the summer of 1989, and its stake is now worth as much as US$1.6 billion, not bad considering Alcan's original grubstake in the enterprise and reinvested retained earnings total US$150 million. "Nippon nearly went down and is back from the dead, hoping to work together with us. It will be our instrument in Japan and Southeast Asia," says Hodgson.

Little wonder, then, that Alcan listed itself in 1989 on the Tokyo Stock Exchange. Listing costs may prove to be its best investment yet. Few shares trade there, but the company is seeking a higher profile among Japanese institutions and analysts. After all, if Nippon with all its financial woes trades at 40 times its earnings, Alcan should be worth US$200 a share, or 40 times its US$5 per share in net income. While that's hardly likely, Alcan's unique partnerships with Japan's establishment giants may rate it a higher multiple (price in relation to earnings) in the future as Japanese analysts realize the benefits of buying Alcan stock at considerably lower multiples than Japanese aluminum companies trade for. North American averages are from 10 to 12 times earnings and 50 times in Tokyo.

Another piece of blue sky may be an increase in the market for aluminum itself. While plastic has been replacing aluminum siding in home construction, Alcan has been spending a great deal of money with several auto makers to produce an aluminum auto body frame that weighs 250 pounds, or half the weight of steel frames now in use. This would more than double the average 155 pounds of aluminum now used on North American cars.

To this end, in 1990 a limited edition Jaguar, consisting of 200 cars worth $450,000 apiece, rolled off assembly lines. Their frames were aluminum. Ferrari did the same and Honda announced it would make

5,000 up-market sports cars using large amounts of the metal. With 32 million cars manufactured annually around the world, the market potential is mind-boggling. If each car added 250 pounds of aluminum, that would increase worldwide aluminium demand by 4 million tonnes. It may take several years before we see this happen.

Whatever the future holds, Alcan is a remarkable Canadian success story, a company that is a play on the country's greatest natural, renewable resource, hydro-electricity and manufacturing know-how. Alcan is poised to benefit, ironically, from the environmental movement and, more importantly, it is an enlightened player, sponsoring research and conferences into pollution problems, striking an environmental committee of its directors and earmarking about $1.8 billion to replace all its Quebec smelters over the next two decades with relatively benign operations. Some $1.2 billion worth of new smelting operations are finished or in progress. With a new Francophone president, Jacques Bougie, at the helm, Alcan can take on the world with confidence. And win.

Caveats: This company is extremely cyclical and investors must have a grip on the outlook for aluminum prices in order to avoid buying when prices are about to tumble and selling when they are about to jump. For instance, aluminum price forecasts are poor during the first half of 1990. Another risk is of a major environmental mishap that may lead to radical politics and rules speeding up Alcan's smelter clean-up in the 1990s, at the expense of the bottom line. High oil prices are good news, but if they are excessive and sustained, they may obliterate Alcan's stake in Nippon Light Metal.

If $10,000 had been invested in January 1980, it would have been worth $21,724 in January 1990. If dividends were reinvested, the total would be $27,734.

AMERICAN BARRICK RESOURCES CORPORATION

Head Office: Toronto, Ontario
Incorporated: July 14, 1984
Ownership: Major shareholder Horsham Securities Ltd.

Revenues in 1989: US$206,069,000
Net Income: US$35,765,000
Earnings per share: US$0.30
Employees: 1,300
Year End: December 31

Deep in toniest Toronto resides the most unusual headquarters for a mining empire anywhere in the world. Tucked among art galleries, oriental rug showrooms and trendy cafés is a red-brick Victorian house with B-A-R-R-I-C-K spelled out in silver serif letters over an archway. This is mining chic, a glittering gold company called American Barrick Resources Corporation, which is run by an eclectic group of executives. But this is no flaky enterprise. In just five years, Barrick has North America's second largest gold reserves.

Normally, I don't like gold stocks. Most gold companies come and go with the results from their latest drill hole. I'm leery because the gold business has been known to be populated by frauds who have propelled stocks ever upward through salted assays or cleverly worded press releases. I also don't understand the intrinsic, magical value attributed to gold. After all, its only commercial value is cosmetic or dental.

The precious metal's glitter is rooted in history. Only enough gold to cover a football field three feet deep has ever been produced in all of history. Its attractiveness combined with its scarcity made it the ideal currency, or the standard to back paper currencies. Gold was hard to find, so rivals couldn't dilute the value of existing currencies, and it is

20

impossible to counterfeit. In the 20th century, the world's central banks abandoned their gold standards to back their bucks but continued to hoard it, which is why Nigerian businessmen and French housewives or Hong Kong welders do too. It is tradition, combined with fear that inflation will lead to monetary collapse, that fuels the world's constant search for gold.

Unfortunately, most gold stocks are offered by single-product companies whose prices swing violently along with bullion prices or inflation rates. Such cyclical stocks should be avoided by most investors and left to pro traders or gold bugs who enjoy second-guessing prices and playing the swings. But Barrick is different. Not only does it look forward to a three-fold jump in gold production at an average cost of only US$205 per ounce, but its stock price will not move in lock step with bullion price swings. An average of 75 per cent of its production for the next five years has been forward-sold, or hedged, at US$433 an ounce. This means that even if gold prices fell to an average of US$350 over the next five years, Barrick's compound annual rate of profit growth would be 30 per cent. Conversely, if the price rose to US$450, profit growth would be 45 per cent a year.

Barrick also has a unique background. It was founded in 1980 by Peter Munk, a Hungarian Canadian who jet-setted his way to a fortune in the hotel business with the initial financial backing of the Khashoggi family (no longer involved) and other wealthy Saudi Arabians. But commuting between homes in London, Sydney and Toronto left Munk concerned that his children would never live a normal life, so he returned to Canada in December 1979. "I didn't want my kids to be nomads like I had been. I came to Canada in Grade 12 and my youngest was just beginning school so I wanted them to be brought up in one place, in Canada," he recalls.

He and his investors cashed in their hotel chips (resulting in Australia's Targest hotel) and decided to invest it in the high-flying oil and gas business in Canada. Their timing couldn't have been worse. Oil prices hit their peak and a recession followed. The cartel collapsed, oil prices tumbled and interest rates soared. "Nothing we did went right. So I examined my failure and decided it was because we got in at the very top of the cycle. So I decided to get into the gold business instead. Gold was down at $250 an ounce, its lowest-ever price, and I figured Europeans would avoid South African gold investments and come over here. We decided to build a one-product company."

Munk was right, and he has never looked back. He merged his oil business with a gold company in 1983, sold the oil assets and then launched a series of acquisitions that hit pay dirt, landing exploration prospects that bigger mining companies had turned down but now wish they hadn't. The basis for Barrick's entry into the big leagues in so short a period of time is its Goldstrike mine in Nevada, acquired in 1986 for US$62 million from small Canadian mining company Pancana Minerals Ltd. and its U.S. partner. Pancana was run at the time by the talented mining man, former Dome Mines Limited head Malcolm Taschereau, and it was controlled by Toronto fuel oil baron Joseph Rotman, now a Barrick director.

Munk was talked into the Pancana purchase by Robert M. Smith, American Barrick's crew-cut president and chief operating officer, whom Munk had inherited along with the first gold company he acquired, Camflo Mines. The two are the odd couple, but it works. Smith was born and raised in Haileybury and comes from a mining family. His grandfather was Ontario's first mining recorder. Stocky and a chain-smoker, Smith is a sharp contrast to the urbane Munk in his $1,200 suits. The two stuck by their decision to buy Goldstrike even though it was heavily criticized at the time, mostly because U.S. giant Newmont Mining Corp. had declined it.

As things turned out, it was a brilliant coup and catapulted Barrick into the big leagues. In 1983, Barrick had gold reserves of 163,000 ounces and by 1989 they stood at 18 million ounces and growing. In 1983, its first year of full production, Barrick produced 34,000 ounces of gold but by 1988 it had produced 341,000 ounces and by 1992 will produce about 1.16 million ounces annually, mostly from the Goldstrike mine. Better yet, estimated costs by then are US$205 an ounce. If those projections come true, Barrick will earn $2 a share in profits, compared to 1988's 63 cents per share. While anticipation of higher earnings already account for the high multiple at which American Barrick has traded since its January 1989 announcement about Goldstrike's massive reserves, many believe as I do that there is still room to grow. There is, however, a lawsuit against Barrick that may create problems with its Goldstrike holdings.

Mining analyst Patrick Mars, president of Bunting Warburg Inc., points out another reason why Barrick is the best buy. The lion's share of its production is in the United States, in Nevada and Alaska. "The labor rates are lower, taxation is lower and politics are better in Nevada than in Canada or a Third World country. Effective tax rates for corporations in Nevada are half that in Canada."

Those are the reasons Barrick has been a darling of mining analysts and portfolio managers around the world. This is a gold stock with a unique upside and a protected downside, suitable for individual investors to participate in. My only concern is that Barrick's chairman-founder and CEO, Peter Munk, has already attracted enormous attention to the company, and stock prices have risen meteorically. Now that Barrick is established as a senior mining company, spectacular gains may be for others. Even so, American Barrick offers relatively secure growth for investors in the future. As First Boston, the U.S. brokerage giant, said in 1989, "Barrick will emerge in the 1990s as one of North America's largest gold producers."

Investors should note that 21.8 per cent of American Barrick is owned by another public company, the Horsham Corporation, listed only in Toronto. Munk controls 57 per cent of Horsham's voting stock and, despite my dislike for subordinated share situations, I think this company also provides an interesting opportunity for the more speculative investor.

Buying Horsham shares is three bets in one. Owners are betting on Barrick's success; they are betting that Munk and his holding company will astutely find bargains in the future; and they are wagering that Horsham can successfully turn around the medium-sized U.S. oil company, Clark Oil & Refining Corporation, obtained in November 1988 through a leveraged buy-out for US$330 million. Clark was protected from bankruptcy through Chapter 11 protection, and the U.S. court blessed Horsham's leveraged buy-out of Clark, meaning that the acquisition cost is a lien against Clark Oil's assets, not Horsham's.

The first two bets are easy to place. Barrick is a solid investment and Munk looks more and more like a genius. But Clark Oil presents one of those classic, high-risk-high-reward propositions, a gutsy gamble that will pay off only if Munk's team can do what great

Canadian companies like Canadian Tire, Dylex and Imasco failed to do: turn a sow's ear into a silk purse south of the border.

For its US$330 million, Horsham obtained 60 per cent of Clark, with an option to buy another 15 per cent by 1993. Clark is a medium-sized regional operator in the U.S. midwest and owns a dozen refineries, pipelines, distribution terminals and 920 gasoline stations. Small by U.S. standards, it nonetheless pumps a staggering 1 billion gallons of gasoline per year, making it two-thirds the size of Texaco Canada Inc.'s downstream (refining and reselling) operation. Clark is also a valuable real estate investment and some 803 of its gasoline-station sites and buildings are owned outright by Clark and most operate convenience stores that sell cigarettes, candy bars and beer.

Almost immediately after taking control of Clark Oil, Munk lured Ralph Cunningham away from giant rival, Tenneco Oil Processing and Marketing, to act as Clark's chairman and chief executive officer. Better yet, stock options at considerably higher prices were set aside to compensate Cunningham and his executive team, a shareholder-friendly incentive designed to maximize share values. Cunningham's capture, along with the prices fetched for similar assets, led respected oil analyst, Jim Doak of Toronto's First Marathon Securities Limited, to recommend Horsham as a buy. Cunningham left on good terms in May 1990 after righting the ship.

"Clark went into Chapter 11 because of a $98-million inventory and trading losses suffered in the oil price collapse of 1986. Clark uses almost 4 million barrels of crude per month and inventory losses triggered the banks to withdraw operating lines," wrote Doak before the deal was consummated in January 1989. "In other words, Horsham has the opportunity to buy Clark because of the oil price crash, not because the assets have fundamental operating problems."

Figures in 1989 were nothing but promising. In 1986 and 1987 the company lost US$96.4 million. In 1988 things began to turn when revenues hit US$1.5 billion and operating income (before depreciation and taxes) reached US$81 million and net profits of $22.46 million, thanks mostly to huge gains made during November and December after Horsham's purchase. By the end of 1989, Clark's revenues for nine months hit US$1.4 billion and earnings hit $32.2 million (before extraordinary items) compared with $4.2 million in the same period the year before. Clark has also been paying down debts. An analysis by Gordon Capital Corporation says if Horsham were valued as other management companies were, it would be trading at $13.50 based on these figures. At the time of the analysis, it remained at $9, partly because of the unresolved Barrick lawsuit and partly because it may be dangerous to assume that Clark is completely out of the woods or can thrive against the U.S. gasoline retail giants. This is not inappropriate. After all, betting on management companies like Horsham is more of a bet on jockeys than on horses. Investors are backing Horsham's five employees who do nothing but read countless financial statements and listen to countless ideas from countless investment bankers. Horsham's "asset" is its collective ability to recognize value and collective agility to act quickly. Even more important is its access to what the three-piece suits call the "deal stream," the constant flow of business opportunities offered to those who have the smarts and the money and the contacts.

And Munk, a cosmopolitan globe-trotter who speaks many languages ("All of them with an accent," he jokes), plugs into as many "deal streams" as does any tycoon in Canada. Perhaps even more. His jet-set connections not only bring deals to his doorstep but also help him raise capital more readily than others. Probably his greatest achievement was his success in building a hotel empire with Arab money in Australia, New Zealand and the South Pacific. That's why his money-raising savvy also led him to strategically list American Barrick on three Swiss exchanges (where the Arabs like to keep their money) as well as on New York, Toronto, Montreal and Paris exchanges. As a result, Barrick's investors are Canadians, Americans and Europeans in equal parts. He plans to do the same with Horsham.

As for "deal streams," he has put together an eclectic and far-reaching board at Horsham Corporation. Its directors include C. William D. Birchall, a wealthy investor living in Nassau; Dr. Roberto Gancia, a wealthy Italian from Milan; Joseph Rotman, the wealthy controlling shareholder of Roy-L Group Inc. in Toronto; Hany Salaam, chairman of the Kuwaiti investment arm, Gulf Resources Corporation in London; Andrew Sarlos, a fellow Hungarian who serves as investment counsellor to Canada's richest families; and Samuel Zell, a billionaire from Chicago. Another large investor is American takeover artist, Carl Icahn, chairman of TWA. And these guys know a great deal more than you and I know. That's why I believe Horsham is one of those "special situation" stocks that punters should ponder. So is American Barrick.

Caveats: Barrick's nagging lawsuit involving a junior mining company in Utah suing for mega-bucks looks as though it has little merit. But anything can happen in courts and the case resumes in fall 1990. More importantly, investors should watch quarterly production figures and costs per ounce like a hawk, to insure that forecasts become reality. Also, gold prices become more critical as Barrick gets closer to the date when its forward sales at US$433 an ounce runs out. If prices collapsed tomorrow, the stock might pull back slightly but nowhere near as much as would others. Clark is still a crapshoot but an interesting one. It exposes Horsham to losses if the Canadian dollar is too high.

An investment of $10,000 in 1983 was worth $76,042 in January 1990. With dividends reinvested, it totalled $76,979. Over the decade prices ranged from a high of $20 to a low of 75 cents, adjusting for splits.

ANDERSON EXPLORATION LTD.

Head Office: Calgary, Alberta
Incorporated: 1968
Ownership: Major shareholders
Kerr Addison, J.C. Anderson, B.C. Sugar

Revenues in 1989: $51,048,000
Net Income: $10,988,000
Earnings per share: $0.61
Employees: 86
Year End: September 30

John "J.C." Anderson is the last of a vanishing breed, an oil man who still owns a sizeable chunk of his company. Most of the others, such as Sulpetro's Gus Van Wielingen, Dome's Smilin' Jack Gallagher or Turbo's Bob Brawn, were blown away by bad breaks or by banks. But J.C., with his easy wit and southern drawl, continues to build one of the oil patch's most interesting companies, not coincidentally called Anderson Exploration Ltd.

"Sorry I can't offer you a view," says J.C. slyly when I enter his office. The building is in the low-rent district of town but his office is a semi-circular wall of windows 30 feet across; they frame a panorama of spectacular snow-capped Rockies in the distance. A better view would be, quite simply, impossible.

This is the headquarters of Anderson Exploration, a relative newcomer to the investment scene, having been public only since July 12, 1988. At that time, its stock traded at $10 3/8 and has more than doubled since. But J.C. has been building an impressive outfit for 25 years with private funds, thanks to his unique ability to find money as readily as he finds oil and gas. Among other accomplishments, he discovered one of Canada's biggest, most accessible gas fields, the Dunvegan, with an estimated 1.5 trillion cubic feet, worth $2.25

billion at current depressed gas prices. As natural gas prices continue to climb during the 1990s, as I believe they will, this company and its shareholders will win big.

Anderson, born in Nebraska in 1930, arrived in Calgary on New Year's Eve in 1966 to take up his post as chief engineer for Amoco Corporation of Chicago. "I realized this was the place. I couldn't believe the opportunities that were here. There was lots of stuff to find and I still feel that way. I quit Amoco in August 1968 and six Texas investors and I put up $400,000. Two were bought out eight years later for $10 million."

On September 19, 1970, Anderson found Dunvegan, an elephant gas field that single-handedly catapulted him from a one-man band with ideas to a medium-sized oil outfit. Next followed some clever financings with U.S. mining companies until the Foreign Investment Review Agency made it important to find Canadian ownership. In 1976, Anderson convinced B.C. Sugar to enter the oil business; the 1981 National Energy Plan, which taxed foreign-owned oil outfits and rewarded Canadian-owned ones with grants, forced Anderson Exploration to switch passports, even if J.C. himself wouldn't. That's when Kerr Addison Mines Limited, controlled by Noranda Inc., bought 34 per cent for $80 million.

Now the witty and chain-smoking Anderson finds himself in bed with two Canadian giants – B.C. Sugar with 20.3 per cent of Anderson Exploration and Kerr Addison with its 34 per cent. J.C. still owns 20.5 per cent and his Texas investors another 7.9 per cent. At first glance, this company is another Bronfman-Hees-Noranda takeover candidate, particularly since there is no successor. Anderson's eldest son, also John, is only 22 years old. (He was on Canada's equestrian team at the 1988 Olympics.)

Clearly, Kerr Addison bides its time, making no secret of the fact it would like to take over the company. "We're not fighting. There is not much question Kerr would like more," is J.C.'s only comment.

Tellingly, however, Anderson's plans in early 1990 to sell $60 million worth of new stock included limiting owners to their current proportion of stock. That means the only takeover would be a friendly one. Of course, Kerr may get frustrated and cash out but not as long as Anderson's stock keeps rising, which it will because there is not a lot of stock available for the public and institutional demand remains high for good finders such as this one. J.C.'s 20.5 per cent is exactly what Kerr would need to control the company. So is B.C. Sugar's 20.3 per cent stake, but J.C. has the first right of refusal. Then there's the 7.9 per cent of stock held in hands friendly to J.C. All three add up to 48.7 per cent of the stock, a form of poison pill that puts J.C. a nudge away from absolute control, lest anyone have ideas unacceptable to him.

The point is, however, that Anderson may one day strike a friendly deal himself. After all, he is no spring chicken. But sale or not, he still runs the show and must put in place management that can carry on the business. Commenting on the fact there is no successor, he says, "I recognize that as a problem but there is a group of guys here who are learning the business side and the search for a chief executive officer is on my plate as a project. There is a guy on the board who could run things on a temporary basis if he had to."

Obviously, Anderson needn't worry about control because he is firmly in charge. And his is a tight ship. Operating an oil company is like running a factory. The raw material is land and the product is oil and gas. The cost of manufacturing is critical, and Anderson enjoys the lowest overhead costs in town on a per-barrel basis.

He is also one of the oil patch's most aggressive explorers, with a track record of finds as impressive as that of Renaissance Energy Ltd. Better yet, Anderson produces a great deal of natural gas and receives the highest price on the continent, recently getting $1.96 per thousand cubic feet when others were getting $1.35. This is because 75 per cent of his volumes supply Calgary pipelines as part of a long-term contract that lets him avoid the cost of transporting gas over long distances. His gas serves mostly the growing northern California market.

"We have the lowest overhead in town and are good finders. To be good, you have to be persistent and patient. We drill dry holes, but if one out of 100 wells finds a Dunvegan, what do you care?" he says. "We have a good team of 46 people who operate 87 per cent of our production. I'm proud of this bunch."

Ironically, Anderson has always stayed in Alberta, disdaining the U.S. oil world he knows better than most. Even after the hated National Energy Program, he resisted the trend among angry Canadian explorers to go to the so-called greener pastures south of the border. "They called them snowbirds and couldn't wait for them to come off the plane. Some of the Canadians – like Home Oil Company Limited [owned by Hiram Walker Resources at the time] – paid ridiculous prices. I don't blame the Americans. Some guy with a Size Two hat and 48-inch belt offers you three times for it so why not sell it to him? They eventually came back. Then the grants ended. Grants brought into the business a lot of people who shouldn't have been. This is a technically driven business. You can't just throw money at it. Nowadays, the good ones get better and the dogs continue to bark."

Anderson and Renaissance are among Canada's exciting new breed of oil cat, committed to Alberta and committed to finding the stuff, not buying it. They are not appendages to large, non-oil conglomerates usually interested only in the bottom line. These companies are run by experts in their fields who also happen to be great businessmen – they have flourished even during the bad times. Now good days are around the corner as OPEC slowly regains its pre-eminence. As Anderson, with four decades of oil smarts behind him, puts it: "The free world outside OPEC is producing at full capacity. The U.S. is at 50 per cent oil imports now and declining. North America, Western Europe and Japan produce 26 per cent of this oil and have only 8 per cent of reserves."

Caveats: This is a company with a small public float that requires investor patience when buying or selling. The biggest concern is that the company is a one-man band. Risks include the lack of management depth or succession plans, the possibility of a scrap with the Hees group, who want the company, and less than bullish oil and gas prices.

An investment of $10,000 in July 1987 was worth $14,804 in January 1990. No dividends have been paid.

ARBOR CAPITAL INC.

Head Office: Toronto, Ontario
Incorporated: 1973 Canadian Memorial Services Ltd.,
1975 changed to Arbor Capital Inc.
Ownership: Controlling shareholder D.J. Scanlon

Revenues: $85,641,000
Net Income: $11,464,000
Earnings per share: $1.47
Employees: 1,000 (seasonal)
Year End: October 31

Canada's population relentlessly ages. According to estimates, there will be only three workers per pensioner by the turn of the century, compared with the current ratio of five to one. Demographers claim that the effect of Canada's current low birth rate will be felt in 20 years, roughly by 2010, when our population will peak before starting to decline. As a result, for the next two decades, there will continue to be a profound consumer shift away from day care, cribs and sports cars toward smaller homes as well as services in medical and pharmaceutical care, fitness, travel, leisure, post-secondary education, nursing homes and other specialized retirement services. Although it sounds ghoulish, there are a number of companies that are so-called "grey" investments, among them MDS Health Group Limited (discussed later). But two companies stand out because they provide an inescapable service that every single Canadian must one day purchase: cemetery and funeral-home services. Two companies in this business are Arbor Capital Inc. of Toronto and the Loewen Group Inc. of Vancouver, described later in this book.

Arbor's wholly owned operating subsidiary, Memorial Gardens Canada Ltd., owns 49 cemeteries and 25 crematoria in all provinces except Newfoundland. Arbor also has interests in 52 funeral homes that provide interment rights, memorials and associated products in Canada and four cemeteries and four funeral homes in the United States. Typical is its flagship cemetery in Oakville, 200 acres of rolling hills and low-rise mausoleums for urns or coffins. Like other such businesses, Arbor has designed tasteful places of rest for a death-denying society, park-like spaces where plaques embedded in the ground above burial sites replace old-fashioned upright tombstones.

Like its understated cemeteries, Arbor indulges in euphemisms. Its annual report and executives refer to "incidents" (deaths) and "pre-care" services (the purchase of burial and funeral services ahead of time as opposed to "post-care"). Arbor is part undertaker, part landscape company and part real estate developer, employing landscape architects and engineers to design everything from buildings to berms and drainage. Cemetery maintenance is paid for by new sales as well as by the proceeds of carefully invested funds in trust, set aside when burial or resting places are purchased. But regulatory hassles, zoning restrictions and land costs convinced Arbor founder, Daniel Scanlan, to halt future cemetery developments and to aggressively diversify his company into the funeral home business. He plans to buy or build another 100 funeral homes in Canada within 15 years.

"It will take us 15 years and we will concentrate in high population areas like Toronto. We estimate its death rate will go up by 31 per cent from 1986 to 2006 because of its aging population," says Scanlan. Existing funeral homes are slowly acquired because most are sole proprietorships that are unavailable until their owners retire or die. Fortunately, Arbor has few, if any, rivals in Canada for these properties. Scanlan also plans to build funeral homes at the cemetery in provinces outside of Ontario (which forbids this) and build homes near cemeteries in Ontario. To pull this off, Arbor will need $200 million.

Ironically, the decision to abandon plans for new cemeteries will go a long way toward paying for his ambitious strategy. Some analysts estimate Arbor is sitting on some $80-million worth of surplus lands – about 3,000 acres near highly populated areas – which will be sold for huge profits to other developers. This is the result of restrictions but also the happy result of the massive switch to cremation from burial by the Canadian public, a change in consumer preference that was spurred in great measure when the Roman Catholic Church lifted its ban on cremation in 1965.

"We sell the services so we know the trends. Cremation is now over 50 per cent in major cities and it used to be less than 6 per cent," says Scanlan. "Cremation costs about $300 and people still place the ashes in niches or bury them. This change affects the economics of cemeteries. It means a 20-acre cemetery for principally cremation would never fill in 100 years. It used to be the fate of cemeteries to get filled, be abandoned and yet maintenance had to continue on perpetually. The trend toward cremation is worldwide, but Italians, Portuguese and many Chinese don't like cremation."

The Canadian way of death has changed in other ways. Wakes are one day in length instead of the traditional three, and services are mostly held at the funeral home rather than in a church. In about 80 per cent of cases, funeral directors must search for a minister because people aren't affiliated with a church but want a clergyman to lead the service.

Interestingly, Arbor's stock price in terms of its multiple to earnings is less than half the multiple of its competitor's, Loewen Group. This may change as the more complex cemetery business is diluted, better understood or more profitable as funeral homes are added to the fold. Many investors are spooked by the requirements for perpetual cemetery maintenance. Others are concerned about Ontario's restrictions, aimed at Arbor, which forbid on-site funeral homes as well as telephone solicitations. There is concern that these restrictions could spread to other provinces. Scanlan blames Ontario's "funeral home lobby" (comprised of rivals) and points out that restrictions have frightened off rivals.

Scanlan, a tall, patrician engineer, launched Arbor in London, Ontario, in 1949 after immigrating to Canada from Detroit with his Canadian wife. He happened upon the cemetery business by accident. "There weren't many jobs after the war, and a friend of mine was building cemeteries and asked me to join him. I started in the U.S. but wanted to go to Canada."

Now he runs his no-frills operation from an office building that Arbor owns in suburban Etobicoke. The annual report is printed in one color of ink, furnishings are early 1970s motif, and only a modest sign in one of the building's entrances hints that the company "serving families across Canada" resides there. Scanlan's six children all work at Arbor in various capacities from marketing to managing ceme-teries. A fit septuagenarian, Scanlan still plays tennis with a pro and works out three times weekly but, like his past and present clientele, can't live forever.

There are two classes of stock, and a Scanlan family trust owns 53 per cent of Arbor As, or shares with votes, equally divided among his six children. In addition, the family owns 1.1 million of the 5 million B stock or non-voting shares. "If anyone were to make an acceptable offer for the As – voting stock – they must also include Bs with the same terms and conditions. I have no intention of making a disposition."

There is little doubt to me that Arbor is a takeover candidate. Rivals Loewen Group and some American funeral-home chains have their eye on it. But there are plans for succession. Arbor has always had a professional president and Scanlan thinks it will stay that way "unless somebody shows great talent." The family trust allows each heir to cash in over a period of time, but the control block has right of first refusal. "One or two might sell, but right now they all have the same feeling I have for the business. They love it."

Caveats: Although Scanlan has always had a professional president in place and is in excellent health himself, succession could be a problem. His children are not yet senior managers and may or may not have his vision or skills. If they sell out at a premium, they may not abide by his pledge to extend a takeover bid to all shareholders, including those with non-voting shares. Until his verbal promises are put in writing in the form of legal coattail provisions, voting stock is preferable to non-voting shares.

An investment of $10,000 in January 1980 was worth $175,000 in January 1990. With dividends reinvested, it totalled $181,400. Over the decade prices ranged from a high of $18.50 to a low of 85 cents, adjusting for splits.

BCE INC.

Head Office: Montreal, Quebec
Incorporated: 1970, reorganization April 28, 1983
Ownership: Widely held

Revenues in 1989: $16,681,000,000
Net Income: $761,000,000
Earnings per share: $2.43
Employees: 125,000
Year End: December 31

As any Canadian schoolchild should know, the world's first telephone call was made in Canada, between Paris and London, Ontario, by Scottish immigrant Alexander Graham Bell. At that time, however, Canada was a fledgling Third World country with insufficient capital and an agrarian mentality. So Alexander Graham Bell sought, and found, his fortune down among the Yankees, who bankrolled his invention. And the rest is, as they say, history.

Now decades later, Bell would be proud of his Canadian namesake, BCE Inc. (which stands for Bell Canada Enterprises). It has become his first adopted country's most profitable enterprise and its third largest with $15 billion in sales and $28 billion in assets. BCE consistently makes more money than all other enterprises in Canada because it owns two-thirds of the country's telephone utilities, the country's monopoly natural gas pipeline, an oil and gas giant with $1.8 billion in assets, Canada's fourth-largest trust company, 21 per cent of Quebecor Inc. (a media and forestry conglomerate that is also North America's second largest commercial printer after Chicago's gigantic R.R. Donnelley & Sons Company), a cellular phone outfit, as well as telecommunications superstar Northern Telecom. Profits flow in at the rate of $20 million per week or $1.1 billion in one year. BCE's profits alone are equivalent to the entire stock market value of the Molson Companies Limited or Bombardier.

With cash flow that a Third World finance minister would covet, it is little wonder BCE is buying up the country. So are other conglomerates, in a form of concentration of economic power known as aggregate concentration – simply, more and more owned by fewer and fewer. By 1989, only 12 of Canada's 100 largest corporations were widely held. These include Canadian Pacific, BCE, Moore Corporation Limited, Alcan, Inco, Nova Corp., Dofasco, Stelco, Varity Corporation, PWA Corporation, Federal Industries Ltd. and Dominion Textile Inc. Combined, these 12 controlled 23 per cent of the assets of all 100 corporations, or $80.48 billion out of $344.74 billion.

The result is that there are few "pure investment plays" available. It also means that investment choices in Canada mostly consist of choosing which conglomerate or conglomerate's conglomerate to buy. Investors must therefore deal with several issues before making one investment decision. For instance, when deciding whether to buy stock in the BCE conglomerate, you must evaluate whether BCE's phone business will continue to perform well or face deregulation; whether BCE paid too much for companies it controls; whether all the companies it controls will prosper in their sector; and whether BCE will manage the lot wisely and profitably. Investors must also determine whether it is better to invest directly in a management company or whether to buy stock in some of the companies it controls. (Unfortunately, sometimes conglomerates are the only route because some assets are not sold to the public, such as BCE's telephone company or Canadian Pacific's wholly owned railway, its hotel chain or its Fording Coal.)

Buying BCE is mostly a telephone-telecommunications bet. If you think that its entry into financial services is particularly inspired or that oil and gas prices may make its Encor Inc. soar faster than others, those stocks should be bought separately. Buying Canadian Pacific is a different matter because it is not dominated by any one sector but is a mixed bag of mining, oil, real estate, railway, telecommunications, school-bus, waste-management, security services, auctioneering, hotel, manufacturing and forestry assets. Those seeking pure plays because of unique sectoral prospects should also consider CP's Pan-Canadian Petroleum Limited, Marathon Realty Company Limited, Laidlaw Inc., Laidlaw's ADT Canada Inc. or AMCA International

Corporation manufacturing outfit. Then there are other conglomerates I admire such as Scott's Hospitality Inc., Federal Industries Ltd., Gendis Inc. and Imasco Limited which mostly own outright all their diverse operations.

Investing in BCE or Canadian Pacific is different from investing in Brascan Limited or Hees International. Brascan – unlike BCE or Canadian Pacific – is strictly a holding company without operating income. This means that it is highly leveraged and its success is based on the income derived from its underlying operating entities. In good times this is great, but in tough times such holding company stocks collapse more dramatically than operating stocks. To me there is a world of difference between management companies, with wholly or partially owned entities, and leveraged holding companies such as the type favored by the Toronto Bronfman empire. Safest bets are those companies with operations.

Nonetheless, a management company or conglomerate is only as strong as its weakest link. Besides, the whole is almost always worth less than the sum of the parts, which is why management companies almost always trade at a discount to net asset values. Canada's pre-eminent management company analyst, Harold Wolkin, with Nesbitt, Thomson Inc., says investors must buy management companies because they have outperformed most other indices over the last ten years and will in future.

He's perfectly right. In essence, the takeover mania that swept Canada reduced the float of stock available and shifted it from shares in operating companies to shares in management companies that own all or part of formerly independent operating companies. "Management companies like Canadian Pacific Limited or BCE Inc. are asset plays and over time investors have got to be in them. They have a wealth of assets and won't retreat in price because they are fundamentally sound. If the difference between their stock values and net asset values widens enough, they become vulnerable to a takeover if widely held," says Wolkin.

My winning list of management companies includes BCE, Canadian Pacific Limited, Federal Industries Ltd., Imasco Ltd., Noranda Inc. and Scott's Hospitality Inc.

Some are better than others and in 1990 BCE got two black eyes. Its real estate investment, called BCE Development Corporation, nearly went under. BCE made an agreement with work-out artist, Carena

Developments Limited (part of the Peter Bronfman empire) and the two announced a $600-million writedown of assets in early 1990, a cash infusion of $500 million and a restructuring of operations. Angry preferred shareholders organized and protested through my *Financial Post* column and elsewhere because of the unusual writedown, which was designed to create tax losses and some value. Although a clever attempt to regain values, the writedown gave BCE Development a negative value of $72 million. This infuriated many because it came months after the Reichmanns offered $700 million to BCE Development common shareholders and weeks after "unqualified" Touche Ross (now Deloitte & Touche) audited financial statements, meaning that there was no mention of an impending writedown or of any problem with the asset valuations. Then in spring 1990 BCE was stuck with another problem investment concerning its $300-million-plus loan to Kinburn Corp., a troubled Ottawa high-tech group. Bell set aside out of earnings a $20-million provision against Kinburn loans. Concern is more provisions may follow, thus lowering profits.

Such poor investments have hurt Ma Bell's lily-white image among investors and will continue to dog the company and be a drag on stock prices for some time to come. On the other hand, it presents a buying opportunity for those who believe, as I do, that this cash cow is too good to pass by. Even if the BCE Development rescue falls apart and never turns around, BCE's writedown is equivalent to just nine months' BCE Inc. profits.

"It was not one of our most brilliant coups," admits BCE's chairman, Raymond Cyr. "We tried to get out of real estate which was in the wrong markets. That was the problem. Houston rebounded and we thought Denver would rebound faster but it didn't and it has horrendously low office occupancy rates. We paid too much because deals were badly financed with a partner and the partner never showed up. Now there is a shortfall."

Investing in Ma Bell has almost become a Canadian institution among conservative, income-minded investors, and Cyr ably explains why. It is also an institutional favorite because it pays healthy dividends and pension funds do not pay income tax on that revenue or capital gains either. "Bell pays significant dividends. It is not for people looking for quick appreciation but for those looking for long-term appreciation. It has outperformed the TSE 300 for most of the past ten years and is good ballast in a portfolio. It includes positions in important sectors," he says.

BCE's latest foray is into financial services with its purchase of Montreal Trustco Inc. in 1989 from Paul Desmarais's Power Corporation of Canada. "We bought it to give us entry into financial services because this is the fastest-growing field in the economy. With deregulation there are all sorts of tremendous opportunities for growth. We already have a significant in-house trust business in the form of our employees' pension fund management organization. After some time digesting, we will no doubt look at a number of other opportunities."

Would he also buy Desmarais's Investors Group Inc. mutual funds? "We may look at it some day, but it is not for sale. We would like Montreal Trust to grow larger, more national. Desmarais sold because he wants to be international. Banque Paribas [a European merchant/investment bank in which Desmarais is a small investor] is a different sort of operation. In an operation like that, you do one big deal every three months then sit around. It is not like operating a branch network. We have had talks with six [trust company operators] to test out interest. We never do an unfriendly takeover. We do not get involved in those messy things. Sometimes it just takes time for them to express their interest. We had discussions with Desmarais long before we did the deal."

That is one of BCE's greatest strengths, financial staying power, which allows it to bide its time and cherry pick when the timing's right for both parties. There's little doubt that in a decade BCE will own Canada's largest trust company network as the owners of potential takeover targets decide to cash in their chips. The list is obvious: National Trust Company, Central Capital Corporation, Counsel Corporation, Standard Trustco Limited and First City Financial Corp. "Montreal Trust could not survive without a significant owner. Nor will the others be able to against the six big banks and foreign groups," says Cyr.

BCE also has a large stake in oil and gas through Encor Inc. and TransCanada PipeLines Limited, both of Calgary. The price outlook is bright, but even if it isn't, pipeline companies like TransCanada still make money moving bigger volumes of less expensive gas. Since gas prices plummeted in 1986, pipelines have been filled to capacity and profits are healthy. In fall 1989, BCE made a smart move and sold off a minority interest in Encor, dividing exploration from pipeline assets. It turned out that it added $600 million in additional market value to both because investors favor "pure plays." The division meant that TransCanada became a pure utility once again, and Encor an oil play.

"B.C. Mobil has turned out to be a great investment worth $1.5 billion or $5 a share underlying value which was not there three years ago," says Cyr. "Northern Telecom is doing well in terms of sales, however margins eroded and we rationalized some operations. It still has 50 per cent market share in switching equipment and is now getting into the new generation of transmission via microwave, fibre optics and cable."

The telephone business still represents 60 per cent of the bottom line, but the goal is to reduce that to half. There is little doubt that BCE's phone profits could be capped by partial, or even total, de-regulation. A decision by BCE's regulator, the Canadian Radio-Television and Telecommunications Commission forced BCE in early 1990 to rent long distance transmission at a discount to small wholesalers who repackage phone services for small businesses. Although only a tiny crack, it nonetheless marks a change in attitude by the Commission to open up the business more than before. It will take at least one year for hearings to determine whether to scrap the current cross-subsidization system whereby long-distance profits subsidize local residential use. The Americans scrapped most cross-subsidies in 1986 and precipitated an expected drop in long-distance charges and huge hikes in local fees. Rogers Communications Inc. in partnership with Canadian Pacific Limited are proposing a regulated duopoly, opening up long-distance competition to two players.

Whatever happens, BCE will retain its pre-eminence (one such duopoly exists in the private-lines commercial area and Rogers and Canadian Pacific have only a 10 per cent market share). Cyr and other telephone executives are going to argue, with success, that competition is a myth and will not help consumers. "In the U.S., there are fees in many states on each local call. In Georgia, for instance, a phone installation costs US$100 and you also need an electrician to wire your house. It only costs $30 here. Some local rates there are twice as expensive as here and some long-distance calls 30 per cent higher," says Cyr.

In anticipation of a partially successful attack by Rogers Communications and its partner, BCE positioned itself in late 1989 in Rogers' cable business by investing in Canada's second-largest cable operation, Groupe Videotron of Montreal. The two have also formed a partnership to start operations in several United Kingdom franchise areas. Videotron, featured later in this book, has developed an interesting cable system called "interactive television," which performs a number of functions for viewers, such as providing a dating service, restaurant listings, house listings and, eventually, banking services. BCE is also in the process of introducing to consumers its "Alex" system, a computer that will allow consumers the ability to access data banks, dating services, banking services and the yellow and white page listings. "Videotron's interactive television to me is similar to the Alex. It can do certain tricks. But we have faster software in Alex. Someday there may be mutual interest and I think we would be interested in Videotron if [Videotron chairman and founder André] Chagnon keeps his cable network up to snuff," says Cyr.

With a piggy bank like BCE has, why not? Cyr can buy the whole damn country eventually if he wants to.

Caveats: BCE is good ballast, or a base, for a portfolio because it moves in lockstep with the market increases. There is concern that BCE's bread-and-butter telephone business may be eroded through partial deregulation in Canada in the 1990s, that its BCE Development or Kinburn fiascos may worsen and that it may blow its brains out buying assets at hefty prices when a little patience would do the trick. It has not proven to be a particularly astute bargain-hunter in the past.

An investment of $10,000 in January 1980 was worth $21,642 in January 1990. With dividends reinvested, it totalled $32,979. Over the decade, prices ranged from a high of $45.63 to a low of $16.63, adjusting for splits.

BOMBARDIER INC.

Head Office: Montreal, Quebec
Incorporated: June 19, 1902
Ownership: Controlling shareholder
Les Entreprises de J. Armand Bombardier Ltée.

Revenues in 1989: $1,396,000,000
Net Income: $68,300,000
Earnings per share: $1.03
Employees: 12,200
Year End: January 31

In the beginning there was the Ski-Doo, an expensive toy created by a clever Quebec mechanic in the 1920s. Out of that idea sprang Quebec's first multinational heavy-manufacturing corporation, Bombardier Inc., which now produces subway cars, buses, trains, tramways, monorails, army jeeps, planes, military reconnaissance aircraft, water bombers, diesel engines, tails for 767s, motorcycles, autos and Challenger jets. The lion's share of its customers are governments, and Bombardier's talented chairman, Laurent Beaudoin, has shown an aptitude for the politics of business. His savvy has allowed Bombardier to capitalize on the privatization trend sweeping both Canada and the United Kingdom in order to launch Bombardier into the aerospace big leagues in just four years. Now 62 per cent of sales is aerospace, and it's growing.

Bombardier entered the aerospace field in 1985 with its $120-million purchase of Ottawa's profitable Canadair, maker of the Challenger jet, which cost taxpayers $1.5 billion to develop. Then Beaudoin signed a similar deal in 1989, buying the world's oldest aircraft manufacturer, Short Brothers PLC of Belfast, Northern Ireland, from the British government for $60 million. Britain agreed to write off $780 million of Short's debts and to invest another $720 million in loans, research grants and retraining programs. In April 1990, Bombardier also snagged a bargain when it bought Learjet Corp. assets out of bankruptcy for "only" US$75 million.

Bombardier's willingness to take over government enterprises is a cunning strategy. Short has been propped up by the British government for years because, with 7,000 workers, it is the largest employer in a country where unemployment has averaged 20 per cent. That is why Bombardier can look forward to future defence and plane contracts from the British government to help turn around the troubled firm. Similarly, Quebec and Ottawa aim to make Bombardier-Canadair a success. Just how far Ottawa was prepared to go to do this became evident in 1986 when it unleashed a firestorm of controversy by shamelessly choosing Canadair for its $1.4-billion CF18 military maintenance contract over a Winnipeg company with a lower bid. Like successful aerospace companies worldwide, Bombardier knows that it helps to have a sugar daddy or two, such as the Canadian and British governments.

All this global wheeling and dealing is amazing considering that in the mid-1970s, Bombardier was a smallish, troubled company with one product that was virtually obsolete in an era of meteoric oil price hikes. By the time the oil crisis came along, thanks to the cartel's gouging, the gas-guzzling Ski-Doo was threatened with going the way of the dodo bird. Ski-Doo sales fell from 226,000 units in 1971 to 110,000 in 1974, eventually hitting a rock bottom of 60,000. Beaudoin rescued the company by taking over its arch rival in Quebec and then diversifying in earnest.

Beaudoin had been in charge since 1964 after the death of the company's founder and his father-in-law, Joseph-Armand Bombardier. Bombardier tinkered with his *moto-neige* during the 1920s without knowing his name would become a brand name like Kleenex or Xerox. Beaudoin became the chosen heir, instead of any of Bombardier's five children, then took the company public in 1969 mostly as an estate planning move, to give them the ability to cash in their inheritances if they wished.

(Family members still belong to a voting trust that retains the right of first refusal over each member's stock. The family has been in the process of transferring the control block from a company to individuals in a complicated manoeuvre designed to avoid the "deemed disposition" and capital gains taxes in January 1993 I described in the introduction. This may not be possible, however.)

Beaudoin now oversees a worldwide empire with $2 billion in sales and 12,900 employees from his 17th-floor office in Montreal's Celanese Building. A former management consultant and chartered accountant from Quebec City, he's one of the most important Francophone businessmen in Quebec. He and his wife, the former Claire Bombardier, enjoy a 90-acre estate in the Eastern Townships. In his Mercedes 560, he travels on weekends from Montreal to the estate, where he plays tennis and fox-hunts. Handsome enough to be a matinée idol, Beaudoin has steered a steady, if speculative, course.

Its aggressive entry into the mass transit rail car business has been most profitable to date. Bombardier also got into this business through government connections and before Expo 67 in Montreal was invited by the Quebec government to tender for the construction of 423 cars for the city's French-designed subway. It won the $117-million contract and now has a 30-per cent market share of North America's $1-billion-a-year mass transit market. This market has been static during the 1980s as low energy prices removed the imperative to build mass transit systems. But in the 1990s, aging systems must be replaced in a number of cities, opening up new opportunities. Bombardier's competitors in this field are the Japanese and UTDC (a former Ontario crown corporation sold to Montreal engineering outfit, Lavalin Industries Inc.). Most of the American competitors have been snapped up by Bombardier; they bought Pullman Technology Inc. of Chicago in 1986 for $5 million, then the rail passenger car division of German-owned Budd Company for another $17 million, giving it exclusive right to the technology designs for the U.S. rail passenger line AMTRAK's 1,700 car fleet.

The biggest mass transit market is in Europe, where $4 billion is spent annually. To get at this business, Beaudoin took over French, Belgian and Austrian companies. "You have to be inside Europe to do business. This is paying off. We were able to get involved in the chunnel project and now Canary Wharf."

The beauty of mass transit contracts is that products are not designed and built on speculation, neither is there inventory to finance. The only up-front cost is the expense of tendering, which is sometimes as much as $300,000. Production occurs only if a contract wins and, presumably, winning bids include enough for a healthy profit. Theoretically, barring production problems or tendering mistakes, this is no-lose heavy manufacturing with few rivals.

Analysts generally like Bombardier, but their optimism ranges widely. Fred Schilling, with broker Nesbitt, Thomson Inc., thinks Bombardier could be worth $45 a share by 1994 based on earnings projections of $2 a share in 1992 and $4 in 1995. He thinks the Short deal is a "steal" and will reap a windfall. A more sceptical fan is Alison Ironside-Smith who was with Deacon Morgan McEwen Easson Limited in Toronto, who recommended buying only below $14 a share throughout most of the past year then selling when the stock is increasing in price. She cites lacklustre profits due to increased competition in all of Bombardier's marketing niches, fewer mass transit contracts in the short term and problems integrating and modernizing Short, while at the same time bringing more Catholics into its work force as part of a local affirmative action program.

Beaudoin is confident Short will turn around and estimates that by 1994 revenues will double to $4 billion annually and profits will more than double. "Almost all Short's contracts are losing money. We set aside a four-year acquisition reserve fund to cover losses in meeting contract obligations. Our goal is to make a profit before the four years is up."

Ireland is key to future success, but also important is Canadair's RJ (Regional Jet), a 50-seat commuter jet bigger than the nine-seat Challenger executive jet. The new entrant was put into production in 1989 after 56 orders were received. To be profitable, however, Beaudoin says 200 must eventually be sold into a market that, thanks to air deregulation, may need 1,000 such jets over the next ten years. With the market too small for a company like Boeing to enter, the competitors in this niche were Short and Brazil's Embraer. Obviously Short is sidelined and Embraer is years behind, unable to take orders on a completed product until 1992, when the first RJ will be delivered. The Brazilian jet will have only a five-foot, ten-inch ceiling compared with the RJ's six-foot, one-inch cabin height.

The Challenger continues to enjoy great success, with 200 sold and more on order. Bombardier churns out two $14-million planes per month, up from 16 per month when it took over in 1986. The aircraft is more comfortable and US$5 million cheaper than its arch rival made by Gulfstream. Facing a growing order book and limited facilities in Canada, Canadair plans to subcontract assembly and maintenance work to Short Brothers, where excess capacity exists.

"We are quite well-positioned and are recession proof," says Beaudoin. "Executive jet sales and snowmobiles are hurt in such a scenario but not our defence or airplane commuter businesses. We have long-term contracts for mass transit and defence and during recessions, governments put money into these areas."

The defence products are mostly maintenance and surveillance remote-control systems, which will continue to sell even during détente. Aerospace accounts more roughly for 62 per cent of revenues and is growing; mass transit, 25 per cent; and recreational products, 13 per cent. Pre-tax income was another story, and in 1989, mass transit contributed 43 per cent of profits; aerospace, 40 per cent; and recreational products, the rest.

Caveats: Challenger sales are sensitive to economic cycles, falling in business downturns. A continuing high Canadian dollar, compared to the U.S. dollar, is harmful because mass transit contracts are mostly south of the border and jets are paid for with U.S. dollars. Beware of any sustained jump in energy prices, which will hurt aircraft, Ski-Doo and Sea-Doo sales and stock prices even though it would create more mass transit projects. Big worry also is the IRA which has planted several bombs at Short Brothers because it mostly employs Protestants. Bombardier has pledged an aggressive affirmative action program and bolstered plant security.

An investment of $10,000 in January 1980 was worth $117,753 in January 1990. With dividends reinvested, it totalled $123,434. Over the decade prices ranged from a high of $18 to a low of 97 cents, adjusting for splits.

BRITISH COLUMBIA TELEPHONE COMPANY

Head Office: Burnaby, British Columbia
Incorporated: 1916
Ownership: Controlling shareholder
Anglo-Canadian Telephone of Montreal owned by General Telephone

Revenues in 1989: $1,689,600,000
Net Income: $181,000,000
Earnings per share: $1.62
Employees: 14,000
Year End: December 31

One of the unfortunate outcomes of concentration of power in Canada is the near disappearance of that traditional small-investor favorite, the utility stock, pure, solid and dividend-paying. True, there are a couple of dozen gas, hydro, phone and pipeline utilities around to buy, but most are part of a conglomerate or are a conglomerate. This means their income statements are muddied with the earnings, or losses, of other investments in everything from computer software outfits to real estate or printing. Gas utilities own oil companies and pipelines own gas utilities. It all makes for confusion, and the market does not reward confusion.

In the United States, by contrast, there are some 300 utilities that are "pure plays." This makes buying and selling choices easier. A pure gas utility's stock goes up when natural gas prices go down. A pure hydro utility's prices leap if interest rates plummet because its costs go down and dividends go up in relation to other money instruments. Proof that the market likes pure plays was the 1989 hike in Trans-Canada PipeLines Limited's stock price after it spun off its oil and gas subsidiary, Encor Inc.

Canada's near-pure utility play is British Columbia Telephone Company, which also happens to have a great deal more going for it. It is desirable because its franchise is in what promises to be the most buoyant region of Canada in the 1990s. This was not always the case. After leading the Canadian economy, postwar B.C. was clobbered by the recession of 1982 as the price of forestry products took a pummelling and interest payments on loans soared. But in 1989, net migration to B.C. was 48,000, one-third of whom were from offshore and the rest from other parts of Canada. This is nearly equivalent to the net immigration of 55,000 persons to the country as a whole that year. And it should continue because British Columbia is, without a doubt, one of the most desirable places to live in North America. It is scenic, virtually crime-free compared to U.S. cities and a favored destination for Hong Kong immigrants. In a volume-based business such as a phone monopoly, this is bullish news indeed.

"We're on a roll, and B.C.'s economic forecast is better than Canada's," says B.C. Tel's vice president of corporate finance, D. Barry McNeil. "The dollar has been coming down; the fact the province has a balanced budget makes for a good fundamental platform. As for our company, we have positioned ourselves well in technology and our common equity in our capital structure. Our credit rating is improved and so are earnings and volumes."

Like other utilities, stock prices track economic growth, which is why it makes sense to buy into a utility with a monopoly in the area with the biggest projected economic, or population, growth. Add to that the fact that phone companies everywhere are also benefitting from the explosion in the use of facsimiles and automatic teller machines. "New business for us was up 15 per cent in 1989 and of that, 39 per cent was facsimile. B.C. is a very buoyant economy and should be for some time," says B.C. Tel's president, Brian Canfield.

B.C. Tel is not quite a pure play. It has diversified but stuck to what it understands by a practice MBA professors call forward or backward integration. This happens when a company "diversifies" by purchasing a supplier (backward) or a customer (forward). Such diversifications are not ventures into unknown territory and are therefore less risky. That is why B.C. Tel's track record is better than most. It sticks to its knitting which is better than BCE Inc., with its real estate fiasco, BCE Development, written down in early 1990 to a negative value.

Only 5 per cent of B.C. Tel's investment is in its non-phone portfolio, but this yielded 10 per cent of revenues and 20 per cent of earnings on a per share basis. Internal estimates are that within five years it will account for 30 per cent of earnings. Among its non-phone holdings are a small Ontario telecommunications manufacturer; a software company; a telecommunications consulting firm; B.C.'s largest electrical contractor, who also does telecommunication, security and computer installations; an equipment-selling agency and cellular and mobile phone networks. Two small investments, of less than $1 million in total, did not work out well and were sold.

"We are also in leasing," says Lynn Patterson, B.C. Tel's executive vice president in charge of diversifications. "Back in 1982 when the market was deregulated for certain types of equipment, we realized that financing was an important tool for marketing such products. None of the banks had that financing in place. So we got into it. We already knew how to raise money for projects and went out and acquired the expertise to do the leasing. Then others came to us and so we moved into those other types of financing."

B.C. Tel and Québec Téléphone are both controlled by American-owned General Telephone & Electronics Corporation, nicknamed GTE. Both were bought in the 1950s and now GTE owns 50.6 per cent of B.C. Telephone and 55 per cent of Québec Téléphone. Parent company GTE is a giant with operations in 24 states and telephone monopolies in southern California and Hawaii. "We get the benefit of their expertise and they have only two of eleven board seats. They have been very good corporate citizens and very supportive," says Canfield.

An interesting speculation is whether GTE will ever be taken over. Sam Belzberg of Vancouver took a run in the mid-1980s and was paid off with "greenmail," in other words his 5 per cent of GTE stock was bought back by the company at a price that assured him a handsome profit. If another raider is successful, GTE may spin off its Canadian babies. However, this is unlikely.

Another looming challenge for all telephone companies in Canada is the one for long-distance business, a challenge that is to be made by the former CNCP partnership, now Rogers Communications Inc. and Canadian Pacific Limited. They will be asking the Canadian Radio-Television and Telecommunications Commission to grant them the chance to compete against the phone outfits. The phone companies are already preparing their case, arguing that competition means lower prices but an end to the subsidy of local service by long-distance rates. That is true. The price for long distance will drop but local service will jump in cost if long distance is opened up to competition.

B.C. Tel, Québec Tel and all the other telephone companies will be fighting this battle over the next few years. Some feel that at best, it may take until 1992 to resolve one way or the other. I doubt whether a decision will be made for years and I suspect the government and CRTC will allow CNCP into the lucrative long-distance business as they have allowed them in on private lines, or selling to large-volume business customers on private networks. This may affect volumes and, therefore, profits for phone outfits.

The point is, telecommunications is going to change dramatically, as will cable television, in the 1990s. And even though B.C. Tel is not a monolith with a massive research arm, it has the best single franchise area in Canada, which will insulate it from the erosion that may result with new long-distance competition. That is why B.C. Tel is a better buy as a pure phone play than the Bell Canada conglomerate or the small, publicly listed phone outfits such as its sister company Québec Tel, the Island Telephone Company Limited, Maritime Telegraph and Telephone Company, Limited, Newtel Enterprises Limited or Bruncor Inc. Competition will erode their earnings to a critically low point while B.C. Tel should thrive because of the growth in population on the west coast and its special access to innovations from its phone-giant parent, GTE.

Caveats: B.C. Tel's fortunes are linked to British Columbia's, which, in turn, are mostly linked to the forestry and mining industries but increasingly to tourism. A downturn in those areas will cause earnings to ebb, but this company is immune from losses.

An investment of $10,000 in January 1980 was worth $21,642 in January 1990. With dividends reinvested it totalled $31,391. Over the decade, prices ranged from a high of $29.88 to a low of $12.25, adjusting for splits.

CAE INDUSTRIES LTD.

Head Office: Toronto, Ontario
Incorporated: 1947
Ownership: Widely held

Revenues in 1989: $838,827,000
Net Income: $43,154,000(B.E.)/$42,755,000(A.E.)
Earnings per share: $0.56(B.E.)/$0.55(A.E.)
Employees: 12,000
Year End: March 31

(B.E. - before extraordinary items; A.E. - after extraordinary items)

David Race cannot enter part of a New York plant owned by CAE Industries Ltd. even though he is CAE's president and chief executive officer. That is because, as a Canadian, he cannot obtain top-level security clearance from the U.S. military, which uses CAE (an acronym for Canadian Aviation Electronics) to develop "black programs" or top-secret computer training courses. "CAE is cleared to top NATO standards and has security clearance in the U.S. for all our facilities," boasts Race. But only American citizens can achieve the highest level security clearance, so that this portion of CAE's business must be supervised by a special committee of CAE's board of directors, comprised of security-cleared Americans.

Black programs are straight out of James Bond, but most of CAE's business is considerably more mundane. Among other things, it is the world's largest manufacturer of airplane simulators, expensive machines used extensively in pilot training. CAE's ability to carve out such profitable niches has made it a stock-market darling for some time. Then in 1988, it doubled in size when it made a $665-million acquisition of Link, a U.S. defence contractor owned by the Singer Co. of Connecticut. Even though Link was involved in highly sensitive black programs and the like, Link's acquisition by foreign-owned CAE was blessed by the U.S. president as "in the national interest."

However, the stock tumbled in fall 1989 after CAE wrote down $10.5 million in anticipated losses from a handful of unprofitable contracts inherited from Link. Stock prices fell off from a high of $9.50 a share, even though the company stated no more writedowns were anticipated. But the market has been sceptical due to the spectacular failure of Robert Campeau, Canadian Tire, Dylex and others to pull off successful U.S. acquisitions. Another cloud is CAE's US$65-million claim against convicted financier Paul Bilzerian, now appealing a sentence connected with insider-trading offences. CAE claims that certain Link contracts were misrepresented, which led CAE to overpay by US$65 million. The market for defence stocks has also been lacklustre since the fall of the Iron Curtain. Others may regard Link as a continuing risk, but I do not. I would suggest that CAE's disfavor is a buying opportunity to those who like the company.

CAE executive headquarters are in Toronto's Royal Bank Plaza. There David Race and his executives pad around in a conservative, wood-panelled space, more law firm in decor than go-go high tech. That may be appropriate, although unplanned. CAE's largest individual shareholder (with 8 per cent) and chairman of the board is Fraser Elliott, the low-profile founding partner of Toronto law firm Stikeman, Elliott. Friendly and brilliant, but self-effacing, he is easily Canada's wealthiest lawyer. Another 12 per cent is owned by Quebec's Caisse de dépôt et placements du Québec.

Apart from those two stakes, CAE is widely held, which makes it a takeover candidate. Better yet, should a takeover occur, it has in place one of the fairest shareholder rights plans, which will force any bid for stock to be extended to all shareholders, thus avoiding a creeping, or slow, buy-out of stock. CAE is particularly vulnerable to a takeover by a large U.S. conglomerate in the defence field already. That is another reason I think it is an attractive company to invest in.

CAE is not all things to all investors. It is very much a specialized investment. It is also a paradox, poised to prosper from military cutbacks during the 1990s even though it does about half its business on behalf of military forces. Cutbacks translate into profits in two ways. Commercial airlines have traditionally relied on the military for a pool of trained pilot talent, but this number may decline. That means more money must be spent on pilot training. Added to that, both military air forces and airlines have been belt-tightening by using on-ground simulators, rather than costly training flights, to educate their pilots.

And that is where CAE comes in. By 1989, CAE had captured 62 per cent of the world's commercial flight simulator market and 40 per cent of the U.S. military simulator market. Simulators are gigantic mock cockpits that never leave the ground but imitate everything from gale-force winds to crash landings, complete with shaking and shimmying, in order to put pilots through their paces. Simulators are not standardized and must be designed anew to imitate each and every plane model. They are never built on spec, but only if a contract is obtained, thus enhancing profits. CAE also provides the complete training package, including classroom curriculum designed by its staff of psychiatrists, behavioral psychologists, scientists, aviation experts and professional educators.

CAE will also benefit from increasing air travel worldwide, lower fares and powerful pilot unions. "Pilots are no longer willing to turn out at 2 A.M. for training in one of our simulators," says Race. "We used to run simulators 20 hours a day, seven days a week but not any more. That means more simulators. Besides, it is now too costly to train a pilot in a real plane and you can't simulate accidents in a real plane. There's also increasing retirements among pilots, and shorter work hours for them. On the military side, we see two improving areas for us. Cutbacks on expenditures will mean cutbacks on training in actual planes and more training of pilots for commercial airlines with no military training at all."

Forecasts are that 7,000 new aircraft will be delivered by the year 2000 around the free world, and the rule of thumb is that for every 12 aircraft, one simulator is needed, creating a potential demand of 580. CAE took orders in 1989 for just 31 simulators and was happy. Simulators save airlines a bundle because a brief training flight in a 747 costs US$16,000 in fuel, but training in a CAE 747 simulator costs US$1,600 an hour.

With the Link acquisition, CAE has an open-ended contract to train pilots for the world's largest "airline," the U.S. Air Force with 730 aircraft. It also is contracted to work for the U.S. Navy, Canadian and British Armed Forces, NATO and NASA, training its astronauts on the intricacies of operating the Space Shuttle. Link gave CAE a huge foothold south of the border, the world's biggest aviation marketplace.

CAE is the largest supplier to NATO of submarine detection systems and is Canada's second largest aerospace firm (after Spar Aerospace); it designed the controls for Spar's Canadarm used in the NASA space program. It also does research into artificial intelligence and funded a chair in robotics at McGill University. There are also low-tech divisions making forest machinery, fibreglass tanks, railway equipment and aircraft repairs. CAE is highly decentralized and is, in effect, a conglomerate of engineers making a range of products and providing a number of services.

But it has also exited from certain fields. It briefly flirted with airplane manufacturing (it built the doors and fuselages for the L-1011). "Manufacturing is not for us. What we're good at is selling brainpower, not hardware. We turned out a good product but not a good return," says Race.

Indeed, CAE's 12,400 workers are a brainy bunch. More than half have university or university-equivalent education and CAE's research-oriented Montreal headquarters is populated by a sea of video screens on desks as hundreds of engineers and other professionals create products and services and widgets for the world. About 13 presidents run separate divisions quite autonomously with mandates to expand or to make acquisitions. CAE's philosophy is that if a division is not first in its niche, it should be sold. "We have five governing principles: get into a business with a domestic market as a springboard for world markets; diversify; decentralization; research (15 per cent of sales); a strong balance sheet and modern facilities,' says Race.

Caveats: To retain its pre-eminence, CAE must make money so it can invest heavily in research and development. The separation of Quebec from the rest of Canada would be disruptive and force the potentially expensive movement of personnel, particularly those involved in Canadian, NATO or U.S. military contracts, out of Quebec. CAE is also dependent upon a successful free trade arrangement with the U.S. and upon special security agreements with U.S. armed forces that must be renewed in a decade. There was concern in June 1990 that the company may have to make a large writedown of its U.S. purchase. Investors should hold off to see what unfolds.

An investment of $10,000 in January 1980 was worth $44,423 in January 1990. With dividends reinvested, it totalled $49,362. Over the decade prices ranged from a high of $15.50 to a low of $1.05 adjusting for splits.

CAMBRIDGE SHOPPING CENTRES LIMITED

Head Office: Toronto, Ontario
Incorporated: 1975
Ownership: Various institutions and management own 65 per cent

Revenues in 1989: $225,269,000
Net Income: $23,434,000
Earnings per share: $0.84
Employees: 1,100
Year End: March 31

The British tradition of strict and centralized town planning has created financial fiefdoms in Canada. Owners of those indoor esplanades lined with shops, known as malls, typically make more money than their retail tenants. That's because landlords charge retailers for the square footage they use and for the maintenance of common areas they share. Then they skim them for up to 6 per cent of their gross receipts. There is little variation in these levies because mall owners also can easily fend off smaller or less politically connected competitors. One example occurred in the early 1980s when the city council of Brampton, Ontario, approved a new regional mall to be built on its boundary with Etobicoke, but the project was successfully scuttled by Etobicoke politicians, developers and retailers. They took their case to court, and years later the highest court of appeal in planning matters, the provincial cabinet, nixed the mall.

By contrast, U.S. municipalities rarely answer to any higher planning authority. As a result, developers play one assessment-hungry town off against another with the result that there are few fiefdoms and mostly retail warfare. Such competition benefits consumers and retailers. Little wonder that Canadian mall rents are twice as high, on average, as those south of the border.

Of course, what is bad news for Canadian consumers and Canadian retailers is good news for Canadian mall owners. And some 45 per cent of the mall market has been carved up among three outfits, Cambridge Shopping Centres, Trilea (a joint venture between Trizec Corporation Ltd. and its 70 per cent owned Bramalea Limited) and the former Cadillac Fairview, now privately owned by U.S. pension funds. Only Cambridge is a pure shopping mall investment and is not in housing or industrial markets like the others. It owns some office space, but this is strictly "retail-driven," additional development designed to enhance the traffic attracted to the retail space.

Cambridge is a good developer and has grown quickly since 1980 when it was Oxford Development Group Inc.'s $150-million shopping-centre division. Now it has assets of $1.4 billion and owns 25 regional malls with a total floor area of 20 million square feet; 11 community and downtown centres with 16 million square feet; and eight office buildings with 358,000 square feet. It also has two mixed-use urban centres, one each in B.C. and Alberta, making another 2.15 million square feet. All are leased and managed by Cambridge, which developed 25 of the 36 centres.

Cambridge may have most of its eggs in the mall basket, but it is geographically diversified across Canada. However, the company wants to spread its wings into the United States and is actively scouting for reasonable prospects. This can be worrisome, considering how poorly many Canadians have fared south of the border. But Cambridge has traditionally been ultra-conservative and cautious. That is why, to me, it is a worthy investment vehicle, far more profitable than those retailers who rent its space. It has some knowledgeable fans, too. The Canadian National Railways Pension Fund owns 28 per cent of its stock and the Ontario Municipal Employees Retirement Fund has another 9 per cent; the Caisse de dépôt et placements du Québec has 6 per cent; management, 9 per cent; and six financial institutions (banks and insurers) another 26 per cent. The public float is only 35 per cent of the stock.

What is key about Cambridge is that its president, Lorne Braithwaite, is a retail man. He is relaxed and works genially with his chief financial officer, William Tinmouth. The two met me in Braithwaite's gigantic, marble-lined office in downtown Toronto. The foyer, with its hockey player sculpture and oils, is a handsome, glitzy developer's foyer, with expensive marble and top-drawer decor. Braithwaite looks like a bookish schoolteacher, but is a hard-nosed and personable tycoon.

Born in Alberta in 1941, he worked seven years for Eaton's of Canada Limited and three more as vice president of marketing for pre-fab manufacturer ATCO Ltd. before joining the former Oxford Development. Then in 1980 while he was president of Oxford's Cambridge Leaseholds, it was spun off in a $150-million leveraged buy-out with pension financing. Now it has $1.4-billion assets and minimal debt. It is also aggressive.

"Our operating cash flow, the measurement we like to apply to our company, has had a 37 per cent compound growth rate," says Braithwaite. "We are aggressive and have 855,000 square feet under development at the moment in urban areas and 2 million in shopping centres. Over the next two years, we will commence construction on another 500 million square feet. As for the U.S., it's a high risk and we want to buy a good company, with 5 to 15 million square feet. We're particular and have been looking for five years."

Such an acquisition might be the only way Cambridge can continue its expansion pace and growth rate. "It is getting difficult to reach targets beyond that, given our size. We are looking at massaging the retail we have at all times and are looking at other uses on adjoining mall lands. We're looking at public storage, infilling around sites, where we could put up cheap buildings where people in apartments could store boats or small businesses, equipment. In the U.S. there are 40 million square feet of this run as ma and pa operations. The Canadian market is 5 to 6 million square feet," says Braithwaite.

Braithwaite's marketing savvy inspired him to make unorthodox disclosures in an effort to overcome the traditional deep discount that stock markets attribute to real estate stocks. It is the only real estate company to publish an in-depth evaluation of all its properties, which others keep private in order to hide values from competitors or takeover artists. This may be why Cambridge enjoys a slightly higher cash flow multiple than others, an average of 15 times for more than 12 months. Even so, the company estimated in March 1989 that its break-up value was $46.20 a share and in 1990, $50. The stock has hovered around the $36 mark for many months.

Braithwaite's retail expertise has made him an enlightened landlord. Retail is not a them-versus-us scenario. "We lease carefully, looking for unique retailers that will bring something special to a mall. We buy out weaker tenants and put in strong ones. The average payback on this is 24 months and is an ongoing process. We can often help retailers and this has paid off. Look at the history. In 1982, during the worst recession, we only had to restructure ten leases chain-wide," says Braithwaite.

Little wonder then that Cambridge has attracted one of Canada's most successful anchors, Sears Canada Inc., as its joint venture partner in many developments or that it makes so much money. In 1985, Cambridge acquired for $223 million the real estate assets of financially struggling Woodwards Stores. Now worth $414 million, the assets were a bargain. Cambridge also invested a few million dollars in Woodwards' ailing retail operations to help its tenant revamp tired stores into competitive units. In return, Cambridge gets equity in Woodwards. This is a big and foolish gamble to some. But Braithwaite is unperturbed. It is investment in a big tenant and, after all, gambles are Cambridge's stock in trade. Small gambles, that is.

Caveats: Despite its astute caution in the past, Cambridge management's search for U.S. assets may end up a disaster as it has for so many Canadians. Its Woodwards' investment is risky and may sour, and the expected rationalization of Canadian retailing may hurt the bottom line even though Cambridge's malls are prime sites. Its stock has not performed that well because of its large institutional following, which means there's little loose stock available to buy even if something exciting happens.

An investment of $10,000 in January 1980 was worth $21,667 in January 1990. With dividends reinvested, it totalled $23,267. Over the decade, prices ranged from a high of $37.50 to a low of $12.13, adjusting for splits.

CAMPBELL SOUP COMPANY LTD.

Head Office: Toronto, Ontario
Incorporated: 1930
Ownership: Controlling shareholder Campbell Investment Co.

Revenues in 1989: $414,000,000
Net Income: $21,600,000(B.E.)/$17,493,000(A.E.)
Earnings per share: $1.46(B.E.)/$1.18(A.E.)
Employees: 2,800
Year End: July 30

(B.E. - before extraordinary items; A.E. - after extraordinary items)

It is tricky for Canadians to invest in the United States directly, now that potentially punitive death duties apply to foreign holdings. It is also tricky, in an era of freer trade, to invest in Canadian companies who may find themselves in head-to-head competition on both sides of the border with U.S. multinational monoliths. That is why investing in the publicly listed Canadian subsidiaries of successful American outfits with brand name products is a good free trade bet. These subsidiaries enjoy not only the spillover of U.S. media advertising but also the benefits of the parent company's research, marketing skills and managerial depth.

As well, under free trade, they enjoy a powerful new advantage over their Canadian rivals who may find they must enter the risky U.S. market as well as defend their markets at home. These Canadian subsidiaries and their investors – particularly in food processing – can enjoy the fruits of operating a relatively uncompetitive Canadian franchise while their Canadian competitors butt heads in the United States. These subsidiaries are also protected from new Yankee intruders as a result of two unintentional non-tariff barriers, Canada's expensive rules that require labels in both official languages and in metric.

Campbell Soup, like Coca-Cola Beverages, is a case in point. Campbell is one of the world's most recognized trademarks, its familiar red-and-white cans gaze at consumers from grocery store shelves coast to coast. The company was founded in the middle of the 19th century by produce merchant Joseph Campbell; he employed in 1897 a young chemist named John Dorrance who "invented" condensed canned soup. This was a revolutionary food process that, at an affordable price, liberated consumers from some of the drudgery of cooking. The Dorrance family owns more than 60 per cent of the parent company in Camden, New Jersey. The parent, in turn, owns 70 per cent of Campbell in Canada.

Campbell's Canadian subsidiary went public in March 1983 and, after a number of acquisitions, has become Canada's largest producer of soups. It makes prepared foods and distributes and packages frozen meat pies, baked goods, vinegar, apple juice and specialty foods and also services restaurants, hotels, institutions and governments. Its brand names include Habitant, Swanson dinners, Le Menu, Pepperidge Farm, Prego, V8, Gattuso, Franco-American, Bisto and Paxo. In 1989 it made more strategic acquisitions, buying a poultry transport company; Laura Secord; jam, marmalade and syrup makers in Quebec; and Gattuso marinated products. It also owns Quadelco Limited, the leading distributor of high-quality refrigerated delicatessen-style foods sold in supermarkets.

For the past six years, Campbell has been run in Canada by an ebullient Canadian marketing man named David Clark, who was born in 1939. Gregarious and jolly, he cheerfully greets visitors to Campbell's head office in the blue-collar Toronto neighborhood of New Toronto. Tight security greets visitors, due to some 2,000 product-tampering incidents a year, which victimize food processors but which never hit headlines.

Clark's office is dominated by an immaculate L-shaped desk. A trash can in the shape of a Campbell's soup can is in one corner, as are soup mugs and a drawing of the famous cherub. It is a big office and overlooks a school. Beside this plant is another occupied by Continental Can, which Campbell, ironically, does not buy from because it can get cans more cheaply elsewhere. Instead, it sells spare steam heat to Continental Can.

Clark was enticed in 1983 away from rival soup-maker Thomas J.

Lipton Inc., owned by Britain's Unilever. Clark got the job by accident but is a well-plugged-in chief executive officer, chairman and
president, and has steered Campbell profitably through the shoals of
Canadian consumer choices. A country is what it eats. By choosing a
Canadian marketing man, sensitive to the differences in eating habits
between the two countries, Campbell pulled off a coup. "Food is one
of the most culturally influenced decisions anyone makes and yet
elsewhere the attitude at Campbell has been it's the Campbell way or
no way," he says.

Clark says cultural differences are subtle, but to ignore them can
erase a bottom line. Canadians, for instance, buy 40 per cent less
frozen convenience food than do Americans. This is partly because
there is less freezer capacity in the average Canadian store and
Canadian home than in the United States, but also because Canadians
are more health conscious. Whether it is tomato or chicken noodle
soup or a can of pork and beans, recipes for Canadian consumers use
considerably less salt. Canadians live longer than Americans.

Campbell is also on top of trends such as the wholesale switch to
convenience and microwavable food. With the alacrity of the marketing man that he is, Clark rhymes off the statistics. "The number of
one-person households has doubled in 15 years and now represents 25
per cent of all households. The fastest growing part of the population
is the over-50s and half of Canadian homes have a microwave and
seven out of ten will by 1991. Limited users among microwave oven
owners represent 26 per cent; active-lifestyle users, 9 per cent; lazy
users, 23 per cent; and serious users, 42 per cent."

Clark's goal is to make Campbell "the best food company in Canada
with the shortest 'gate to plate' cycle in the business." He is referring
to the period of time it takes from harvesting the ingredients to
preparing, freezing, selling and eating after a reasonable time in a
home freezer. Right now, in the case of a Swanson frozen dinner, the
duration is 20 weeks and he aims to slash this to one-third or only
seven weeks. To do this, manufacturing is being concentrated to
become more efficient.

Free trade is positive in the long run for Campbell because it, along
with GATT, will eventually undermine the supply management
board system in Canada that restricts not only the quantity that food
processors like Campbell Soup can buy from outside Canada but also

the price they pay for it. Here, quotas keep prices artificially high and keep imports out. But in 1989, GATT condemned curbs against U.S. yogurt and ice-cream exports; the condemnation will undermine protection for milk, which costs 50 per cent more in Canada. Since yogurt and ice cream are made from milk, they must be protected too or be undercut by cheaper U.S. imports. "I think we will have a two-price system, one for food processors which will be lower than that paid by consumers. We're not worried in the least and source [buy] most of our ingredients here in Canada where prices are comparable anyway," he says.

Free trade is costly to Campbell in the short term. It is closing operations in Manitoba and Quebec and will invest $40 million in a bigger, better plant in Toronto. "We are now 25 per cent less efficient than the most efficient U.S. plant, but with added volumes in 1991 we will be within 3 per cent of the most efficient plant in North America and our plant will serve the whole Canadian market and part of the New York, Chicago and Washington, D.C., triangle too."

Caveats: The stock has been trading higher than earnings would dictate on the speculation that the Canadian subsidiary may be privatized and bought out by the U.S. parent. The U.S. parent is also the subject of takeover speculation now that a dozen or so members of the Dorrance family have opted out of the family voting trust. Privatization would benefit Canadian investors, but a leveraged buy-out in the United States could rob margins if the new owner hiked its royalty, trademark and management fees. Growth in the mature food industry is slow, due to slow, or no, population growth. Expect to see a fight for market share in the future.

An investment of $10,000 in January 1980 was worth $30,000 in January 1990. With dividends reinvested it totalled $32,606. Over the decade prices ranged from a high of $26 to a low of $6.38, adjusting for splits.

CANADIAN IMPERIAL
BANK OF COMMERCE

Head Office: Toronto, Ontario
Incorporated: 1961
Ownership: Widely held

Interest Income in 1989: $2,937,000,000
Net Income: $450,000,000
Earnings per share: $2.28
Employees: 36,000
Year End: October 31

The first thing that struck me years ago as an immigrant to Canada was how a few banking chains seemed to be as commonplace as McDonald's. Virtually all Canadian intersections had a bank branch on each corner. Even in Toronto, the country's financial capital, bank towers dominated the skyline. They still do. Canada was, and remains, a nation of bankers, in great part because Canada was, and is, a nation of savers. The result is that Canada has created a handful of profitable, well-managed, global banking giants.

Frankly, there is not a bad one among the big six Canadian chartered banks. Each is a worthy investment, certainly better for a number of unique reasons than are investments in most of the world's large banks. Three stand out, to my mind: the Toronto-Dominion Bank, the Royal Bank of Canada and Canadian Imperial Bank of Commerce, each for differing reasons. They can provide their investors with a long-term, safe and profitable stake in our economy. They are Canada's best banking bets.

Apart from the endorsement of Canada's darling, singing star Anne Murray, not a lot went right for this bank in the early 1980s. The Canadian Imperial Bank of Commerce found its stock, and its following, dogged by such financially troubled Companies as Massey-Ferguson Limited (now Varity Corporation), Dome Petroleum Limited, Turbo Resources Limited and dozens more. Most of these companies were eventually "worked out" but, while the trouble lasted, the Commerce received the brunt of the bad publicity because it was lead lender and head negotiator involved in the Turbo mess, as well as with Massey and Dome's high-profile government bail-outs. Since then, and partially as a result of those negatives, the entire upper echelon and structure of the bank has altered. Now, like its rivals the Royal Bank of Canada and the Toronto-Dominion Bank, it offers investors an even safer and more solid investment opportunity than before. "The I.Q. at the Commerce is just as high as it is at the Toronto-Dominion [Bank]," says Hugh Brown, respected bank analyst with Toronto broker Burns Fry Ltd. "It has turned around nicely."

One of the best things that happened to the bank was the appointment of Donald Fullerton as chairman of the bank. Even though he was a "lifer" and involved in the former executive team at the bank that was blamed for so many high-profile lending mistakes, he brought a uniquely aloof view for an insider, partly because of his personality and partly due to the senior jobs he had held along the way. Back in 1983, Fullerton was one of the top four executives of the bank and was asked to pull together a major "strategy plan." This task took him around the world. "It was not difficult to identify weaknesses, and the board approved a plan. One of the elements was to narrow the span of control enough so that objectives could be attained. Before, everything funnelled through the top and there were bottlenecks," says Fullerton.

Fullerton ended up implementing his own plan and lopped off huge portions of the bank's operations, trimming products offered in regions such as Europe and beefing up others at home. He cashed in or wrote off all the bank's troublesome loans to lesser developed countries (LDCs). He also restructured the executive branch of the bank and created what he calls a "president organization with global business units." Beneath his chairmanship, four presidents have been delegated a great deal of authority to deal in their areas. This was done to attract and keep talent, including non-bankers, which is unusual at Canadian banks because they rarely recruit outside bank circles, and to create a group of presidents from which an heir can be chosen. Every morning at 8:30, Fullerton and his presidents meet to discuss their units and plans with appropriate support staff. By all accounts, the group works well together even though personalities are very different.

The man at the top, Fullerton, began with the Commerce as a mail clerk in 1953. Born in Vancouver in 1932, he is a contemporary of his counterparts at the T-D Bank and Royal Bank. He is, like the others, a no-nonsense banker. He also serves on the boards of IBM Canada Limited, North American Life Assurance Co., Amoco Canada Petroleum Co. Ltd., the Dominion Realty Co. Ltd. and on the Financial Post Corp. advisory board, as I do. In board meetings, he shows his true colors. He's built like a linebacker. He does not talk very much but, when he does, he speaks unequivocally, stating his case with the brevity and clarity of a headline writer.

That is why his spartan offices on the Commerce Court West fifth floor are not surprising. A guard behind a desk greets visitors. The only wall decoration is two woven wall hangings, and visitors sit on mustard wing-back chairs that look as though they came off the set of "I Love Lucy." The Commerce's executive headquarters are the antithesis of flamboyance – appropriate for a group handling other people's money carefully.

Unlike in other banks, Fullerton employs top executives from outside his bank. "There is not a number-two man in this bank but four presidents, all capable of stepping into this job if a truck hits me tomorrow," he says proudly. The four include Commerce veterans Al Flood and Warren Moysey. Non-veterans include Paul Cantor, president of the bank's investment banking operations (which includes Wood Gundy Inc. and its 1990 acquisition of the retail arm of Merrill Lynch Canada Inc.). Cantor worked for the federal department of finance and Polysar Inc., among others, but was recruited to the Commerce ten years ago. Another president is Ian Ronald, a retailing executive formerly from Zellers Inc. and Markborough Properties Ltd. Other key executives were recruited from Cadillac Fairview Corp. Ltd. and RJR Nabisco Limited.

"The T-D has enjoyed excellent performance and has every reason to be proud. You look at this bank and our performance record is not so good. But there has been steady upward movement and we're confident there will continue to be an improvement in our performance," he says. "Ten years from now, I'd like to see a fairly well-integrated component operating in North America. No question. Canadian banking strength has been in the Canadian sector. Our strength is our national network and its strong base of personal support. We have 6 million customers."

The Commerce is also proud of its worldwide operations. "We are number one among Canadian banks in Hong Kong and Singapore. Gundy's the only major Canadian dealer in Japan and is well positioned in Europe and the Far East."

The Commerce also has a unique relationship with Hong Kong's richest citizen, Li Ka-Shing, now a Canadian citizen who commutes between his island mansion and Canada where he owns, among other assets, the Expo lands in Vancouver, Husky Oil Ltd. and the Harbor Castle Hilton Hotel in Toronto. "That relationship began 17 years ago with a handshake between Mr. Li and Russell Harrison (Fullerton's predecessor). Canadian Eastern Finance is CIBC's company there and is in real estate, investment banking and merchant banking. It shares with Li Chung Kong, a public company listed there in real estate and venture capital," says Fullerton.

The Commerce is actively looking at potential U.S. acquisitions such as banks or thrifts (savings and loans that are similar to our trust companies) but is going to be very cautious because deregulation there has created uncertainties and problems for thrifts. Its current U.S. operation is small and focused on communications, real estate, utilities and oil and gas. Each branch office specializes in one or two sectors.

Similarly if deregulation is allowed in Canada, Fullerton said the Commerce will consider buying into the trust and insurance company business. "The trust business may offer opportunities but insurance we will not bother with if there is no power permission to distribute insurance. We are not rushing to get in. Doing it right is more important than just doing it. That is our overall strategy in North America."

Caveats: Bank stocks are cyclical. Prices fall during higher interest-rate periods and rise along with rate declines. Longer term holds are advisable. Risks include revisions to rules governing financial institutions in both Canada and the United States; these revisions may lead some banks to make unwise acquisitions or may open up the Commerce and others to more competition in the lucrative corporation lending side from trust or insurance outfits. But the Commerce, under Fullerton, is very cautious, which is good.

An investment of $10,000 in January 1980 was worth $25,392 in January 1990. With dividends reinvested, it totalled 39,940. Over the decade prices ranged from a high of $33.63 to a low of $8.13, adjusting for splits.

CANADIAN PACIFIC LIMITED

Head Office: Montreal, Quebec
Incorporated: 1881
Ownership: Widely held

Revenues in 1989: $11,020,200,000
Net Income: $745,200,000
Earnings per share: $2.35
Employees: 75,500
Year End: December 31

Canada left Third World status when the tiny federal government nearly went bust by providing loan guarantees to build the Canadian Pacific Railway. That east-west ribbon of steel opened up the hinterland and ushered in nationhood, but in return Ottawa gave away enormous land grants in the form of easements along rights-of-way. That land bank, the size of half of Nova Scotia, formed the basis for the creation of one of Canada's largest conglomerates, Canadian Pacific Limited, with $18 billion in assets, $11 billion in revenues and profits of $15 million a week.

William Stinson is Canadian Pacific's current chairman, president and chief executive officer, a "lifer" with the company who started off washing rail cars during summers off school. After graduating from the University of Toronto he joined the firm permanently in 1950, has filled most of the important positions and has been a prime booster of its prospects ever since. Canadian Pacific is a management company, a combination of wholly owned and partially owned divisions. The railway, mining assets and hotels are captive subsidiaries, and dozens more are controlled with varying stakes. Canadian Pacific's head office employs only ten key people; they function as the group's central bank and policy advisor. Stinson and two vice presidents sit on the various boards of the companies. A third vice president is in Europe looking for acquisitions. They also manage Canadian Pacific's $4-billion railway pension fund.

Typically, such management companies trade at a discount to asset value unless companies are spun off to the public partially. When that happens, the value is there for all to see. For that reason, Canadian Pacific embarked on a new strategy to enhance shareholder value in 1989 by distributing to all shareholders 80 per cent of the stock in its Marathon Realty division, then scuttled the deal after an adverse court decision. This distribution was designed to trim the sails and to address the management company malaise that occurs when wholly owned divisions are undervalued unless their stock trades separately.

Canadian Pacific has been repositioning itself in businesses with a future while jettisoning others considered surplus such as Canadian Pacific Air Lines, Maple Leaf Mills Limited, Cominco Ltd., Algoma Steel Corp. Ltd. and Steep Rock Resources Inc. Its latest investments have been in waste-management and school-bus conglomerate Laidlaw Inc., which in turn owns British conglomerate, ADT Inc., a security and auctioneering play. It has also undertaken a potentially risky partnership in telecommunications with the visionary and risk-taking Ted Rogers.

"We have no current plans to spin off more assets, but we feel CP is a collection of businesses all in strong competitive positions," says Stinson. "And we are well-positioned in waste management and telecommunications, two of the biggest growth areas in the 1990s. The strength of this company has been in oil, gas and forestry where it has been pre-eminent since 1881 and, to my mind, is as dynamic now as it was then."

Ted Rogers and his Rogers Communications Inc. replaced Canadian National Railways as 40-per cent owner of the tired old telex network, CNCP, which was destroyed by the explosion in facsimile transmission via phone lines. Canadian Pacific and Rogers hope to get into the long-distance telephone business against Bell Canada Enterprises by expanding upon CNCP's existing nationwide network of fibre-optic and microwave transmission facilities. If competition is opened up, CNCP could offer a package of cellular phone and cable services too. It is undoubtedly due to Canadian Pacific's partnership with Rogers that Bell Canada is cozying up to Groupe Videotron, with its cable and interactive-computerized television concept.

Both are to square off at hearings in 1990 and 1991 into this issue of long distance before the Canadian Radio-Television and Telecommunications Commission. "We are positioned to be another MCI [a U.S. long-distance service created after deregulation]. We think there will be deregulation in two years," says Stinson.

Interestingly, Canadian Pacific may have created Canada as we know it, but it was British-controlled until the Second World War when U.S. investors obtained most of its shares. Since then it has been gradually repatriated, thanks to large-scale institutional interest at home by pension plans and mutual funds. Ironically, however, more foreign participation is wanted, primarily to raise the conglomerate's profile and to enhance shareholder values. The largest shareholder is Quebec's Caisse de dépôt et placements du Québec with 5 per cent of the stock. "After the National Energy Program, which hammered us, the U.S. ownership left. But we are on the New York and London Stock exchanges and are 65 per cent Canadian-owned, 35 per cent U.S. and 5 per cent European. We want to get that up and we're happy that now eight or ten U.S. railway analysts and others are following the company," says Stinson.

The Marathon spinoff gained a great deal of attention in 1990 as did a stock jump, rumors of an impending foreign takeover and also AMCA International's turnaround. CP owns 51 per cent of AMCA, which announced record earnings in 1989. "AMCA reshaped and sold off assets. We gave Processed Minerals Incorporated to Fording Coal to run with $23 million in revenues and $7 million in profits. It has the world's largest deposit of an asbestos substitute called wollastonite. AMCA is in three businesses: BOMAG in Germany which has 40 per cent of the world market in compacters used in waste sites and highway construction; Cherry Burrell, which makes dairy and food processing equipment; plus a prefab warehouse business with the leading market share in the U.S. All are strong businesses."

Besides Marathon with its $4 billion in real estate, CP owns 100 per cent of a hotel chain that includes some of the country's best known landmarks: Le Château Frontenac, Banff Springs, Chateau Lake Louise, Jasper Park Lodge, Le Château Montebello, Chateau Whistler Resort, The Algonquin in St. Andrews-by-the-Sea, Victoria's The Empress, the Royal York Hotel and the Deerhurst Inn. The

Whistler, in British Columbia, was built for $70 million and, only weeks after its completion, 80 per cent of the hotel was bought by Japanese interests for $80 million plus a 15-year management contract. Some hotels, such as Banff and Jasper, are almost priceless.

Forestry and mining are also important components and are really what's known as a backward integration designed to enhance the railway's operations. Forestry and coal mining use rail transportation and through ownership are captive customers. And both are good operations. Canadian Pacific's wholly owned Fording Coal mines have made money during the 1980s when most others were hit hard by a worldwide drop in demand and prices for metallurgical and thermal coal. Fording's success is partly because it is the world's third-lowest-cost producer and also because Canadian Pacific reduced its dependence upon the ruthless Japanese, who have beaten down the price, by pruning Japanese sales to 30 per cent from 100 per cent of revenues.

Canadian Pacific Forest Products Limited is the result of a merger between two forestry companies that Canadian Pacific owned. Now Canadian Pacific owns 80 per cent of this forestry giant which makes Facelle tissues, among other products. CP Forest is now Canada's third-largest forestry outfit with $3 billion in sales, behind Abitibi-Price Inc. with $3.3 billion and Noranda's two companies, Noranda Forest Inc. and MacMillan Bloedel Limited, with combined sales of $7.9 billion. The current outlook for all forestry companies is pretty grim as the forestry cycle heads downward.

But counteracting that is Canadian Pacific's wonderful, debt-free oil giant, PanCanadian Petroleum Limited of Calgary, with the biggest land spread of any privately owned oil company on earth. Its 8 million acres of subsurface mineral rights along old rail easements make its land bank the size of some members of the United Nations and considerably bigger than Prince Edward Island. Canadian Pacific owns 87 per cent of PanCanadian, one of western Canada's most aggressive explorers. And PanCanadian is as safe as a bank, with $2.35 billion in assets and less than $100 million in debts, half the amount of profit it rings up annually. Speculation has long swirled around this company that it might be privatized by its parent but that's unlikely. Some feel, however, that PanCanadian is too conservatively managed and could leverage itself greatly and earn more in the long haul by snapping up for a song some of the tens of billions of dollars of oil and gas assets on sale.

Such interests in forestry, mining and petroleum products help CP Rail prosper. What will help even more will be the planned privatization of the now-profitable Canadian National Railways, not likely until the mid-1990s. The pruning of VIA Rail has had virtually no impact because CP Rail was not getting much income by renting lines to it. Stinson thinks CP Rail needs to be better positioned under free trade, which is why it bid, unsuccessfully, for a large U.S. railway and is hunting another. "We folded in the Soo Line and took out minority shareholders to get permanent access to Chicago. We tried to bid for another in Delaware but failed. We want more railway access," he says.

Some feel that Canadian Pacific's 53-per cent interest in the voting stock of Laidlaw Inc. is its greatest asset. Laidlaw is indeed a great company, but is such a small portion of the overall portfolio of this conglomerate that I consider it elsewhere in this book as a separate case also worthy of investor consideration. Laidlaw, in partnership with CP Forest, also hopes to cash in on environmental concerns and will build two newsprint recycling and de-inking plants, one in each of Quebec and Ontario. There are other connections too numerous to mention between its many affiliated companies.

"Canadian Pacific is an asset play and over time investors should be in it. You can't afford not to be there. It is a slice of Canada with a wealth of assets," says Harold Wolkin, management company analyst with Nesbitt, Thomson Inc. "It is better to be in management companies than mutual funds. If the gap in earnings performance widens enough, shareholders will get break-up values."

To me the bottom line is that Canadian Pacific is, like BCE Inc., impossible for investors to ignore. Both provide great ballast and represent an investment in Canada itself. Unlike BCE Inc., which committed a major blunder with BCE Development Corp. and a $600-million writedown in 1990, Canadian Pacific has been more ably and conservatively managed. That is no small achievement in an era of leveraged buy-outs and escapades by gamblers such as Dome Petroleum's Jack Gallagher or Robert Campeau. Boring old Canadian Pacific is a pretty good bet, all things considered.

Caveats: This is not a get-rich-quick stock, but a solid play on our country. Canadian Pacific shares tend to track the economy in general.

An investment of $10,000 in January 1980 was worth $19,586 in January 1990. If dividends were reinvested, it totalled $23,927. Over the decade prices ranged from a high of $30.25 to a low of $11.50, adjusting for splits.

CANADIAN TIRE CORPORATION, LIMITED

Head Office: Toronto, Ontario
Incorporated: 1927
Ownership: Controlling shareholders
D.G. Billes, A.W. Billes & Martha G. Billes

Revenues in 1989: $2,956,842,000
Net Income: $149,616,000
Earnings per share $1.65
Employees: 25,000
Year End: January 2

Most Saturdays I am a Canadian Tire widow. My husband disappears for an hour or two into one of those familiar, free-standing Canadian Tire stores that are always hopping busy despite a generally lacklustre retailing scene. His dresser is piled high with Canadian Tire money, which is carefully saved but rarely cashed. Canadian Tire catalogues, more popular when home renovations are underway, dot our living-room landscape. Although he may be a trifle unusual, ask yourself: Can you name one able-bodied, handy, home-owning male in Canada who does not know where the nearest Canadian Tire store is?

I rest my case. This company has carved out a brilliant franchise that rings up $48 million in weekly sales, rain or shine, recession or rebound. Its sales have grown steadily while retail sales have generally slumped. Its sales increased in all regions, even those experiencing slow, or no, growth due to high interest rates or plummeting commodity prices. That's because it sells items that people need, recession or not. When times are tough, do-it-yourselfers go to Canadian Tire for materials. When times are good, they go there still.

Canadian Tire has been a tremendous growth stock and a good defensive stock during downturns. There was one lapse, due to a disastrous foray into U.S. retail, which led Canadian Tire to hire an

American-born chief executive officer to take them south profitably. Ironically, Tire president Dean Groussman thinks Canada affords the greatest opportunities for expansion, and by 1994 he will have put roughly $2 billion where his mouth is. And, oh, how the money will roll in. "Canada's the best kept secret in North America," he says.

Canadian Tire's modest head office is blocks away from the site of its original store on Toronto's Yonge Street, where funny money was handed out and clerks on roller skates fetched products for customers. It was an eccentric retailer in the 1960s, but is much imitated now, after having grown coast to coast into a vast network of 408 stores, as well as a chain of 165 gasoline stations. About 372 of those stores are owned by dealer-franchisees who invest $450,000 these days to buy their first, small-town franchise. It is significant that only one dealership in the company's history has ever closed and that was following a fire that destroyed a marginally profitable store in a remote Newfoundland region.

"Tire went to the U.S. because everyone thought this was a mature company here in Canada. I came here with a lot of people telling me that, so we looked for acquisitions as a way to expand," says Groussman, who left a top position with profitable Zale Corp. in Texas for this position. "Fortunately, we didn't find any acquisitions that looked like they made any sense. So we analyzed our market and all the evidence pointed to the fact that this business was not mature."

In 1987, when Groussman took over, Canadian Tire's retail space was growing by 1.25 per cent annually, one of the lowest growth rates among major retailers. Expansion and modernization of existing operations to allow better display and better traffic flows inside stores started in 1988 and sales jumped dramatically whenever this was completed. In August 1989, Tire's board of directors looked at the figures of sales increases, projections as to potential by independent consultants and approved Groussman's plan to spend up to $2 billion over five years.

"We are looking at multilevel stores, better land use, more variety of products, better display areas, $243 million in gasoline chain expansions and we might add 40 stores in the next five years," he says. Groussman, a confident and competitive executive with a brilliant track record in the United States estimates Canadian Tire in 1994 will have doubled its sales to a staggering $5 billion annually, bigger than Hudson's Bay Company or Sears Canada Inc.

Canadian Tire was the brainchild of two mechanic brothers, John and Alfred Billes, who sold automotive parts out of their repair garage directly to the public. Part of the secret of its success is that it has spread into other areas and is now attracting women and children to its stores, to buy housewares, sporting goods, toys and garden implements.

"I like Tire. It's a proven concept – competitors from every quarter – but nobody can beat it," says Marty Kaufman, a well-respected brewery and retail analyst with broker Nesbitt, Thomson Inc. in Montreal. "It is recession-proof and the upside is getting women involved by diversifying products. It has room for growth compared to department or fashion or food stores. It will also benefit from the increase in autos and the fact that people cannot postpone repairs, recession or not."

Another upside potential is Groussman's commitment to the gasoline and car-servicing business. Currently about 20 per cent of revenues and a smaller portion of profits, the gasoline game will be more profitable in the 1990s now that Ottawa has allowed Imperial Oil Limited to take over Texaco Canada Inc., a merger of the third-largest retailers. The company plans to add 22 new gasoline stations to its chain of 165 outlets located at store sites and may expand into off-site locations. It is also experimenting with a scaled-down Tire store attached to gasoline and automotive services. "In London we have 5,000 square feet of retail called Auto Plus with four service bays, gasoline and a quick lube. We're going to do a few locations in the north central U.S.," says Groussman.

Despite its track record and ambitious plans, Canadian Tire stock continues to trade at a discounted multiple relative to many other merchandising companies. Kaufman thinks this is due to the misconception that it's a mature retailer with little room to grow. But Tire is already proving that untrue, with the modernizations it has already completed. And the market still doesn't reward its hidden real estate value of some $540 million.

The company's reputation was also blackened after it took a $250-million bath in the United States when it bought a poorly positioned retail operation that couldn't be turned around. That was followed by a public squabble among the three Billes family heirs over a share transaction that gave control of the voting stock to the Canadian Tire dealers. Now the Billeses and the dealers share voting control as part of an agreement until the mid-1990s, thus eliminating the possibility that dealers could get control and drop wholesale prices to themselves at the expense of corporate profits for the rest of shareholders. Even though the dealers are held at bay, it still remains offensive that the three Billeses, who didn't build the company, control it with just 3.5 per cent of the equity dollars. But like it or not, Canadian Tire is too good an investment to ignore.

Caveats: Billes family and dealer squabbles appear to be buried but may loom again as dealers may balk at the company's expensive modernization costs, much of which they must bear. An acquisition in the United States would also be bearish, and a lengthy recession would harm stock prices even though the company is virtually recession-resistant. This is not a company for those who disdain non-voting, or restricted shares, even though there are coattail provisions protecting minority shareholders. Only 10 per cent of common shares, with votes, is available for public purchase.

An investment of $10,000 in A shares in January 1980 was worth $44,907 in January 1990. If dividends were reinvested, it totalled $48,556. Over the decade prices ranged from a high of $69 to a low of $4.60, adjusting for splits.

CARA OPERATIONS LIMITED

Head Office: Toronto, Ontario
Incorporated: 1961
Ownership: Controlling shareholders are Phelan family trusts

Revenues in 1989: $308,346,000
Net Income: $32,272,000
Earnings per share: $0.86
Employees: 20,000
Year End: April 2

While families like the Bronfmans and Reichmanns capture headlines with their every corporate twist and turn, a relatively unknown family group is responsible for starting and sustaining two of Canada's most successful enterprises. Both are unique Canadian success stories, both are old Toronto money that has been invested in creating two worthy investment vehicles with excellent managements, bullet-proof balance sheets and splendid future prospects. They are Cara Operations Limited and Scott's Hospitality Inc. which may one day be merged, that is if Paul J. Phelan has anything to say about it. A chapter on Scott's follows later.

Paul Phelan runs his food-service empire, Cara Operations Limited, in a friendly house hidden behind a Swiss Chalet and a Harvey's on Toronto's fashionable Bloor Street West. A narrow walk-way between restaurants leads to a wrought-iron gateway and a tiny courtyard. This is the only head office in Canada that smells like barbecued chicken. Inside, visitors walk on a melon carpet and view a collection of handsome portraits of former Cara presidents. Lining one wall is a glass case filled with impressive silver sailing trophies.

Commodore Phelan greets his visitors in a huge, comfortable office that resembles a Rosedale sitting room more than a tycoon's lair. He commands a ship that is more than a century old and without a mortgage of any consequence. The ship is Cara Operations, but the trophies are Phelan's. When he is not steering Cara's varied operations, he is setting sail somewhere as the well-known and generous patron of a number of Canada's entries into the America's Cup.

Homespun and with a twinkle in his blue eyes, Phelan is clearly to the manor born, a man thoroughly satisfied with his life, his family and his accomplishments. Yet he is also imbued with the modesty of the good steward who inherited great advantage and took it to even greater heights.

"In 1962, I bought out 50 of my relatives, settling their estates by giving them half cash and debentures earning the same interest they would have gotten in dividends. I asked five of my executives to become my allies and gave them stock. It's nice to know they're all millionaires," he says. "I own the business and have 57 per cent of the voting shares and 37 per cent non-voting control. The family – and by that I mean my four children and 12 grandchildren – function through Cara Holdings Limited, but as an ex-squadron leader and commodore I know there has to be a commander. I'm that. My son is vice chairman of the company and chairman of the executive committee. I worry about my son because I'm not going to retire. I'm now 73 and, God willing, I'll be around for quite a little while. He says, 'Don't worry, dad, hang in there and when ready I'll take over.' He sails with me. We're great pals."

Cara was launched six generations ago in 1883 by Thomas Phelan, and by the end of the century it was prospering as the caterer on steamships and the country's fledgling railway. Now it is Canada's largest food service company; its work force of 17,500 makes 56,000 meals daily in 12 massive flight kitchens and some 400 restaurants. Cara's chains are Wellington's Lounge, Hershel's Deli, Swiss Chalet, Harvey's and Steak & Burger. It also owns the 200-room The Days Inn in Toronto and operates railway and airport gift stands, tobacconists, stationers Grand & Toy Limited, newsstands and a small chain of upmarket craft shops.

Beside Phelan's Forest Hill mansion is the museum-like chateau owned by his brother-in-law, his wife's brother George Gardiner, a brilliant stockbroker and founder of Scott's Hospitality Inc. Phelan's wife, Helen, owns about 12 per cent of Scott's shares. She sits on the Scott's board as well as on the Percy R. Gardiner Foundation.

The Gardiner fortune, like the Phelan fortune, was in food services. George and Helen Gardiner's father owned Bowes Lunch, a
popular Toronto chain during the Depression. George took it over on
behalf of himself and his sister and it became the basis for Scott's.
Now Helen (and her four children) own 19 per cent of Scott's stock,
while George Gardiner's three children control 41 per cent of shares.
(George Gardiner was also in business for many years with the late
Mary Hunter, of Maclean Hunter Limited. The two owned, among
other property assets, control of the famous Arizona Biltmore Hotel
in Phoenix.)

Phelan and his brother-in-law are good friends, but opposites.
Phelan is easygoing, chatty and a jock who loves tennis, swimming
and sailing. Gardiner is a more formal person whose passionate hobby
is collecting artifacts, antiques and artwork. He bequeathed his world-
class collection of ceramics and donated it to the building around it
called, not surprisingly, the George R. Gardiner Museum of Ceramic
Art near Toronto's Royal Ontario Museum.

Phelan explains their differences. "We have two big golden re-
trievers, a tennis court and swimming pool. There is always chaos in
our house with kids and dogs running through the place all the time.
He lives next door in a French chateau and it is like a museum."

Even so, Phelan has wanted to merge Cara Operations with Scott's
Hospitality for some time, but Gardiner nixed the notion. However,
things may change in the future; the cousins get along, having grown
up together. "I had a lovely talk with George [Gardiner]. I think a
merger is a very natural thing but we operate in our own individual
ways and we both want to run our companies. He studied it and felt
that a merger was not a good idea," says Phelan.

The big difference is that after March 1989, Gardiner was no
longer in control; his son Michael Gardiner is. "George's kids threw
him out [in spring 1989] after he divorced their mother and remarried.
His son, Michael, is the major shareholder and head of the family.
There's no desire [there] but I would merge the two. It's a natural
thing. I think it's possible but not probable. One of my daughters, Dr.
Gail Regan, said we have two good horses pulling for us now. Why
join them?"

Phelan says he cannot be kicked out of Cara by his kids. "My four
children and I share equally the control block, with 20 per cent each.
My kids can't keep me out. I wanted to give all the shares of my

company to the kids and remain chief through preferred shares, but my wife and lawyer said, 'Don't do it.' She said, 'Should our son be chairman? Maybe not.' I think he's a natural leader."

Despite his septuagenarian status, Phelan still runs an aggressive ship. Cara joined Unicorp Canada Corporation's George Mann (a Forest Hill neighbor) by bidding $300 million to take over Dunkin' Donuts in the United States. They were spurned after an ugly court battle. Cara also bid, and lost out, to buy Canada's premier retailer, Canadian Tire Corporation, in 1985.

"Tire was too big for us but I could've run it – no problem. I would've made it a wholly owned subsidiary. It's big but magnificent and the family only had 6 per cent. The Ontario and Quebec Securities Commissions got into the act [blocking it]. I would have slowly bought up to 50 per cent. We decided to go looking for a nice Canadian outfit. There was not much left. Then along came George Mann, who's a neighbor of mine, and Dunkin' Donuts."

Phelan describes his corporation as a "beautiful garden" and points to an office map with squares, triangles and circles showing where his 400 restaurants are located in every province. Succession is not a question here, because it has already taken place with Commodore Phelan skipper and his officers fully in place with their duties firmly in mind. "I've achieved everything I've wanted to achieve," says the mischievous Phelan. Then he winks and says, "Oh, I wouldn't mind winning the America's Cup one day."

Caveats: Succession questions always nag in family businesses even though the company has been professionally managed for years. Cara has subordinated stock without votes and no coattail provisions protecting minority shareholders. This means the family can cut a side deal – including a merger with Scott's Hospitality, for instance – which could leave other shareholders out in the cold. Cara may be considered pricey, but I think it is a Cadillac among a lot of corporate clunkers.

An investment of $10,000 in January 1980 was worth $67,969 in January 1990. With dividends reinvested, it totalled $71,756. Over the decade prices ranged from $20 to a low of $1.55, adjusting for splits.

COCA-COLA BEVERAGES (FORMERLY T.C.C. BEVERAGES)

Head Office: Toronto, Ontario
Incorporated: 1949
Ownership: Major shareholder Coca-Cola Ltd.

Revenues in 1989: $932,348,000
Net Income: $15,867,000
Earnings per share: $0.39
Employees: 4,000
Year End: December 31

If every single Coca-Cola bottling plant burned to the ground tomorrow, the company would easily rise again from the ashes. This is not just because its bottlers are insured, as they undoubtedly are, but because Coca-Cola is the most recognized trademark in the world. And that pinnacle of marketing success makes Coke the world's most indestructible asset even though it's just some water with a little flavoring. With the world's most recognized brand name, Coca-Cola is pure black gold.

Coca-Cola Beverages (formerly called T.C.C. Beverages Ltd.) is Canada's largest soft-drink bottling company and is 49 per cent owned by Coca-Cola Inc. of Atlanta, Georgia. The public owns the rest. Coke's marketing operations in Canada have been run since 1978 by a couple of talented executives from South Africa: president and chief executive officer, Neville Kirchmann, and senior vice president and chief financial officer, Frank Graham. The two branched out into bottling here, then began acquiring fellow bottlers. In September 1987 they took the company public and now operate Coke's far-flung Canadian operations out of a Don Mills low-rise with a – what else – gigantic sculpture depicting a Coke bottle. Besides Coke and its sister drink, Diet Coke, the company also bottles Sprite, Fanta, TAB,

Fresca, Minute Maid, Hi-C fruit juices, Canada Dry, Schweppes and A & W beverages.

The stock is pricey, but blue-ribbon. It trades at a higher multiple than its U.S. parent even though its parent is the subject of takeover rumors. Contrary to popular belief, Coca-Cola is both a growth stock and a defensive stock, able to withstand recessions handily and increase its market share mightily. One of its biggest assets is the fact that as a publicly traded arm of one of America's most successful multinationals, Coca-Cola Beverages also enjoys the expertise, advice, management support, marketing help and research only monolithic multinationals can muster.

"There are three entities. Coca-Cola Beverages is a bottling operation which buys concentrates from Coca-Cola Inc. which has 49 per cent of us," explains Kirchmann. "Then there is Coca-Cola Ltd., the parent's wholly owned entity in Canada which handles distribution and marketing and quality control. Coca-Cola sells concentrate plus the trademark. Media support is covered in the cost of the concentrate which can range from 28 per cent of cost to 58 per cent. The concentrate is shipped in tanks, then diluted by bottlers, five parts water to one part concentrate. Only two people in Atlanta know the final formula."

Even though this has been a stock market darling for these and other reasons, the market is far from mature here in Canada. Canadian drinking habits provide a huge upside potential. For some reason, Canadians are a nation of coffee drinkers and consume far fewer soft drinks annually than do our American cousins. "People consume 150 gallons a year of liquid," says Kirchmann. "In the U.S. there are 44 U.S. gallons of soft drinks consumed per person per year, followed by coffee, then milk. In Canada, coffee, milk and soft drinks are the order. We drink 400 soft drinks each per year and the Americans, 700. About half of soft drinks are colas."

Health concerns are causing a switch away from coffee and milk and toward diet soft drinks, sparkling water and juices. This is where Coke can capitalize, especially in Canada, where growth is 6.7 per cent compared to U.S. increases each year of 4 per cent. And Coke is king in Canada with a 60-per cent market share in Ontario and 50 per cent nationally compared to arch-rival Pepsi Cola's 30 per cent. The two are virtually neck-and-neck south of the border.

Coke started as a soda fountain business and has carried that tradition on through exclusive arrangements with chains such as McDonald's, Wendy's, Harvey's, Swiss Chalet and Hardee's (Imasco's hamburger chain in the United States). Another marketing ploy is vending machines and, once again, Canada lags behind the United States. "We're investing heavily here. In Canada there are only 34 machines per 10,000 Canadians and 74 vending machines for every 10,000 Americans," says Kirchmann. "Every machine costs $2,000 and sells 500 cases a year. It pays for itself in 2.8 years. We're installing our own and installing them through third-party vending companies. We added 12,000 in 1987 and 1988 and 7,400 in 1989."

Coke is also taking aim at the coffee break in offices. Kirchmann shows off his company's compact, table-top, Breakmate soda fountain, complete with a carbonation canister and syrups for three drinks. It costs $1,000 and is the size of a coffee maker. Right now, about 60 per cent of sales is cans bought in packs of 24, but movie theatres and retailers are all being encouraged to carry and sell large bottles or cups of Coke.

Besides such techniques, Coke marketing research has found that if large quantities of Coke are bought for home inventories, household consumption increases. "To facilitate this, we offer volume discounts and are also selling it in non-traditional and non-food outlets such as drug stores, Canadian Tire and gasoline stations," says Kirchmann.

Special event marketing gimmicks are handled by U.S. Coke and in Canada have included Coke as the exclusive soft drink in Toronto's SkyDome, at the Economic Summit and at the XV Olympic Winter Games in Calgary. Apart from such organic growth, Kirchmann and Graham have embarked on another growth strategy, sure to enhance returns as time marches on. Little by little, it is gobbling up family-owned bottlers of its products when, and if, they come up for sale. So far, $150 million has been spent making such acquisitions and at least another $150 million is on hand to finish the job. The goal is to wholly own all bottlers (there are 23 independents left in Canada who bottle 18 per cent of Coke's line) thus completing a vertical integration unheard of in Atlanta, Georgia, or anywhere else for that matter. Atlanta has a veto over such sales.

The Free Trade Agreement is great news for franchises such as Coke because their market is protected from American marauders while they can shop in the United States for cheaper suppliers, particularly packagers and can manufacturers. "We can't ship to Buffalo but Buffalo can't dump surplus Coke here," Kirchmann says. "We move 40 million cases of cans and in Toronto we have the fastest can line in the world – 6,000 cans a minute are filled. That's better than the U.S."

That may be why Coca-Cola in Canada trades at significantly higher multiples than does Atlanta's Coke. This is a quality operation run by two gentlemen who also happen to know a whole lot about how to peddle black gold. A great bet if you ask me.

Caveats: A leveraged takeover of the parent company by a corporate raider may result in higher concentrate costs, which currently rise along with the rate of inflation. The company also exists by the grace of God and the parent company, which can pull licensing in 20 years, but this is unlikely. That is why its 49 per cent stake is a comfort to investors.

An investment of $10,000 in September 1987 was worth $24,410 by January 1990. With dividends reinvested, it totalled $25,275. Since 1987 prices ranged from a high of $12.88 to a low of $4.50, adjusting for splits.

CORBY DISTILLERIES LIMITED

Head Office: Corbyville, Ontario
Incorporated: 1979
Ownership: Controlling shareholder
Hiram Walker-Gooderham &
Worts owned by Allied-Lyons PLC

Revenues in 1989: $106,600,000
Net Income: $13,500,000(B.E.)/$21,500,000(A.E.)
Earnings per share: $1.96(B.E.)/$3.12(A.E.)
Employees: 570
Year End: February 28

(B.E. - before extraordinary gain; A.E. - after extraordinary gain
resulting from the sale of assets of McGuinness Distillers)

Most people are not part of the oat-bran-and-jogging crowd. But there is general concern about health and fitness, particularly as Canada ages. There is also concern about drinking and driving and, for the last four or five years, consumers have been switching whole-sale to wine and beer or fizzy water and away from distilled spirits. Volumes are down and will continue to fall. Even so, there's money in selected liquor companies, and both the Seagram Company Ltd. and Corby Distilleries Limited remain worthy investments. But for very different reasons.

Seagram is a good bet because it has diversified and is now the largest shareholder of chemical giant E.I. du Pont de Nemours & Company, America's 11th-largest industrial enterprise. Corby is a good bet because it has not diversified, but has taken over competitors and trimmed operating costs dramatically. That makes it a privatiza-tion target. Already in 1989, its largest shareholder, Allied-Lyons PLC of Britain, made a $32-bid to buy all the stock of Corby it didn't already own, but it failed. (Allied-Lyons owns 55 per cent of Corby.) Eventually as the liquor business as a whole shrinks, Allied-Lyons will return and entice minority shareholders away with a premium price for their stock. In the meantime, owners can enjoy nice profits and dividends because, health concerns or not, there's still money to be made in the liquor business. And Corby peddles brand name products that are at the so-called "top end," or expensive, portion of the market. Sales of these liquors are not declining, in dollar terms. "Consumers for the last four or five years have been drinking less but drinking better. Sales of premium brands are increasing," says Corby's Roger Lachapelle, who retired in 1990 as Corby chairman and CEO.

General figures tell the tale. Between 1981 and 1988 the steady increase in spirits' consumption reversed itself and declined from 3.34 litres of pure alcohol per capita to 2.50 litres. At the same time, wine increased marginally from 1.10 litres per capita to 1.16 litres and beer fell slightly from 4.30 litres to 4.14 litres. "In 1982 we could see what was happening. The switch to beer and wine," says Lachapelle. "Then there's the drinking and driving legislation. In total between 1982 and February 1989 industry volumes declined by 28.4 per cent but dollar figures increased slightly."

Corby's head office in Montreal is the grandest in the land. Kitty-corner from Montreal's Ritz-Carlton Hotel, offices are housed in a mansion built in the 19th century by a wealthy plumber. This was part of the area known as "The Square Mile," where Canada's rich and famous ran the country in the 19th century when it was a Third World nation with blue eyes. The foyer is a magnificent wood panelled area with stairs wrapped around a large shaft and leading up to an opaque glass roof. Rooms have 15-foot-high sculpted ceilings and the chairman's office is, without a doubt, Canada's most handsome with its carved stone fireplace large enough to roast a deer.

Lachapelle's successor is Donald MacMartin, a marketing man from Montreal with a vast amount of experience from Canadian Canners Limited, RJR Nabisco Limited and Robin Hood Multifoods Ltd. As its chief, he will head a distillery operation that owns such brand names as Tia Maria, Wisers, Lamb's Rum, Silk Tassel, Beefeater and Wisers Deluxe 10-year-old Whisky, among others. "Wisers Deluxe and Lamb's Rum are gaining volume while generally volumes are dropping," says Lachapelle to underscore his point that distilling is now a quality, not quantity, business.

Corby's trick will be to manage a slow shrinkage of business volumes without losing profitability. Its strategy of takeovers at bargain prices is necessary to gain market share in a shrinking market. "We want to do more acquisitions within and outside our industry. But we are taking our time. There are one or two in Canada we are interested in. Some in the U.S.," he says.

Such rationalization goes on in all declining markets and the winners are those who gobble up the smaller fish, cut duplication and push onwards. That is why a bet with Corby stock is a bet that its management will continue to buy wisely, never overpaying and always watching expenses. So far, that has been the case and there is little reason to believe, with a tough-minded board of directors, things will change. "We are a good stock to buy. We do not go into fields we don't know because that is bound to backfire. This company has a pre-tax return on capital of 22 per cent," says Lachapelle.

That excellent return, and industry rationalization, is why it may be inevitable that Corby is eventually taken over by its controlling shareholder, Allied-Lyons. Corby is a medium-sized fish gobbling up little fish and it is just a matter of time before the big fish gobble up the medium-sized. Interestingly, the obstacle to Allied's $32-bid in 1989 is Square-Mile denizen and investment counsellor Stephen Jarislowsky, an outspoken advocate of shareholder rights. His office is across the street from Corby and Jarislowsky is on a friendly basis with all of Corby's directors. He also manages the Corby employee pension funds and waded into the controversy in 1989 because he is a custodian of a large block of Corby minority shares for his many clients. He balked at the $32-offer and insisted that Corby stock was worth at least $45 a share. He said he would not tender to the offer. Allied-Lyons backed off. For the moment anyway.

Despite the contretemps with Corby's chief shareholder, Jarislowsky still handles the pension portfolio for Corby's 450 employees. "And he does a good job too," says Lachapelle. "Allied won't come back with a bid in the foreseeable future. They made a fair proposal and it would be wrong for them to say they did not offer proper value." I would guess that Allied-Lyons will bid for Corby before 1995.

Caveats: The large discrepancy between U.S. and Canadian excise taxes on liquor and cigarettes has fuelled the rise of cross-border smuggling and shopping. The world's longest undefended border is a sieve and a crackdown is probably impossible. This will continue to hurt anything that is not a name brand.

An investment of $10,000 in A shares in January 1980 was worth $57,414 by January 1990. With dividends reinvested, it totalled $69,114. Over the decade prices ranged from a high of $31.50 to a low of $4.67, adjusting for splits.

CORPORATE FOODS LIMITED

Head Office: Etobicoke, Ontario
Incorporated: 1911
Ownership: Controlling shareholder Maple Leaf Mills Ltd.

Revenues in 1989: $202,493,000
Net Income: $12,743,000(B.E.)/$14,243,000(A.E.)
Earnings per share: $0.67(B.E.)/$0.75(A.E.)
Employees: 16,000
Year End: December 31

(B.E. - before extraordinary earnings; A.E. - after extraordinary earnings)

The current health and fitness fad will continue into the 1990s and beyond as yuppies age and try to postpone their mortality. This is hurting red-meat producers and distilleries, but making some foodstuffs big winners. One of the triumphant is turning out to be the lowly loaf. Fuelled by the search for fibre, there has been a mini-boom in the sale of bran-laced breads, along with organically grown vegetables and fruits. The bottom line is that bread is good for you and Corporate Foods is Canada's pre-eminent baker of bread, among other products. It is well-positioned on grocery store shelves with brand-name breads like Dempster's, Bamby, Sunshine, Rainbow, Canadiana and Grains Natural, Sun-Maid Raisins or Gainsborough pastry products. It also provides the ingredients used by most in-store bakeries and sells 700,000 bagels daily.

"Bread is now considered one of the best foods you can eat," says Corporate Foods' president, Bob Bonus. "We were the first with a 'light' bread for weight-conscious consumers. There are demands for light breads and fibre in our daily diets. Now bread has fewer calories and three times the fibre of regular bread. About 45 per cent of our sales are variety breads and 55 per cent the old-fashioned white bread. But we feel this will switch soon. Non-white bread sales have doubled in ten years and margins are higher than margins on non-white."

The switch back to non-white bread is ironic, considering Dempster's Bread began as a tiny ethnic bakery in Toronto. Now decades later, boring old bread may never be the same and Corporate Foods is on top of trends. Some 55 pounds of bread per person is consumed a year in Canada, with young families the biggest users. But changing demographics mean less bread, but more value-added bread, is going to be the future. Packages will be smaller in the 1990s, due to smaller household units, and packaging will be biodegradable due to the concern about the environment. Corporate Foods intends to cash in on all these new trends.

Corporate Foods is 68 per cent owned by Maple Leaf Mills Limited, which used to be public but was bought out by British food conglomerate, Hillsdown Holdings plc of London. Hillsdown bought Maple Leaf from Canadian Pacific in 1982 and also owns Bluewater Seafood, one of the country's largest seafood processors and exporters. Maple Leaf Mills' president is Norman Currie, who is Corporate Food's chairman of the board. The seafood and bakery businesses are run separately. In spring 1990, Maple Leaf Mills merged with Canadian processing giant Canada Packers Inc., through a complicated $1-billion share swap. At the time, Maple Leaf spokesmen said Packers, Corporate Foods and other operations it controls would remain separate. However, down the road I believe Maple Leaf Mills may buy the shares of Corporate Foods it does not already own and fold the assets and operations into Canada Packers. This could eventually be very profitable to Corporate Foods shareholders, but may be quite some time off.

Corporate Foods is a superstar, posting dramatic gains in earnings, sales and dividends since 1984. Bonus and his team of executives run their far-flung empire out of a no-frills suburban Toronto high-rise. It is part manufacturer and part marketer and increasingly an acquisitions specialist. It also enjoys an advantage over its principal competitor, George Weston Limited, because Corporate Foods is not in competition with customers for its baked goods. Weston, on the other hand, controls Loblaw Companies in competition with chains that are also approached to buy Weston bakery products. Most do not.

Corporate Foods also has an edge due to its unique distribution system. It has franchised the country to self-employed businessmen. "Some 90 per cent of our sales are through independents with their own routes. They are self-employed and self-financing but we assist them in systems for accounting and inventory. We are committed to this because we feel it is important that they have an investment in their operations. We now have 250 of these entrepreneurs working with us in Ontario and 200 in Quebec."

Corporate Foods owns 25 per cent of Multi-Marques Inc. (its management owns the rest). Multi is Quebec's largest baker and just formed a joint venture with Corporate Foods to cover the Maritimes. At the moment the west is untouched, in bakery items, and Bonus says opportunities to enter that market in a big way through an acquisition or two is limited. The company's entry into western Canada was in early 1988 with its purchase of all of Olivieri Foods Ltd., a family-managed fresh pasta and sauce producer in British Columbia.

Another joint venture arrangement is between Corporate Foods and Dough Delight, which sells 700,000 bagels per day, as well as English muffins, crumpets, breads, dough and pastries to in-store bakeries run by all the supermarket chains. Corporate Foods owns 49 per cent of Dough Delight and the rest is owned by its two East Indian founders who run the operations.

Corporate Foods also does business with its parent, Maple Leaf Mills and deals with its flour, rendering, poultry and grocery products businesses. "We manage grocery products for them, distributing cake mixes, retail flour, icings and drink mixes," says Bonus. "We are also looking at whether or not to start marketing Hillsdown products such as teas."

However, Bonus keeps his distance from Maple Leaf Mills' re-tailer, Buns Master. "I don't want it. It's a conflict. Buns Master is a retailer and I'm a supplier to retailers competing against Buns Master."

Maple Leaf Mills was public until ten years ago, then it was peddled to the Brits. But Corporate Foods will likely remain a public company, says Bonus. And to keep profits and dividends up for the parent company, future acquisitions are very much in the cards. "Our man-date is to be profitable and if you want to grow to any extent you must do acquisitions. The population growth is only 1 per cent and if you can pick up an added market share of one or two percentage points, you are lucky. So we are continually looking at acquisitions. There is nothing in Canada, so we are looking to expand our customer base by going into the United States," says Bonus. On the other hand, Corporate Foods is cautious because, as Bonus says, "we don't want to bruise that 20 per cent return on equity by paying too much for something."

Caveats: The core business is slow-growth and the secret to future success will be acquisitions and market-share increases. Overpaying or buying a dog in the United States could harm this company's outstanding track record. Under free trade with the United States, supply-marketing boards still leave bakers at a slight disadvantage to their U.S. competitors when it comes to buying flour, but the gap is minimal and may disappear as boards are unravelled.

An investment of $10,000 in January 1980 was worth $247,283 in January 1990. With dividends reinvested, it totalled $271,522. Over the decade prices ranged from a high of $12.25 to a low of 44 cents, adjusting for splits.

DEPRENYL RESEARCH LTD.

Head Office: Toronto, Ontario
Incorporated: 1987
Ownership: Schulman family interests 18%; Chinoin 8%

Revenues in 1989: $1,800,000
Net Income: $1,600,000
Earnings per share: $0.70
Employees: 19
Year End: December 31

The two-storey, red-brick building is on the corner of Marmaduke Street and Roncesvalles Avenue in a working-class section of Toronto's west end. Frann's Fish & Chips is a few doors away, as is the storefront office of the weekly Polish newspaper. On the side door of the building, a sign reads: "Deprenyl Research Ltd." It used to read "Dr. M.P. Shulman, Physician and Surgeon." Inside, up a few stairs and to the right, is a storage room where a computer terminal allows Shulman to call up stock and commodity trading results from around the world in seconds. To the left is his small physician's waiting room. This is where Morty Shulman – financier, author, politician, television personality, philanthropist, and now pharmaceutical magnate – works most days of the week.

Shulman has had a lifetime of accomplishments but he says that in 1987 he was ready to commit suicide after Parkinson's Disease struck, leaving him slightly crippled, listless and shuffling. A neurologist colleague at Toronto Western Hospital prescribed a Hungarian drug widely used in Europe and elsewhere but, as yet, unlicensed in North America. Called Eldepryl from the generic family of drugs known as Deprenyl, the pharmaceutical relieved Shulman's symptoms within 24 hours. It is no cure.

Shulman liked the relief so much that he bought the rights to the pharmaceutical in Canada as well as 30 per cent of Somerset Pharmaceutical, a private U.S. company with the U.S. rights. He then launched Deprenyl Research Ltd. which retained the Canadian rights and was listed on the Toronto Stock Exchange in 1989. That year, Somerset was bought out, giving Deprenyl more than $10 million for its stake. By January 1990 Deprenyl was given the nod by health officials in both countries for Parkinson's patients. (It can, and is, being prescribed for "humanitarian purposes" in other diseases, notably Lou Gehrig's Disease, Alzheimer's and even multiple sclerosis.) Estimates based on first quarter sales are that Deprenyl's revenues will hit $12 million in fiscal 1990 and earnings, $6 per share. The U.S. sales have been running at $2 million a week. Shulman and his family own 16 per cent of Deprenyl's shares; Toronto Western Hospital, 5 per cent (donated by Shulman); Hungarian-born money manager Andy Sarlos, 6 per cent; and the Hungarian government, 15 per cent.

Deprenyl is a risky proposition, but an interesting, pure investment geared to changing demographics. (An older population is more susceptible to the diseases Deprenyl treats.) Now no longer a speculative stock, it graduated in 1989 into a mature company with a real product and actual sales. While it has been trading at a premium multiple there is incredible potential here, too. Many prominent scientists believe that this drug is a medical breakthrough. (For instance, the stock of Mylar Laboratories on the New York Stock Exchange, one of two owners of Deprenyl's U.S. rights, jumped US$400 million in value in fall 1989 after the drug was allowed for use by health officials.)

Meanwhile here in Canada, Deprenyl Research has enjoyed huge increases in two years from $3 to around $21 a share, predicated on its exclusive right to sell in Canada. Deprenyl's monopoly on this drug will last until 1993, after which generic drug producers can make it. "This is a ten-year opportunity with this drug, but this company also has the rights to other drugs discovered by the Hungarians," adds Shulman.

Deprenyl Research Ltd. has Canadian rights to other drugs developed by Chinoin, Hungary's state pharmaceutical company, which makes Deprenyl. This is significant because some believe Deprenyl is the beginning of a new generation of pharmaceuticals which have, for the first time, actually slowed the damage caused by both neurological diseases and aging. "The Hungarians are ahead of the whole world on this one," says Shulman. "They have some 600 researchers working under Dr. [Josef] Knoll."

Knoll is Hungary's eminent physiologist and pharmacologist, who "rediscovered" Deprenyl, an anti-depressant which had fallen into disrepute over perceived adverse side effects. Knoll says that man's potential lifespan is 120 years, barring disease or accident, and that Deprenyl slows the aging process which is, physiologically speaking, self-generated brain damage. "A resting animal becomes restless and searches for food. He needs bursts of energy to hunt and to escape predators. With aging the ability to surge declines, as does sexual activity, the ability to learn and to work. In nature that means the organism will become a victim of a predator. Animals in natural habitats never get old. It's a built-in suicide mechanism."

Aging is caused when substances that trigger activity also generate toxins which destroy brain neurons. Knoll determined in 1980 that Deprenyl protects the brain cells from the naturally generated toxins. When those findings were corroborated in the summer of 1989 by an independent California study, they triggered headlines around the world and a jump in Deprenyl's stock price.

Knoll himself has been taking Deprenyl twice a week, since 1985, five milligrams at a time, with benefits. "The first experiment destroyed a bacteria in 1905, paving the way for immunology and chemotherapy. Antibiotics came along in the 1930s, but now's the time to approach another question. How to devise tools to reach the maximum lifespan? Deprenyl is a start."

The drug's supposed life-extending property is the reason why Colgate-Palmolive has been testing it for use in its Hill's Science Diet pet foods. This application was dreamed up by Shulman and is ignored by many market players, but Deprenyl Research has the North American rights for such use and there are 200 million cats and dogs, many of which are pampered by their owners. If that use ever took off, in addition to its application for other human diseases, Deprenyl's stock price could take off through the stratosphere. Such pie-in-the-sky speculation aside, Shulman says of his company, "This is no longer a promotion. This is a business. It's wonderful."

Caveats: Shulman himself says his health, and the gradual and inevitable return of his Parkinson's symptoms, are negative factors, because promotion has been pegged to his recovery. But he is stepping aside with the appointment of a new president hired away from Connaught BioSciences Inc. The pet food sideline could be spectacular, but is highly speculative. Deprenyl's new president must be able to recognize promising drugs in order to rescue this company from being merely a one-drug company.

An investment of $10,000 in February 1988, when the stock was issued at $3 a share, was worth $69,993 by January 1990. Another $499.95 worth of dividends would have been collected on the original purchase.

DOFASCO INC.

Head Office: Hamilton, Ontario
Incorporated: 1917
Ownership: Widely held

Revenues in 1989: $3,908,300,000
Net Income: $217,900,000
Earnings per share: $2.88
Employees: 23,000
Year End: December 31

Hamilton, Ontario, has always had a bum rap, considered by the rest of Canada as a smelly, polluted cesspool far removed from the glitzy, sparkling towers of Toronto where financial decisions are made. As if to defy such off-base criticism, the low-rise head office of Dofasco Inc. squats amid stacks and flares that shoot out of state-of-the-art mills and foundries. This 900-acre site of industrial might contains what many feel to be the world's pre-eminent steel maker. Fans cite the fact that Dofasco was the only steel company in North America to make a profit during the bleakness of the early 1980s when the world was gripped in economic recession.

Originally Dominion Foundries and Steel Limited, Dofasco is dubbed the "biggest small company in Canada." It is easily Hamilton's biggest employer, with 13,400 employees, $2.98 billion in revenues and operations that are about as diversified as a steel company's could be. Even so, investors must realize that this macho manufacturing business is ultimately cyclical, tracking the economic upswings and downturns. Besides that roller-coaster ride, steel is uniquely subject to protectionist measures, chiefly in the United States.

Canadians like Dofasco were exempted in 1984 from voluntary restraint agreements imposed by Washington against 29 countries accused of dumping steel below cost. Even so, our companies have trod lightly ever since, agreeing to abide by unofficial import quotas that leave them with their traditional sliver of only 3 per cent of the U.S. market. This market share is paltry despite the ability by Canadians to undercut American producers easily due to significantly greater efficiencies and quality. Meanwhile, the United States has 8 per cent of Canada's steel market.

The Canadians have chosen not to rock the boat – and for good reason. Their deference to American sensitivities is ironic considering Dofasco's "American" roots. It was founded in 1912 by two brothers from Chicago, Frank and C.W. Sherman, who immigrated to Hamilton to start a foundry for rail castings because the city was a big railway hub. The enterprise prospered under their unusual brand of paternalism, which included pioneering by-laws enshrining generous profit sharing for all workers. The result is employee relations that are the envy of any corporation, little turnover and two- and three-generation workers. Typical of the loyalty is Dofasco's own gentlemanly, soft-spoken president and chief executive officer, Paul Phoenix. His father worked for the firm, Phoenix's first job at 15 years of age was as a foundry inspector and he joined the firm straight out of university in 1949 after graduating as an engineer with an MBA.

Dofasco's motto is "our product is steel. Our strength is people." Every year, the company's paternalistic tradition translates into a full-blown Christmas bash for 38,000 people – the workers and their families. Profit sharing is an important perquisite and has kept out unions. By early 1990, a Dofasco worker reaching retirement age could look forward to a pension of up to $40,000 a year, including Canada and Old Age Pensions, and a lump sum of $300,000 in cash besides. Benefits are equally dispersed among employees every year, irrespective of position or salary, and consist of 14 per cent of profits plus profits from prior investments on the accumulated total. The result of this mandated generosity is a corporate love-in that translates into an enviable turnover rate each year of only 2 per cent, absenteeism of only 4.7 per cent and a morale rivalling the enthusiasm found in Tokyo factory workers or first-year fraternity brothers.

Dofasco even looks after its retired work force of 1,500, providing a social club, staging annual events and generally treating them generously. The company is a personnel pioneer, employing the only corporate social worker and providing unmatched recreational, educational and medical services. Such sensitivity was also unmatched even during troublesome layoffs of 2,200 workers in November 1981 in order to retain profitability. Workers were laid off strictly according to seniority with those having less than three years' service targeted, regardless of shortages created in specialized areas. They were given individual counselling and were recalled in the same way, regardless of specialty. "My secretary was recalled and the only job open was as a sweeper. She took that until a secretarial position suiting her opened up months later," recalls Dofasco spokesman Bill Gair.

Such superlative labor relations have enhanced profits, but labor represents only 20 per cent of the cost of making steel. Besides, it acquired 9,000 unionized workers when it bought rival Algoma Steel Corp. Ltd. in 1988 for $560 million. Dofasco bought Algoma to avoid investing in massive facilities itself but has found it a drain on earnings. Some operations have been merged to save money, but the two cultures remain poles apart and rationalizations, including assets sales and layoffs of hundreds, have been in the works during 1990 due to the excessively high Canadian dollar. "Prospects for Algoma are, at best, dismal." This was the prediction in early 1990 of Jay Gordon, a steel analyst with Toronto brokerage firm McLean McCarthy Limited.

Algoma is part of a long-term strategy. Dofasco realized before many that the world's steel makers are rationalizing, as cement makers did during the 1970s and 1980s, to realize economies of scale. The purchase of Algoma, along with other acquisitions, integrations and joint ventures, is part of an ongoing process to retain pre-eminence in the long haul. A similarly inspired move, say some analysts, was its purchase from U.S. Steel of half of Quebec Cartier Mines, an iron-ore mining operation that assures cheap supply for the future.

Dofasco has also joined rivals in other ventures. "We are the largest galvanizer in Canada and are building a plant in a joint venture with Sidbec [Quebec corporation]. The market in Quebec has grown rapidly due to industrial outfits like Bombardier and Canam Manac [maker of truck trailers]," says Phoenix. "We are in a joint venture with National Steel NKK of Japan in southern Ontario to make automotive-grade galvanized steel bodies. With five-year auto warranties against rust, this is necessary and we apply a zinc coating on steel to prevent rust. We will see more and more joint ventures on a global basis."

Phoenix says Dofasco is going to stick to North America, spurning the complicated Japanese market and Europe where "cartels are already there, legalized and getting stronger through mergers before 1992." Now 40 per cent of its business is auto-related; 25 per cent, energy-related; 15 per cent, consumer-related (tinplate, pop cans, food cans); and the rest, construction-related. "Algoma now comes into the play because we were out of capacity in terms of front-end steel-making blast furnaces."

The cyclical nature of Dofasco has made investors cautious. So did its shareholder rights plan imposed in early 1990, which made a takeover bid at a premium impossible. Even so, Dofasco is a great Canadian success story and deserves investment support. As Phoenix says, "This is a technologically up-to-date plant, with a solid customer base and differing products, no matter which cycle. The auto pact created an important customer base for us in southern Ontario and you don't make money shipping steel umpteen miles and Ontario and Quebec are solid and growing."

Caveats: Although Dofasco is on top of technological changes in the business, steel may be replaced in automobiles by aluminum and plastics to an increasing extent. Dofasco's Algoma is especially vulnerable to a high Canadian dollar, and slumping energy prices and problems led to lower Dofasco earnings and stock prices in early 1990. High debts incurred to make acquisitions also make Dofasco vulnerable to high interest rates until assets can be sold. Dofasco is a cyclical stock, so buy carefully. Another danger zone is the free trade deal, if there is renewed protectionism south of the border, or moves north of it to rescind the deal. It is unlikely to happen but would be a disaster if it did.

An investment of $10,000 in January 1980 was worth $21,075 by January 1990. With dividends reinvested, it totalled $28,895. Over the decade prices ranged from a high of $32.63 to a low of $9.00 adjusting for splits.

FCA INTERNATIONAL LTD.

Head Office: Westmount, Quebec
Incorporated: 1945
Ownership: Major shareholders Fairfax Financial Holdings Limited

Revenues in 1989: $71,682,087
Net Income: -$2,804,802
Earnings per share: -$0.27
Employees: 1,700
Year End: June 30

Mark Lubotta is not central casting's version of the guy on the other end of the phone at a collection agency. Soft-spoken, tactful and slight in stature he usually pads around FCA's executive headquarters dressed casually in a sweater. FCA's presence is a surprise tucked above a storefront in suburban Westmount. But the elevator drops you off at a tastefully decorated area. Lubotta's own office is an attractive suite filled with Oriental art and ebony furnishings, sculptures and screen dividers. Hardly the outpost of the stereotypical knee-breaking collector. But Lubotta says diplomacy, not threats, is the art of collection, contrary to popular belief. And he ought to know. The firm his father founded, FCA, is the biggest collection agency in the land and North America's second largest.

FCA stands for Financial Collection Agencies and employs an army of salaried agents in 68 offices in North America, and another three in the United Kingdom. Essentially, FCA and other collection agencies are an extension of credit departments for merchants, banks, airlines, oil companies, car rental firms, telephone companies, other utilities and even governments. FCA in 1989 was given $1.5 billion worth of bills by hundreds of companies and can keep 25 per cent of whatever it collects. If, on the other hand, its collectors strike out, it makes nothing. But FCA is good at what it does and its recovery rate leads the industry's, 13.2 per cent of what it is hired to recover.

Collections is a people business. Techniques and training are critical. But the name of the game is also to attract "quality" late bills, or those with the greatest chance of collection. Recovery rates vary greatly from industry to industry, depending upon how well the seller screened the buyer to whom he gave credit. It also depends upon the collection efforts of the company before accounts were handed over to an agency. For instance, mail-order subscriptions have the lowest recovery rates because anyone can fill in a card and order a magazine to be delivered. Publishers do not check credit, ask for references or even determine if the mailing address is accurate. They simply ship out the magazines and hope for the best. Credit card companies, on the other hand, get references and have legally binding contracts in their files, which help net recovery rates of as much as 13 per cent.

The paradox in this business is that FCA and others could not exist unless most people were basically honest. "We listen to their excuses. They say they don't like the service or that they have lost their job and cannot afford to pay whatever the bill is for. Most people want to pay, but just need reminding. The basis of our business is that most people are honest," he says.

Lubotta says about one-third of "late accounts" can be collected just by sending out a reminder letter. The next third requires a follow-up phone call, another sixth requires more mailings and the final sixth is made up of people who cannot pay because they have financial troubles or who have disappeared. "You find them and talk to them, using the third-party psychology approach. We say we are unbiased, we are not the oil company, Mr. X, but you have no choice. You received the merchandise and you must pay now. Most listen to this and are not out to beat the system."

FCA's spanking new computerized system reminds agents to make calls (up to four) and send letters (up to four). Under its former system, accounts were entered onto index cards, which could be lost or forgotten. Sometimes accounts piled up and agents spent too much time on hopeless collections. Although the computer helps, it also created some enormous problems. After its initial installation in 1986, FCA went from being a stock market darling to a dog, with little or no earnings.

The company lost money in 1989 and this year began a turnaround. "We took $20 million in cash, which was earning interest, and turned it into hardware and software and $5.5 million of depreciation off income," he says. Savings and operating improvements as a result of the computer were insufficient to recoup that flip-flop. Besides, employees balked at it or used it as an excuse. "Looking back on it, the company went on hold for three years. People would say if it was a lousy month, it was the computer's fault. To blame the computer is a little unfair. We grew quickly through acquisitions and by opening new offices. We sometimes ran faster than we wanted to. It was a combination of several things."

Conversion became expensive because agents had to work with both systems. Old, uncollected accounts were on index cards while new accounts were entered into the computer system. Some 20 offices were pruned during 1988 and 1989 and a professional operations executive, Steve Levy, was hired to slash head office expenses, too. At the same time, FCA became more selective in the accounts it would take over. Raising standards hurt revenues; so did a jump in the Canadian dollar *vis à vis* the U.S. dollar. That is why some analysts see the light at the end of the tunnel this year because despite upgrading, accounts accepted for collection have grown 8 per cent year over a year, a good sign that once expenses are in line, profits will return. "New, better-quality business is starting to go up and so should collectibility ratios. The system is also more efficent and we are starting to see each collector handling more accounts," says Lubotta.

Perhaps due to problems, Mark Lubotta and his father, Jack Lubotta, sold their 24.3 per cent of FCA in early 1990 to financial services holding company, Fairfax Financial Holdings Limited. Mark and his management team will remain in the saddle to steer the company toward restored profitability and renewed good prospects. Fairfax owns insurance, trucking, farm, underwriting and claims adjustment businesses and has a 37 per cent interest in Toronto broker Walwyn Stodgell Cochran Murray Limited. The 24.3 per cent of FCA was divided among 16 institutional clients.

FCA is an interesting turnaround play. It also has an advantage in getting some accounts because it is the only large, sophisticated collection agency with operations in the United States, Canada and the United Kingdom. Growing pains caused by the computer may prove to be a simple case of taking two steps back to leap forward. The sale of control to Fairfax Financial may be viewed as a positive step because Fairfax could generate collection business as well as provide guidance and discipline at the board level. But only time will tell.

Caveats: This is a counter-cyclical play that does better during hard times. Once this company returns to the black, the multiples could reap huge benefits. But it is not there yet and is therefore speculative. Believers in the long run should accumulate.

An investment of $10,000 in January 1980 was worth $45,064 in January 1990. With dividends reinvested, it totalled $48,498. Over the decade prices ranged from a high of $11.75 to a low of $1.33, adjusting for splits.

FEDERAL INDUSTRIES LTD.

Head Office: Winnipeg, Manitoba
Incorporated: 1967
Ownership: Widely held

Revenues in 1989: $2,281,000,000
Net Income: $45,600,000
Earnings per share: $1.57
Employees: 14,000
Year End: December 31

Tucked away in Winnipeg, John F. "Jack" Fraser and his Federal Industries Ltd. are virtually unknown except to stock market sophisticates. Despite a name that sounds like a crown corporation, Federal is far from being some lacklustre civil service outfit. It is a sleeper and one of Canada's most successful and diversified companies. To get that message across, its president, chief executive officer Jack Fraser, practically lives on airplanes and commutes weekly from his prairie head office to tell Federal's story in central Canada.

The result of such strenuous work is that Federal under Fraser's watchful eye has grown from sales of $100 million in 1978 to a $2.3-billion baby. After assuming the reins that year, he ditched most of its holdings, except for trucking businesses, to assemble a different, more profitable, conglomerate. He sold off its businesses in men's clothing, fuel oil distribution, aerospace manufacturing, poultry processing and pre-fab home construction.

Through acquisitions, he quietly created Canada's largest trucking company, Yellow Roadway Freightway (ranked fifth in North America); a lucrative steel distribution business for a song; an industrial products division; and a specialty retail powerhouse as owner of Regal Greetings & Gifts (a catalogue-driven sales organization with agents selling gifts to workplace colleagues), Cashway Building Centres, Jelinek Sports equipment, Willson Stationers stores, W.H. Smith Ltd. books and Classic Books. Naturally, the secret of such a mixed-bag enterprise is to obtain assets at everyday low prices. And Fraser has proven capable of shopping wisely.

However, such diversity has resulted in a lacklustre stock price. Investors don't buy confusion or unknown quantities in highly competitive businesses. But a number of changes loom on the horizon. Federal shareholders may be offered stock in some of its businesses directly in return for Federal stock to create more pure plays, to leverage the company by freeing up cash through the sale of equity and as a weapon against takeover. This is what Canadian Pacific Limited has done through its sale to the public of 80 per cent of Marathon Realty Company Limited. "Stock prices have been poor due to the cyclicality of the steel business. Investors think we are more cyclical than we really are. We feel reasonably balanced between specialty retailing, industrial products, steel distribution and trucking," says Fraser.

Ginger-haired and blue-eyed, Fraser makes some 60 trips a year to Toronto to deal with bankers, brokers and investors. His Commerce Court office is virtually bare because he merely camps there for two or three days a week. His headquarters is in Winnipeg and that is where he intends to keep it. Part of the Winnipeg "mafia" headed by grain baron, broker George Richardson, Gendis Inc.'s Albert Cohen and Global Television's Izzy Asper, Fraser admits that staying in Winnipeg means he must travel excessively to keep in touch. It's important to plug into what's known as the "deal stream," transactions that are shopped around by investment bankers. Being outside the deal stream when you are a conglomerate such as Federal means you see the opportunities last and bid on them only after they have been cherry picked, chewed over or missed. Those outside the "deal stream" starve for good acquisition candidates, so Fraser quite rightly networks constantly in central Canada, particularly in Toronto. Personable and energetic, the 60-year-old Fraser also sits on important boards to this end, notably as a director of the Bank of Montreal and Thomson Corporation, among others. Thanks to such contacts, hard work and the inspired acquisition of Russell Steel Inc. in the early 1980s, Federal is approached routinely by investment bankers with deals.

It hasn't always been the case. In fact, Federal catapulted into the big leagues when it bought a basketcase in the recession of 1982 that others, ahead of it in the deal stream, had spurned. That year, it paid a fire-sale price for Russell Steel from Joe Tanenbaum's sinking YRI-York Ltd. after making a leveraged buy-out at 22 per cent interest rates. A handful of years later, Federal bought Russell rival Drummond McCall, bringing steel distribution sales to some 60 per cent of Federal's revenues. "Russell in particular was one of those opportunities you get once in a generation," says Fraser.

Fraser has drummed up a great deal of institutional support over the past few years for his stock. "Our largest shareholder is the Mackenzie Financial Corporation with nearly 10 per cent of the stock, then there's Investors Syndicate, Canada Life and OMERs (the Ontario Municipal Employees Retirement Fund), which just bought a lot of our stock," he says. "We get clustered with management companies like Brascan, Canadian Pacific or Power Financial. They are true holding companies but we own all our businesses 100 per cent."

Another difference is that those holding companies compete globally, whereas Federal is mostly a service-sector conglomerate in operations that are more shielded from gigantic foreign competitors than are resource or manufacturing companies. Its steel distribution, trucking and retail divisions are in the service sector. Only its industrial products division manufactures, but it is somewhat insulated from global competition because it specializes in niche operations.

"This is our highest performing group with return on net assets of over 30 per cent. Why? Because each business is a major player in small specialty niches. They are neat little manufacturing companies with $10 to $40 million in sales and nobody's heard of them. There's Delhi Industries Inc., which is a major manufacturer of all the little fans that go into air conditioners in Canada. Northern Pigment makes dyes and inks for bricks and tile and is the only one in Canada. Milltronics, in Peterborough, makes electronic measuring devices used to measure bulk commodities like flour, coal."

Federal is one of the few widely held conglomerates left in Canada that has not been a takeover target. Perhaps there are those who feel it may have problems with its steel and trucking businesses in light of the free trade deal. But Fraser says detractors are wrong and that, in fact, free trade is a benefit. However, he says to be well-positioned he hopes that by 1995 half of his conglomerate's revenues will be from

U.S. operations, in all divisions. And to this end, he admits that Federal is not plugged into the American "deal stream" and that most sales are "shop worn" by the time they reach Winnipeg. Even so, his strategy is to expand into the United States.

"We now see 15 per cent of our revenues from the U.S. Our mental attitude is that the 49th parallel doesn't exist any more, both in terms of growing our businesses and acquiring new ones," he says. "In trucking, there has been an appreciable switch to north-south traffic as opposed to east-west traffic. Our edge is that as imports north-south – particularly in Ontario – increase, we have the contacts to bring loads back to the U.S., so we won't go back empty, which allows us to undercut them in costs. In the first year, we found that even though the Ontario and Quebec economies were slowing with ton-nages off 5 per cent, our business was up by 10 per cent."

However, Yellow Roadway with its 75 Canadian and 20 U.S. terminals must be still larger to prosper. Essentially, there are only four giants in Canada now after a number of buy-outs and these are Motorways, Reimer Express Lines Ltd. and Canadian Pacific Lim-ited. "There is rationalizing among the smaller players, and the industry is in a period of turmoil. I don't want to sound like a buzzard, but this is heavenly in terms of acquisitions. We are looking at U.S. acquisitions with good U.S. management at the right price," he says.

How will Federal avoid the catastrophes that have befallen so many Canadians south of the border? "If they were buying in France or Turkey, they would have worried about nuances, languages, customs and nervously studied the situation carefully. But most assumed that if it works in Brampton it works in Dallas. That is wrong. Americans play harder ball and markets are different. We understand that at Federal."

Caveat: Federal is somewhat confusing for investors due to its mixed bag of assets and may always trade at a discount to net asset value. However, as it grows in importance and profile, the discount may decrease. Steel and trucking are still most important and both are cyclical. Although doing well now, Fraser may be frustrated in his attempts to find U.S. acquisitions to round out his North American strategy. Future profits will depend upon astute acquisitions in the

United States, something Canadians rarely demonstrate they can pull off. Another problem is that this company is very much Fraser's creation and succession is uncertain.

An investment of $10,000 in A shares in January 1980 was worth $41,538 in January 1990. With dividends reinvested, it totalled $49,692. Over the decade prices ranged from a high of $20 to a low of $3.19, adjusting for splits.

FINNING LTD.

Head Office: Vancouver, British Columbia
Incorporated: 1933
Ownership: Widely held

Revenues in 1989: $903,965,000
Net Income: $42,197,000
Earnings per share: $1.36
Employees: 3,652
Year End: December 31

In deepest, darkest, Republican Illinois sits a scenic little city called Peoria. Apart from the vaudevillian "I played Peoria" line, this city of 200,000 is best known as the place where comedian Richard Pryor grew up in his grandmother's brothel. But to anyone in the earth-moving business, Peoria is famous as the world headquarters of Caterpillar Inc. And "Cat," as it is known in the corn-and-Bible-belt region, is the world's pre-eminent heavy-equipment manufacturer. It even wipes the floor with the Germans and Japanese. The secret of its success is that it makes quality products and also that it has built one of the world's best dealership networks. The biggest Caterpillar dealership in the world, and probably the best of the lot, is a publicly listed Canadian baby called Finning Ltd.

The company was started in 1933 by Earl B. Finning, the same year that Caterpillar launched itself in a modest little garage in Peoria. For decades Finning was like other Cat dealers – a family-owned agency with a restricted, smallish franchise area. The deal was, Caterpillar made the stuff, provided the specs and priced equipment to sell. Finning sold trucks and tractors to his friends, neighbors and business acquaintances in a portion of British Columbia, then fixed things if they went wrong. Finning has two major shareholdings, 9 per cent held by the founder's daughter, Mrs. Joanne Barker, and another 9 per cent owned by employees. A shareholder rights' plan was in place in 1989, allowing management to dilute a raider if he does not make an acceptable bid to all shareholders.

What sets Finning apart from other Cat dealers is that his business grew meteorically, along with British Columbia and its forestry industry. Finning prospered thanks to the forestry industry, which represented 75 per cent of his sales by 1969. His franchise area spread to the entire province as Caterpillar fashioned custom-made equipment for the loggers and haulers and forestry giants.

In 1969 Finning became the first Cat dealer to go public, thanks to its former president, who died in 1989 of a sudden heart attack. The late Vinod Sood was a talented manager with an engineering doctorate from the Massachusetts Institute of Technology. He had run the company brilliantly. It has never lost money since going public, an envious track record brought about by technological innovation that is now emulated by other Cat dealers around the world. But Finning has also grown through aggressive acquisitions and is now an eclectic mix of franchise areas: British Columbia, Alberta, the Yukon, the western third of the Northwest Territories, the northern half of England, Wales, truck franchises in Holland and rights in Poland. For a good portion of the 1980s, Finning was a franchise of convenience to Iran, selling to a country that U.S. Caterpillar was forbidden to deal with directly.

Now the forestry industry represents less than 10 per cent of Finning's sales, with the rest to mining, construction and public works. It is a play on British Columbia's continuing prosperity, the prospects for higher oil prices in Alberta's economy, Britain's $20 billion road improvement program (over the next ten years), Alberta's $5 billion worth of forestry mega-projects under construction plus the burgeoning Eastern Bloc, newly opened for business and exploitation. Finning is positioned in all these areas and already capitalizing. A tantalizing prospect is that Finning can serve Poland via its U.K. operation and the Eastern Bloc is probably up for grabs as far as Caterpillar is concerned. Finning, therefore, has a toehold in an exciting franchise frontier.

In 1989, the firm grew by one-third in one fell swoop when Caterpillar gave it reluctant permission to buy neighboring franchise

R. Angus Alberta Limited of Edmonton for $220 million in 1989. But Caterpillar's reluctance to bless the Angus deal may prove to be limiting to the continuation of Finning's exponential growth. "We were already the largest dealer in the world – equal to the Cat dealer which has all of France – and the Angus acquisition put us over the top. Our problem was dealing with Cat and convincing them to allow us to expand," recalls Finning president Don Lord, a Harvard grad and former B.C. Lions football player. He took over briefly after Sood's death, stickhandled the troublesome bid-approval process for R. Angus, masterminded the merger, then announced plans to retire.

"We said to Cat, 'What is your concern? We are probably your best dealer in the world so why don't you want more of a good thing?' Traditionally Cat has dealt with family-owned dealers who are small. Here we come along and we're a publicly owned company with no shareholder that owns more than 9 per cent. We're professional managers. But the best argument we had was the succession question which they face every time a dealer dies," says Lord.

To put it into perspective, Cat has $11 billion a year in sales worldwide and Finning with Angus will top $1 billion. "But it will be tougher next time around to get Cat's permission," he says. "They see a dealer becoming quite good and large and possibly down the road we might not want to be a Caterpillar dealer any more and we might twist the tail of the tiger."

Either side can cancel with 90 days' notice, but the two are so entwined that it would be equivalent to shooting off feet. That is because selling equipment is only a small portion of what a dealer like Finning does. It sells 300 different models made by Caterpillar and tens of thousands of different moving parts. It also services that equipment in a way that is the key to its selling success. "We maintain a substantial competitive advantage because we guarantee turnaround time on parts and service if something goes wrong. If we don't meet that deadline we pay our customer as much as $1,000 to defray the cost of his downtime. We also provide unique operating leases as a form of financing. If a machine is worth $100,000 and after three years it is worth only 35 per cent of that base, our lease is based on amortizing the 65 per cent and then we buy back that residual at the end so the customer doesn't have to pay for the whole thing," says Lord. Leasing, by this method, is an "incredible profit centre."

More importantly, Lord says the secret of success is Caterpillar's superior line of equipment plus Finning's cost-consciousness. For instance, its inventory management system saves a bundle and consists of a fleet of 14 trucks that deliver parts between its 30 service centres 24 hours a day, seven days a week. This provides good service and reduces inventories to a central warehouse.

Caterpillar dealers mark up products by roughly 20 per cent and Caterpillar prices its models based on worldwide market share. If it gains 80 per cent in one product, it raises prices in recognition of the fact that the price is probably too low. Prices are also based on making dealers profitable based on dealers who are considerably smaller than Finning. Cat's prices result in higher margins for Finning than for its smaller dealers who cannot realize economies of scale that Finning can. Slightly higher margins also mean Finning can gain more market share against competitors because it can afford to cut prices.

"It is a simple business. We own our own buildings and pay for heat and lights. We have no manufacturing base, no plants to have to shut down or mothball. All we have is people and inventory. When business goes up, we add more people and borrow more money. When it goes down, we do the reverse," says Lord. "It's simple, but execution is the key. We delegate authority out to the customer sites and keep a very lean head office."

Caveats: Finning is vulnerable to a downturn in western Canada which is unlikely. Until it acquired Angus, nearly half of its revenues were earned in pounds sterling, exposing earnings to currency fluctuations. This is a reduced factor now.

An investment of $10,000 in January 1980 was worth $28,919 in January 1990. With dividends reinvested, it totalled $32,768. Over the decade prices ranged from a high of $24.25 to a low of $4.25, adjusting for splits.

FOUR SEASONS HOTELS INC.

Head Office: Toronto, Ontario
Incorporated: 1978
Ownership: Controlling shareholder Triples Holding Ltd.

Revenues in 1989: $207,787,000
Net Income: $15,036,000
Earnings per share: $0.74
Employees: 10,000
Year End: December 31

Four Seasons Hotels Inc. owns and manages the world's foremost five-star hotel chain. Customers are pampered and catered to. No detail is too small. Stand at any of the brass elevator doors in a Four Seasons Hotel and peer down at the standing ashtray. Someone actually picks out the butts then leaves the ashtray sand with an impression of the distinctive Four Seasons logo. Awaiting you in your room are flowers, a welcome note from the manager and fruit or candy. Go into the bathroom and you'll find an electrical outlet you can plug a curling iron into, not one of those "razors only" outlets found in most hotels, who do not consider the possibility that females stay in hotels, too. For these and other reasons (the food is indescribable), I have become a devout patron of the Four Seasons chain, providing my employer pays. Some 15,000 others every single day feel the same way.

Even Four Seasons' head office in suburban Don Mills, Ontario, is the ultimate in taste. Hidden in trees, it is a low-slung structure of green and maroon marble that reclines along a winding road. Its interior is a labyrinth of connecting courtyards, modern sculpture and paintings, windows, skylights, wood and plants. Isador Sharp offers

116

coffee in exquisite china cups and saucers. He is a thoroughly personable, casual and open man whose artistic education has left its stamp on this corporation with its beautiful spaces and exhaustive concern over details.

"Architects are creative people, not business driven. They are driven to be creative," says Sharp, who graduated with honors in architectural design 30 years ago from Toronto's Ryerson Institute of Technology. "I don't consider myself a designer. I'm just a good critic, I guess. I recognize my strengths and I didn't for a moment entertain entering the field as a designer. I wanted an education for my immigrant parents."

Sharp is an oddity among the world's five-star hoteliers. Many are real estate financiers or successful graduates of the hospitality end of the business. Sharp's father, Max, owned a construction business, and Sharp and his father hired a friend to design a $1.5-million downtown motel in Toronto. It was a high-stakes gamble with an eye-catching and avant-garde design, but it paid off for Sharp and his original backers, wealthy Toronto furrier Eddy Creed and Murray Koffler, a pharmacist who founded Shoppers Drug Mart, now owned by Imasco Limited. Creed is related to Sharp by marriage and Koffler grew up with Creed.

Success was secured when Sharp attracted a top-notch hotelier to run his modest motel, the late Ian Munro, who taught Sharp how to give his hotels cachet. Another unorthodox hotel project followed – a high-rise hotel in the suburbs, Toronto's Inn on the Park. Fresh from that triumph, Sharp took on his biggest gamble, a bold entry into Britain's hotel sweepstakes where he built London's Inn on the Park, considered by many to be the city's finest hotel.

With 22 hotels and 7,000 rooms, the Four Seasons may not be one of the world's biggest hotel chains. But it is one of its best. Buying Four Seasons stock is a bet on Mercedes rather than Ford. In just 27 years, Four Seasons has grown into the largest operator of medium-sized luxury hotels in the world. It mostly builds its own unique hotels, but it has bought landmark luxury palaces such as The Pierre in New York City and the Ritz-Carlton in Chicago. The chain caters to businessmen, which is why it is significant that *Institutional Investor Magazine*'s last survey in 1988 of the 50 best hotels in the world included six from Four Seasons: The Pierre; Ritz-Carlton; Four Seasons, Toronto; Four Seasons (Washington D.C.); Le Quatre Saisons in Montreal; and London's Inn on the Park. It is routinely among the top ten chosen by restaurant and hotelier trade publications as well.

Four Seasons is primarily North American, but it intends to build more hotels in Japan, the Far East, Europe and even Latin America. It is also getting into the resort business and now has a resort in each of Dallas, California and northern Ontario; others are under construction. The aim is to cash in on the reputation of the existing chain by enticing executives who are Four Seasons customers to sign on for family holidays at Four Seasons resorts in order to enjoy the same top-notch service.

"Now we have more opportunities than we can handle. We turn down dozens of deals. We are the premier top luxury hotel chain in the world and sought out as a partner for every luxury hotel deal in the world. But we are careful not to compromise and will expand by internal growth. In five years, we will build 12 to 15 hotels/resorts and will continue to improve existing operations too. We are constantly upgrading," Sharp says.

The meticulous care given to surroundings is also given to staff. "We believe in the golden rule and have a screening process to find people who will treat colleagues the way they expect to be treated. This flows through to customers. Staff keep computer data with information about guests such as whether they prefer a non-allergenic pillow or a rare type of tea. We have the lowest turnover rate of staff in the industry and the highest occupancy and room rates, too. We also withdraw from management of a hotel. In Edmonton our hotel there is better as a Hilton than as a Four Seasons. We wouldn't compromise and the real estate owners weren't happy with their return from hotel operations."

It has not always been easy and Four Seasons' troubles during the recession in the early 1980s led to an interesting, and winning, strategy as to ownership of its real estate. "We started off with 100 per cent ownership (of real estate) but had 100 per cent of the risk. As we got accepted, then we moved into managing other people's real estate. I've always preferred to own the real estate but we have a joint venture method where we own up to 20 per cent so if times turn bad and we need a cash injection, we can reduce our equity in the real estate."

This strategy resulted from Four Seasons' financial woes in 1982 when interest rates peaked at 22 per cent. The company hunkered down and survived by selling the real estate out from under several of its biggest hotels, including half of flagship London's Inn on the Park. "We figured we were creating a brand name. We sold bricks and mortar and invested in a reputation which is worth more than any asset," he says. "We reinvested $40 million in upgrading our hotels during the recession when everyone was running for cover and thought we were crazy."

Some think their expansion into resorts may be a little misguided, but Sharp says the first one, in Dallas, is a tremendous success financially. Debts are relatively low; there's little exposure to downturns in real estate and some protection against downturns in hotel management. When things turn sour, owners must hike management fees. Sharp does not want to get involved, however, in the resort business involving casinos. "It's profitable but there's the possibility of an unsavory element. I wouldn't like to wake up and find myself with new partners I couldn't deal with or get rid of."

Sharp owns all of Four Seasons' voting shares and 28 per cent of non-voting shares sold to the public in 1986 when Creed and Koffler decided to cash in their stakes. He says he would insist that an offer for his stake be extended to all shareholders for the same price and terms. As for succession, two of his three sons are in the business but are too young to take over the reins immediately. "There is management depth and there are trustees who understand my thinking," he says. "This is a long-term stable growth stock. Not one to trade up and down in the short term. I've got everything at stake and we have created a brand-name chain, more valuable than other assets."

Caveats: Only a small proportion of stock is available to the public which makes it volatile in price. Some feel the stock is overpriced at the moment. Non-voting stock could be a problem despite Sharp's coattail promise, as could succession, even though Sharp is in good health and relatively young at 59 years of age. Another problem is that some 70 per cent of its management income is paid in U.S. dollars, good when the Canadian dollar is low but a charge against income when it is not.

An investment of $10,000 in February 1986 was worth $29,643 in January 1990. With dividends reinvested, it totalled $30,054. Since 1986 prices ranged from a high of $43.50 to a low of $11, adjusting for splits.

GENDIS INC.

Head Office: Winnipeg, Manitoba
Incorporated: 1962
Ownership: Controlling shareholder Cohen Family

Revenues in 1990: $748,200,000
Net Income: $25,200,000
Earnings per share: $1.50
Employees: 8,600
Year End: Last Saturday of January

After IBM and Coca-Cola, Sony ranks as the world's third most recognized brand name. And brand names, to my way of thinking, are more bankable than bullion. For starters, they don't suffer from price fluctuations beyond their control. Brand names create their own demand and brand-name owners control supply. But the name "Sony" was not even a twinkle in the eye of Akio Morita back in 1954 when a tall, friendly Winnipeg entrepreneur named Albert Cohen and his oversized translator came to call at Morita's modest Tokyo factory. The name came later, but back in 1954 the two men struck a deal on the spot, forming a mutually beneficial business partnership that has endured for more than three decades. Now Cohen's Gendis Inc. of Winnipeg shares with Sony Corporation the rights to market Sony products in Canada; it is one of the country's most lucrative franchises.

But Gendis is more than a Sony franchise. It occupies a sprawling low-rise building on 23 acres in a Winnipeg suburb. Albert Cohen continues to run this gem of a merchandising empire and its 51 per cent of Sony of Canada Ltd., five retail chains with 507 stores, 30 per cent of medium-sized Chauvco Resources Ltd. in Calgary and dozens of valuable real estate sites across Canada. Gendis is an outstanding investment for a number of good reasons. It makes lots of money; it has solid assets, good management and an enviable track record. But it is also one of Canada's pre-eminent "succession plays."

Albert Cohen and his five brothers built Gendis into the billion-dollar baby it is today. Cohen's greatest asset, apart from hard work, is his ability to form friendly workable relationships with Morita, his five brothers and employees. A self-effacing and likable individual, Albert Cohen says he and his brothers have never had an argument. They also share equally in their accomplishments. Back in 1968, they took Gendis public for estate-planning purposes so that a ready and fair market could exist for their stock. At that time, and until 1989, each brother owned 11 per cent of the stock and the public, the remaining 34 per cent.

The current generation of Cohens is in its seventies and the next generation has little, if any, interest in running the show. Only three out of the current 19 heirs are involved in the family business. Samuel Cohen died in 1989 and another brother, Morley, and his family cashed in their Gendis chips that same year, selling their 11 per cent of Gendis stock back to the company treasury (which has first right of refusal on all Cohen stock) for the then-market price of $16 7/8. This transaction greatly enriched all shareholders because it involved a buy-back of stock in a company that continues to enjoy profit increases. The number of shares are reduced but the profit per share increases. Not surprisingly, months after Morley's family bailed out, Gendis reached $22 per share. Now the four remaining Cohen brothers, and Samuel's estate, own 63 per cent of the company. (It has two classes of shares authorized, A and B, but both have votes and there are no Bs issued.) Albert thinks it's a matter of time before the next generation is diluted out or sells out.

"There is no one to take over the job I'm doing," says Albert. Currently, three Cohens, Daniel, Charles and Mark, are senior officers in three Gendis retail chains, Greenberg Stores Limited, Metropolitan Stores of Canada Limited and Saan Stores Ltd. "I have no illusions. Everything is well run with professional management. There are 19 heirs today and I can see down the road, philosophically, they'll say, 'Why have stock in a company that only pays a 2 per cent dividend? I can put the money in the bank at 5 per cent.'"

The Cohens disdain the type of protectionist measures – from poison pills to restricted stock to voting trusts – that other families have adopted to keep control in the wake of waning interest among the inheritors. "We have not formed a voting trust. I don't believe in it. I don't believe in nepotism. You cannot control things forever."

At best, Gendis will be a first-class takeover candidate, yielding shareholders a premium. At the very least, Gendis stock will increase in price as profits continue and the Cohens cash in, one by one, selling to the company treasury and enriching fellow shareholders. Even if none of the above events occur, Gendis is a well-managed, diversified conglomerate in four businesses: retail stores, real estate development, oil and gas production and its Sony franchise.

The family's climb into the business big leagues began when Albert Cohen, on his honeymoon back in 1954, came across the world's first transistor radio and tracked down its creator, Morita. He offered Morita and his fledgling enterprise, then known as Tokyo Tsushin Kogyo K.K., its first international distribution network, rescuing Sony from the jaws of the Japanese monoliths, known as Zaibatsu, which control Japan's economy, distribution networks and financial assets. Without export success thanks to Cohen, Morita's Tokyo Tsushin would likely have been gobbled up as so many others were.

But Cohen gave Morita a market and, even more importantly, some invaluable marketing and pricing advice that helped him become one of the first Japanese entrepreneurs to successfully tap the North American marketplace. Conversely, Morita's superior products helped catapult Cohen's small family-owned import company into one of Canada's foremost merchandising companies. With profits from the sale of Sony's exceptional electronics technology, Cohen built Gendis into a well-diversified conglomerate. Not surprisingly, savvy investment counsellor Stephen Jarislowsky and his various clients own a great deal of Gendis stock. So does the Canadian National Railways pension plan.

Little wonder that, like a monarch's portrait in government offices, a formal color photograph of Morita hangs on the wall behind Albert Cohen's desk. On an opposite wall in his spacious office is a black and white photo of the two men shaking hands in 1975 when they formed Sony of Canada Ltd., with its exclusive right to sell Sony's inventions such as the Walkman, the compact disc, Trinitron television and Betamax, among others. One of the most visible symbols of Sony's pre-eminence is its $17-million JumboTron video system in Toronto's SkyDome stadium; it is the largest video display system in the world, with a screen measuring 35 feet by 115 feet.

Morita masterminded Sony's incredible rise and is now one of Japan's most prominent businessmen – and also one of its richest. At 68, he remains Sony's chairman and the largest single shareholder with 8 per cent of Sony, which has worldwide sales of US$24.5 billion (equivalent to half of Ottawa's tax revenues). Sony expanded into the entertainment field in 1989 buying CBS Records Inc. and then Columbia Pictures. Morita and Cohen are "like brothers" and Morita asked Cohen if his eldest son and heir apparent, Masao Morita, could serve his apprenticeship in Toronto. He has been under Cohen's wing as an executive vice president with Sony of Canada.

Although lucrative, Sony is only part of the Gendis story. Cohen's entry into the oil and gas business arose after he was asked by former Manitoba premier Duff Roblin to become a director of PanCanadian Petroleum Limited, Canadian Pacific Limited's oil arm. Cohen learned the business and in 1979 decided to take advantage of tax benefits by launching a junior exploration company in partnership with Calgary oil tycoon Bud McCaig of oil service outfit Trimac Limited. The two formed Tripet Resources Ltd. and merged it in 1987 with Chauvco Resources Limited, a darling of oil analysts following two propitious acquisitions in late 1989. Gendis is Chauvco's largest shareholder with 32 per cent, or 5.2 million shares, acquired at $4.50 and trading during the first half of 1990 at around $11.50 per share.

Gendis's real estate division is a lucrative sideline that grew out of retail operations. "A few years back we realized that if someone else wanted to buy and develop our properties, why shouldn't we? For instance, a Saskatoon Metropolitan store occupies a Gendis plaza with a branch of the Bank of Nova Scotia as a tenant. A Saan store in British Columbia leased part of its premises to Scotiabank and also to Shoppers Drug Mart. And in Ottawa, a Metropolitan store faced with being shut out of a neighboring downtown mall was sold to the mall's developer and Gendis was given, in return, an interest in 33,000 square feet of the mall.

Meanwhile Gendis's bread-and-butter retail operations chug along using a Mao Tse Tung approach – to use Conrad Black's military analogy – avoiding clashes against giants by sticking to smaller conquests in the countryside. Gendis is a small-town retailer. Its 95 Metropolitan stores are small department stores with only 30,000 square feet; its 230 Saan stores are sprinkled throughout western Canadian towns selling men's, ladies' and kids' fashion for the middle class in outlets between 8,000 and 12,000 square feet in size; its 25 Saan for Kids stores are 3,000-square-foot outlets specializing in kiddy clothes; and 105 Greenberg stores are a smaller version of Metropolitan stores in western Canada. Sony of Canada also owns 52 stores.

Cohen still runs the whole works as chairman and chief executive officer but has groomed a capable successor by most accounts, G. Allan MacKenzie, a former lieutenant general in the Royal Canadian Air Force who has been with Gendis for ten years. MacKenzie, Cohen and other executive committee members run a decentralized operation, keeping monthly tabs on budgetary projections for each division. "We call in management if goals are not met to find out the reasons why and we watch inventories," says Cohen.

Without a doubt, Gendis would run like clockwork without the Cohens at the helm. But it's been a breathtaking rise to the top mostly due to their knowledge and skills. While ever-modest, Albert Cohen is clearly proud of his family's accomplishments. "We never dreamed of this. We were looking for security but success breeds success. Sales are now $725 million, which doesn't include 51 per cent of Sony. The 51 per cent of profits show but not the revenues. If they did, we'd be over $1 billion a year. Who would've thought?"

Caveats: The public float is tiny which means that shareholders should be patient when trying to buy or sell. Analysts rarely watch it so that investors should pay special attention themselves to important corporate developments, such as the Cohen family's plans or Chauvco's results, which may affect stock prices.

An investment of $10,000 in A shares in January 1980 was worth $75,344 in January 1990. With dividends reinvested, it totalled $85,740. Over the decade prices ranged from a high of $25.75 to a low of $2.63, adjusting for splits.

GREYHOUND LINES OF CANADA LTD.

Head Office: Calgary, Alberta
Incorporated: 1957
Ownership: Controlling shareholder Greyhound-Dial Corporation

Revenues in 1989: $270,629,160
Net Income: $22,102,331
Earnings per share: $2.61
Employees: 2,500
Year End: December 31

VIA Rail cutbacks and the takeover of Wardair by PWA Corporation were bad news for consumers but exceedingly good news for Greyhound Lines of Canada Ltd. This is because as the rail alternative shrinks and air fares increase due to the disappearance of Wardair, an aggressive competitor, the most affordable mode of public transportation in the 1990s for many will be the lowly bus.

Cashing in on an otherwise dim transportation future is Greyhound, a cash cow that typically makes 10 per cent profit after tax, or $22.597 million in 1988 on revenues of $263.38 million. The bus business is particularly attractive in Canada because it is not deregulated and probably never will be. The result is that the country is carved up into non-competing franchises. Greyhound's competitors are other modes of transportation, not other bus companies.

Greyhound is a good investment because it's a name-brand transportation monopoly granted by Ottawa to provide bus service to 2,500 communities from Toronto westward. Its eastern counterpart is Voyageur Inc. bus lines, privately owned by politician Paul Martin, Jr. Then there's significantly smaller Grey Goose, owned by Laidlaw Inc., with 55 buses operating mostly in Manitoba and the Toronto Transit Commission's taxpayer-owned Gray Coach, in Ontario. Like telephone utilities, these bus companies are granted route franchises and fares designed to extend the service to most parts of their respective franchised area. This is done by cross-subsidy: fares on well-travelled routes more than make up for losses racked up by providing bus service to distant, remote areas.

"I would suggest that 70 per cent of these routes would be unprofitable without cross-subsidies," says Greyhound's president Dick Huisman, a tall, angular Dutchman. Huisman's mandate is to boost the image and enjoyment of travelling by bus.

Already, Greyhound's Calgary headquarters reflects the company's marketing emphasis. The city's principal bus terminal has been transformed from a frayed old waiting room into a cheery, airport-like lounge with fast-food kiosks and specialty shops. Valuable real estate for future terminals is being put on the block, if unneeded, and the proceeds are used to revamp the company's computer system and to pay for additions and expensive renovations to its fleet. Its real estate portfolio is valued at around $150 million, but most sites must be upgraded and cannot be sold because they are prime terminal locations in downtowns.

It is significant that Huisman, whose office includes an eccentric antique law clerk's desk at which he stands to work, is a marketing man. He was enticed away from CP Hotels in 1989 where he worked for 13 years as senior vice president of marketing. "We are experimenting with a passenger snack pack and earphones. We want to employ attractive drivers with good people skills and to provide a safe and comfortable environment," says Huisman. "We will not carry drunks or people who are abusive in appearance or behavior. Standards have deteriorated over the years, but this company will be turned into a customer-focused entity."

Computerization promises to reap huge benefits, just as it has enhanced airline profits. Airlines, also regulated, routinely undercut their permitted fares to compete, raising them during peak periods and lowering them to encourage travel during less popular times or to less popular destinations. Greyhound's Huisman says such techniques will be deployed and aggressive advertising campaigns will sing the praises. "This industry has not reached the limits of its potential," he says.

Greyhound operates two more lucrative sidelines. Brewster Travel has a tight grip on the increasingly popular Rocky Mountain bus tours. Brewster dominates the market and carried 5.75 million passengers in 1989, earning revenues of some $22 million. It also owns half of the Mount Norquay ski resort and two hotels. Greyhound Courier Express grows by leaps and bounds, racking up revenues of $45 million from a standstill just a handful of years ago. Courier Express piggybacks the bus routes, and mail or parcels are carried in the bellies of buses to 600 communities. This provides a huge upside potential to the company and may reap a windfall if plans are implemented to gradually offer door-to-door service to customers now getting depot-to-depot service only.

As Greyhound upgrades and expands its bus service, others do the same, providing the company with yet another benefit. About 44 per cent of Greyhound's revenues and 50 per cent of its profits derive from its bus-manufacturing operation, Motor Coach Industries of Fort Garry, Manitoba. It builds between 350 and 500 intercity bus frames annually and renovates existing buses, a market it shares with only two others in North America. Motors are made by Greyhound's parent company, the Greyhound-Dial Corporation, whose gigantic manufacturing facility in New Mexico serves the U.S. bus market. The two share research and development costs.

Greyhound of Canada is 68 per cent owned by Greyhound-Dial, a widely held public corporation that, despite what the name has come to represent, is no longer in the bus transportation business. In the early 1980s, it sold out to a group of Texas investors but stayed in manufacturing and kept its stake in Greyhound in Canada, where the lack of deregulation lessens competition but heightens profits. And oh, how the money's flowed in! Like most companies with a large controlling shareholder, dividends are traditionally generous, another reason why Greyhound's stock is a good bet for individual investors.

About the only cloud hanging over Greyhound in Canada is the question of future ownership and the potential conflict of interest inherent in the fact that the parent and the Canadian operation are entwined in manufacturing. This means that, theoretically, the best interests of minority shareholders in the Canadian operations could be on a collision course with the best interests of Greyhound's U.S. investors. But Huisman maintains that both operations do their own thing. Significantly, and despite a 68 per cent stake, only one director from the U.S. parent sits on Greyhound Lines of Canada's board. Also on the board are three officers from the Canadian company and four out of the eight directors are truly outside Canadian directors, without other links to the company.

Thus far, the U.S. parent says it is happy with its Canadian investment. But similar noises were made before it peddled off its bus company in early 1988. In fact, Greyhound's controlling shareholder is merely a cash-rich holding company, diversifying into other businesses strictly on the basis of returns. And if someone offers the right price, chances are they'll sell. There is concern that it may sell its U.S. manufacturing operations sometime in the future to a competitor or to someone who will discontinue the current arrangements with Motor Coach. But Huisman says a separation of U.S. and Canadian manufacturing would be difficult, which means if U.S. Greyhound-Dial wish to sell U.S. manufacturing, the U.S. parent must also sell control of Greyhound in Canada. "They are very much intertwined in manufacturing. They could sell but it would require a lot of untangling."

Huisman says Greyhound-Dial considers its stake in Canada as a solid, long-term investment. "Greyhound Corp. has made a major commitment to this corporation because of opportunities in the future."

Caveats: Deregulation of the bus business is unlikely but would hurt profits for this and other bus companies. (On the other hand, the also-unlikely disappearance of VIA Rail would help.) Huisman's plans to upgrade and modernize his bus line are risky and there could be concerns if the U.S. parent sells its manufacturing business. The labor troubles at U.S. Greyhound Bus (and its impending bankruptcy) won't affect Greyhound Canada.

An investment of $10,000 in January 1980 was worth $22,956 in January 1990. With dividends reinvested, it totalled $31,941. Over the decade prices ranged from a high of $34.25 to a low of $12.63, adjusting for splits.

(LE) GROUPE VIDEOTRON

Head Office: Montreal, Quebec
Incorporated: 1964
Ownership: Controlling shareholder André Chagnon

Revenues in 1989: $344,880,000
Net Income: $23,683,000
Earnings per share $0.61
Employees: 1,700
Year End: August 31

Le Groupe Videotron is Canada's second largest cable company with 950,000 subscribers, compared to Rogers Cable's 1.2 million and Maclean Hunter's 400,000. It is by far the most innovative. Most of its subscribers are in Quebec, where the the business is not as mature as it is in Anglophone Canada, giving it more room to grow. Only 64 per cent of Quebec households purchase cable services compared to the Anglophone average of up to 80 per cent in major urban areas. (Videotron also serves 30 municipalities in northern Alberta, has two start-up franchises in London, England, and others in Southampton, Paris and Morocco.) Oddly, however, lower penetration levels in Quebec have not translated into lower profits per subscriber. This is because Videotron adds value to its service by offering more services and innovations to its customers than any other cable operator in the world. In fact, Videotron is at the leading edge of new technology, which can bring more services into your living room than exist at the local shopping mall or newspaper.

Videotron is a pioneering broadcast and cable investment. Through its ownership of 99.6 per cent of the voting stock of Quebec broadcaster Télé-Métropole Inc., it is the largest private-sector network in *la belle province,* not to mention the radio stations it owns.

Télé-Métropole, in turn, owns 54 per cent of Pathonique Inc. with four more Quebec radio and television stations. With such assets, Videotron occupies the pre-eminent broadcast position in the province. "Télé-Métropole produces more original French programming than anyone in the world. Bigger than any station in Paris," crows Videotron chairman André Chagnon proudly.

Chagnon is a ranking member of Quebec's New Guard of francophone tycoons. Born in 1928, he attended a vocational school, began his working life as an electrician and cashed in a $7,000 life insurance policy to set himself up in business in order to compete against his former employer. He recognized in the early 1960s the potential of cable television and started installing coaxial cables in houses and offices and buying up cable companies. The Caisse de dépôt et placements du Québec financed him along the way and now he is chairman of an empire with 2,500 workers, $300 million in sales and $550 million in assets. His family owns 63 per cent of Videotron and the Caisse owns 27 per cent.

Videotron's head office is on Berri Street in Montreal's low-rent district. Although respectably high-rise outside, inside the decor is strictly space-age as visitors face 40 television monitors lining the reception area wall. André, soft-spoken and personable, is chairman and his oldest son, Claude, is president. His second son, Christian, vice president information systems, works in the computer section of the corporation.

"Rogers wants to get into fibre optics and expand into telecommunications, a $20-billion business. The cable industry gets about $400 million of the telecommunications business," says Chagnon. "We feel we're in the entertainment business, can develop an information industry, then enter into transactional services. Télé-Métropole is necessary – the synergy. If broadcasters don't do anything like we are doing, they are doomed. Fragmentation (VCRs, satellite dishes) has started to occur."

"Cable is destroying traditional television," Chagnon says. Take the Sports Network on cable. It can go out and negotiate the rights to the best ball games for one year for $125 million, which is only 37 cents per subscriber. HBO movies go into 50 million homes. Cable can outbid networks for programs and rights and are doing so. The economics is changing.

Videotron's control over television networks allows it to offer more targeted information and products than other cable outfits. For two years, its subscribers have been able to scan property listings in their living rooms, complete with photographs of interiors taken in various rooms and at various angles; they can join a dating club and see what prospective companions look like; tune into career advertisements, travel ads or Montreal area entertainment listings. Some 3,500 joined the dating service in its first year of existence and 750 homes sold; Videotron collects nothing if a property doesn't sell but charges a flat fee of $2,000 for each home sold regardless of price.

But Chagnon's secret weapon is his $35-million stake in a unique "black box," a converter that promises to provide a host of new services he calls "interactive television." A pilot project for Hydro-Québec was a great success and shows how cable television can become as essential as the telephone, Chagnon's avowed goal. In the pilot, 200 South Shore cable subscribers were given up to $150 each in potential credits on their hydro bills for the year. To find out about these credits, viewers would tune into a specific channel when the black box had a red light showing. On the screen would be a message from Hydro advising them how many credits they would earn if they avoided heat-producing appliances from 5:30 P.M. that evening until 1:00 A.M. Hydro passed along the savings to these consumers because their conservation saved it the expense of generating extra power or, conversely, allowed them to export the surplus to the United States for a premium.

This is just one of many innovations that may soon become commonplace. The most dramatic innovation is Chagnon's "interactive" television – called Videoway – launched at the beginning of 1990 in 3,000 Montreal homes. It is a proprietary technology that Chagnon can peddle to other cable companies if it is successful. For $12.95 a month, Videoway customers can have all the wiring removed from their set and replaced with a small computer the size of a standard television converter and keyboard. This will give them access to deaf signage for programs; allow them to send personal messages to others; let them access weather reports, lottery and sports results, flight timetables, job listings, recipes, traffic reports and other types of information. Eventually they may be able to summon their bank accounts onto the screen. Already viewers can watch a hockey game or ballet telecast and switch camera angles or watch a delayed broadcast and replay any portion of the show they wish as they are watching it. Videotron also plans game shows where viewers can key answers and win prizes and newscasts where they can "choose a longer treatment of their preferred subject" from among the line-up of news stories that day.

Another future project is called Telecash – electronic green stamps or credits toward purchases if they are made as a result of seeing a commercial on Videotron cable. "We plan to organize a consortium, including print people. You need a special credit card which you would insert into our computer if you were playing a game show for points. You could also earn points if you put the card in while the commercial was being aired or read a Canadian Tire ad in a specific newspaper," says Chagnon.

Videotron has adapted the black-box technology from ACTV, a New York interactive television pioneer with whom it shares a 50-50 stake in the U.S. market. Videotron has the European and Canadian rights. If it succeeds, it could reap the company a windfall. At worst, Videotron continues to run a profitable broadcast and cable conglomerate.

"When interest rates went to 22 per cent, it was important to have a strong partner like the Caisse with $10 million invested. The market value of that is now $250 million," says Chagnon. "It's been very exciting but there's more business ahead. How much, who knows? In eight years, $25 million in profit was achieved and I said $5 million in ten years. For investors, Videotron is a growth stock. We do everything to grow, dividends are always reinvested with the object of planning for medium and long term."

Caveats: Chagnon has been the driving force and his two sons may lack his drive and vision when they succeed him. The family's 63 per cent is split among the two sons and three daughters. A separation by Quebec from the rest of Canada is unlikely, but is another negative aspect if it occurs, even though it may not affect the bottom line. Another question mark is whether Chagnon's gambles in both Europe and his black box will pay off. It may take a few years of investments before that is known. The decision in May 1990 by Ottawa cable regulators to freeze profits made by cable companies for the next few years will limit profits, and therefore stock price increases, to cable outfits with diversified products, new franchises or unique opportunities for incremental growth.

An investment of $10,000 in 1985 was worth $20,806 in January 1990. With dividends reinvested, it totalled $21,194. Since 1985 prices ranged from a high of $20.25 to a low of $7.50, adjusting for splits.

IMASCO LIMITED

Head Office: Montreal, Quebec
Incorporated: 1912
Ownership: Controlling shareholder B.A.T. Industries

Revenues in 1989: $5,724,700,000
Net Income: $365,100,000
Earnings per share: $2.87
Employees: 85,750
Year End: December 31

Canada has taken the most direct aim against tobacco use of any developed country in the world, in part because of the Mennonite background of a former health minister in the federal government. It is also because our government provides open-ended medical services, so it makes financial sense to discourage cigarette smoking because it causes lung cancer and contributes to heart disease. Ottawa has taken aim in several ways. Tobacco-growing subsidies have been deep-sixed, taxes have been piled on cigarettes making them as expensive as a six-pack of beer and everywhere smoking has been banned from the workplace; Canada's 6 million smokers, even in winter, routinely huddle outside offices and schools inside which they are forbidden to light up. Canada's gone smokeless with a vengeance. But, public health or religious views aside, investors can still make dough betting on cigarette companies.

It remains ironic that one of the government's actions, the ban on advertising by cigarette makers, actually blackens their bottom lines. So do tax hikes because, I suspect, those allow companies to mask hidden, and higher, margins. Even so, this is not a business with a long-term future, but it certainly will be fun while it lasts. Cigarette profits increase, and smart companies have reinvested these into diversifications in order to dilute the importance of the weed. One successful conglomerate built by cigarettes is Canada's largest tobacco manufacturer, Imasco Limited.

Nearly three decades after the U.S. Surgeon General's Report fingered cigarettes as a major health hazard, Imasco, like others, has turned itself into a far-flung conglomerate with $6 billion in revenues. Besides cigarettes, which contribute one-third of its revenues but more than half of its profits, Imasco has three other divisions. Its retail division owns nearly 633 Canadian Shoppers Drug Marts as well as the United Cigar store chain. Its food service division has become America's third-largest hamburger chain, after McDonald's and Burger King, and is called Hardee's Food Systems Inc., with 3,916 Hardee's and 7 Burger Chef restaurants. Besides its lucrative cigarette company, which represents more than 50 per cent of profits, is Imasco's 97 per cent of Canada Trustco Mortgage, the country's second-largest trust outfit and seventh-largest deposit-taking financial institution.

"We are not looking for a fifth leg," says Imasco senior vice president, Torrance Wylie, a well-connected Montreal Liberal and sometime-advisor to former Prime Minister Pierre Elliott Trudeau. Wiley is part of Imasco's management inner circle, unlike other executives with that title. "As for Canada Trustco, we assume under new legislation we may have to divest back to 65 per cent ownership."

Imasco, formerly Imperial Tobacco Company of Canada Limited, occupies a modest-looking office tower at 600 de Maisonneuve in Montreal, closer to the city's downtown shopping district than to its office buildings. Controlled by Britain's B.A.T. plc, a large tobacco-retail giant itself which owns 40.4 per cent of the Canadian conglomerate's stock, Imasco remained steadfastly faithful to Montreal despite the upheaval during the 1970s when so many head offices left. And it remains committed. "Canada will continue," scoffs Wiley when asked what the company would do if Quebec separated from the rest of the country.

But B.A.T. may not control Imasco forever. It has been under siege from takeover predator Sir James Goldsmith and has fended off his bid through the courts and also by jettisoning lower return assets. Imasco is a possible divestiture that would reap a dividend to its minority shareholders. Such speculation sent its stock soaring in mid-1989, but it fell back as Goldsmith's attempt looked less likely, leveraged takeovers looked less probable in general and the stock market players realized that if B.A.T. parted with Imasco it would owe Ottawa a huge, possibly unconscionable, amount of tax in the form of a capital gain.

"Our position if there's a change in B.A.T.'s ownership is that 60 per cent of our stock is owned by other shareholders and we're going to look after them, too," says Imasco's chairman, president and chief executive officer, Purdy Crawford. "We could call a special meeting, wage a proxy fight and drag the company through a lot of negative publicity. But that's doubtful. I don't think Goldsmith is unreasonable. We might deal with the block ourselves [management may engineer a buy-out by its treasury or a friendly white knight]."

Crawford is a jolly, cherubic man who is the son of a New Brunswick coal miner. He acted as the conglomerate's lawyer for many years as a senior partner at Toronto's blue-ribbon law firm, Osler Hoskins & Harcourt, but was enticed away when the deal making and legal ramifications of acquisition became more important than an operations or cigarette marketing man at the helm. Even so, cigarettes are the sizzle in this stock.

"Consumption has declined since 1982 by 4.5 per cent per year, [7 per cent in 1989], but the smart money – including Sir James Goldsmith's – is on tobacco today," explains the thoroughly candid Crawford. "Imperial Tobacco benefits in this market from strong trademarks [Player's, du Maurier, Peter Jackson, among others] and we are making market share gains of 1 per cent a year plus. This is phenomenal. The ad ban has boosted operating. We are fighting the ban in court, on principle, but the bans maintain the momentum of brands like ours that are already pre-eminent. It helps international brands but the biggest seller is Marlboro and we own the name in Canada. We have 57 per cent market share in Canada."

Imasco's second-most important asset is Canada Trustco, which will continue to improve through organic growth. However, several proposals to revamp financial institutions in Canada will inevitably lead to forced divestiture down to 65 per cent by Imasco. Such a roll-back was proposed because of concern about links between non-financial borrowers and financial lenders in the wake of several unrelated self-dealing scandals. But the policy is much disputed, particularly 1989 proposed legislation that would have prevented control blocks held by non-financial shareholders from being sold to someone else as a block. Stickhandling issues through Ottawa's political maze is the type of thing that Wiley does as well as anyone in the country. He's also a good friend of Prime Minister Brian Mulroney.

Like so many Canadians, Imasco has had some problems in the United States. It recently sold its 490 U.S. drugstores, called Peoples Drug Stores Inc. It is hoped that the remaining portion will turn around. But its U.S. fast-food entry appears to be a winner and was dramatically expanded through an acquisition in 1989. In Canada, Shoppers Drug Mart and United Cigar continue to crank out profits.

As Canada heads into a potentially troublesome decade, Imasco is considered a solid counter-cyclical entry that may provide investors with long-term growth and meet its management objectives of 20 per cent earnings increase each year. Drug and fast-food retail and financial services compensate for the decline of the tobacco sector.

Caveats: A downturn in the U.S. economy or the Canadian dollar will affect earnings adversely. There is concern that Imasco may have the same problems south of the border as virtually every other Canadian retailer has had, due to differences in the market and considerably more competition. Ottawa will try to speed up the decline of cigarette consumption through public education but will stop short of outlawing the use.

An investment of $10,000 in January 1980 was worth $70,824 in January 1990. With dividends reinvested, it totalled $83,868. Over the decade prices ranged from a high of $40.50 to a low of $5.25, adjusting for splits.

IMPERIAL OIL LIMITED

Head Office: Toronto, Ontario
Incorporated: 1880
Ownership: Controlling shareholder Exxon Corp.

Revenues in 1989: $10,100,000,000
Net Income: $456,000,000
Earnings per share: $2.38
Employees: 12,731
Year End: December 31

Corporate Canada is a high-class club and investors should seek membership in those companies in highly concentrated markets or product lines that are protected by barriers to entry. But recognizing quality barriers can be tricky. Some are fleeting and some are not. Probably the safest, and most profitable, barrier is simply size and success. Take the oil business. Any mechanic can run his own gas station without a great deal of capital. He can rent facilities from a big oil company, use its products and rely on the company's national marketing or public image to bring in business. Starting your own chain is another story. The best corner station locations are already owned by a handful of major oil companies. All the refineries, where you are going to buy your products, are owned by the same bunch. And they also bombard the airwaves and newspapers with their sales pitches. Exxon Corp.'s subsidiary here, Imperial Oil Limited, virtually dominates Canada's oil industry from field production to refining to pipelines and gasoline stations. It is Canada's best integrated oil bet by far and, for a number of unique reasons beside, should handily outperform the oil index.

Of course, size isn't always a guarantee of success or dominance. But Imperial is different. It is Canada's seventh-largest enterprise after General Motors of Canada Ltd., Ford Motor Co. of Canada, BCE Inc., Canadian Pacific Limited, George Weston Limited and Alcan Aluminum Limited. It jumped up a number of notches in 1990 when the Competition Tribunal in Ottawa finally blessed its 1989 takeover of arch-rival Texaco Canada Inc. for $4.96 billion. Months of negotiations with competitions officials and two sessions before the Competitions Tribunal finally resulted in a deal whereby Imperial would sell 636 gasoline stations. It also had to obtain permission from Investment Canada and in spring 1989 agreed to sell up to $550-million worth of upstream, or oil field, assets, to reinvest 70 per cent of upstream cash flow before debt servicing into operations and to protect Texaco's 3,200 workers from layoffs.

"We came out of it all right. We're happy but it was tough negotiations," says Imperial's personable chairman, Arden Haynes, who has two more years left until 1992 when, at age 65, he must retire. His obvious successor is Imperial president, Bob Peterson, born in 1938, who ran upstream operations for many years. The two occupy the 20th floor of the company's executive headquarters on Toronto's St. Clair Avenue West, removed from the city's financial district. The 1950-ish building is in good repair but singularly unflashy. Similarly, Haynes is avuncular in manner, a big, handsome Manitoban with the manners of the preacher's son. A thoroughly pleasant man, he runs a thoroughly pleasant company.

Now that all the regulatory hoops have been jumped through, Imperial is Canada's pre-eminent oil producer, refiner and re-seller with $9.6 billion in revenues. Imperial also makes chemicals and fertilizers and is in the pipeline business. Ottawa's Petro-Canada, with $4.8 billion in revenues, is in distant second spot. Even though Petro-Canada's new stock issue is an interesting proposition, there is a great deal of importance in being significantly in first spot in virtually all markets. This permits economies of scale, lower financing costs and bigger marketing budgets. As a result, Imperial Oil has the lowest finding costs of any oil company in Canada, the biggest inventory of oil on hand in the country, the best refinery in North America, a strong brand-name following and good station locations locked up. Unlike most others, Imperial has 10 years of conventional crude oil and natural gas liquids on hand; 27 years of heavy oil (thick sludge used as highway asphalt) at Cold Lake; 32 years of oil left at its

Syncrude oil-mining operation; and 19.8 years of gas left because of the Texaco acquisition. All of this adds up to the best prospect among any of North America's integrated oil companies. It also has a great deal of leverage should oil prices increase in the 1990s, as many expect they will. "For every $1-a-barrel increase in oil prices, it adds $70 million to our bottom line after tax. Some analysts think we are a better investment than our parent, Exxon," jokes Haynes.

The oil cartel, which skyrocketed prices 12-fold during the 1970s, finally collapsed in 1986 when prices plummeted from US$36 a barrel to as low as US$10. But throughout much of 1990, they have hovered at slightly more than US$20, and concerns that the world's two biggest producers – the United States and the Soviet Union – are running low on inventories are bullish for oil prices. That, combined with the fact that North Sea production peaked and Third World exploration has been on hold due to economic and oil price malaise, has led to a consensus that Persian Gulf producers will be in command by 1995 and prices will reach at least US$30 a barrel. There is little reason to take a contrary view on that. And among North American integrateds Imperial is the most sensitive to price fluctuations.

Not only that but if prices steadily rise, so may the differential between the prices of light and heavy crude such as Imperial produces at Cold Lake. These heavy deposits are tar-like and filled with impurities but can be upgraded into light, valuable crude oil for refinery purposes if there is from US$3 a barrel to US$5 a barrel difference in price. That is enough of a spread to justify the building of heavy oil upgraders (if oil prices are also higher than US$20 a barrel). If that occurs, Imperial could crank up production two- or three-fold, exporting light crude, chemicals, fertilizers or gasolines to the increasingly depleted United States in the 1990s. It has one of the world's largest potential oil resources at Cold Lake where 90,000 barrels a day are being produced out of Imperial's current production of 348,000 barrels daily.

"Our view about OPEC is a fundamental one shared by many oil companies. Saudi Arabia has announced more production, up to 10 million barrels daily and Iraq has made more discoveries. Meanwhile in the Unites States and elsewhere production is declining. As OPEC members cheat on quotas, the Saudis crank up production so the whole situation is volatile and will be for awhile," says Haynes.

"That's why mega-projects are very dicey without government subsidies. That's why these should wait until oil prices go up."

Imperial has escaped the adverse publicity suffered by its parent, Exxon, which has been charged by a grand jury in Alaska with negligence concerning the Valdez oil spill in 1989, a case that may cost the corporation as much as US$2 billion in fines and legal fees. Although that amount seems huge, to the world's biggest corporation (which Exxon is, by far), it is not life-threatening. Even so, some wonder if Exxon may end up like Texaco Inc. which ended up selling Texaco Canada to Imperial Oil because of a multibillion court judgment. Exxon owns 69.9 per cent of Imperial stock. "Analysts are regarding that as a mere blip," says Haynes. "Exxon is huge with huge cash flow and they wouldn't even feel a few billion dollars in fines at all. Exxon has no intention of selling Imperial and regards it as one of its best investments worldwide."

The privatization of Petro-Canada is good news for Imperial because Petro-Canada will be more bottom-line conscious and, therefore, less inclined to lead price wars at the pumps, which hurts profits for both. Similarly, the free trade deal is good for Imperial's chemical business in Sarnia, Ontario, where much of the U.S. market is within a day's drive. Tariff barriers on chemicals are now 10 per cent, among the highest, and as they ease, crude from Alberta and chemicals from Sarnia will undercut competitors in the United States, says Haynes.

Altogether, the future looks bright for Imperial even if demand for gasoline products grows only by 2 to 3 per cent a year, he says. "Shareholders can look forward to a promise Imperial will return at least the equivalent of its cost of capital. It is a secure company which has never cut a dividend. It also promises adequate growth and there are a lot of synergies [mutual benefits] to gain from the merger with Texaco. As crude oil prices go up, it becomes a tremendous investment because of our vast reserves at Cold Lake. With a potential of 1 trillion barrels in reserves and in the Arctic, we have Canada's largest natural gas field, which is going to be produced one day."

Caveats: Imperial's performance tracks the general business cycle, which has been heading downward. A downturn in oil and gas prices would hurt too, although that is considered unlikely. Another problem would be the election of an NDP or economically nationalist

Liberal government in Ottawa. Imperial would become a handy straw man for such opportunists, as has happened in the past, but it has learned how to manage controversy.

An investment of $10,000 in A shares in January 1980 was worth $14,587 in January 1990. With dividends reinvested it totalled $18,131. Over the decade prices ranged from a high of $81.50 to a low of $24.50, adjusting for splits.

LAIDLAW INC.

Head Office: Burlington, Ontario
Incorporated: 1966
Ownership: Controlling shareholder Canadian Pacific Limited

Revenues in 1989: US$1,413,375,000
Net Income: US$210,785,000
Earnings per share: US$1.00
Employees: 28,000
Year End: August 31

A pilot project in my Mississauga neighborhood has been underway for most of a year and consists of home-owners separating their refuse into several categories. Plastic containers, styrofoam, compost, twigs, cans, bottles and newsprint are picked up separately and taken to experimental recycling operations where the economic viability of their re-use is being tested. It is a bold experiment and a complicated system, what with different containers (supplied by the municipality) for different pick-up days depending upon what type of garbage is involved. The project encompasses an area with many socio-economic groups and, to my surprise, has been overwhelmingly accepted. One of the biggest boosters and the designer of the project is Laidlaw Transportation Limited, author of the popular Blue Box program in Mississauga years before. Concern about the environment, combined with the issue of land fill and disposal, is going to dog the 1990s. Enlightened Laidlaw is poised to profit from it because it is North America's most experienced curb-side recycler.

Laidlaw's founder, Mike DeGroote, operates his incredibly successful conglomerate out of a modest one-storey office complex beside the Queen Elizabeth Way in Burlington, Ontario. Inside and out, it is cheerfully decorated in the red, white and blue colors of the Laidlaw logo. DeGroote, a chain-smoking entrepreneur, sold 47 per cent of his control block of Laidlaw's A, or voting stock, to Canadian Pacific Limited in 1988 for a staggering $499 million. The purpose was to lock in value for estate-planning purposes, probably because his four children need the money to pay a huge capital gains tax on trust funds that become due in 1993. He signed a two-year contract to stay with Canadian Pacific but that expired in June 1990.

While the talented DeGroote's departure is disappointing, the incoming chief executive officer, Donald Jackson, promises more of the same prosperity. His self-professed goal is 20 to 25 per cent annual growth and an emphasis on pollution clean-up and waste management areas world-wide. Jackson, himself a talented executive, came to Laidlaw from the presidency of John Labatt Ltd.

DeGroote is a remarkable success story, a Belgian immigrant, who made his first fortune when he was in his early twenties by hauling freight with his small fleet of trucks during the uranium boom in Elliot Lake. A handful of years later he was flat broke, as was Elliot Lake until the lucrative hydro contracts assured its continued existence. But DeGroote moved back to Hamilton, Ontario, paid off all his debts over time, then turned around and built himself one of Canada's most successful conglomerates.

Laidlaw was at first a trucking giant, hauling everything from tomatoes to steel between the U.S. and Canada, but DeGroote abandoned the highly competitive trucking business for more lucrative fields. He swapped highway rigs for school buses and dumpsters. Now Laidlaw has a fleet of 18,500 vehicles that haul schoolchildren and 1,650 vehicles that haul garbage. The beauty of the bus and garbage businesses is that the only up-front risk is the cost of pricing, then snagging a municipal or school board contract. Once signed and properly priced, the rest runs itself like a utility, with amortization of vehicles built neatly into contract prices and a predictable rate of return to boot. Perhaps it was the Elliot Lake experience that taught DeGroote the value of government contracts.

From a standstill just a decade ago, Laidlaw today commands North America's largest school bus business, with 560 school board contracts and sightseeing ventures in 21 states and three provinces. More significant to many investors is Laidlaw's commanding position as North America's third-largest waste disposal company, an enterprise that will become more valuable as the environmental movement and the resistance to dumps makes Laidlaw's 34 U.S. land-fill sites valuable assets. Even so, Laidlaw's U.S. rivals, Waste Management Inc. and Browning Ferris Inc., trade at higher multiples than does Laidlaw. That may change in the 1990s.

Laidlaw's strategy won't change, so that entries into new areas are unlikely. The company is very interested in Europe 1992, and the firm is hunting opportunities. "We will be there," DeGroote commented before his departure in June, 1990. "Maybe in one year or in five. It is a very different market and regulations regarding waste management are still in a state of flux over there, but we believe they will adopt U.S. standards. As for other acquisitions, we will continue to follow our general tendency of service and non-cyclical businesses with high profit margins. We are not interested in manufacturing, even though we are one of the biggest purchasers of buses and other vehicles around."

With most of its operations in the United States, Laidlaw will greatly benefit from proposed U.S. legislation relating to land-fill sites, such as ground-water testing and recycling requirements. Many sites, not large enough to meet criteria, will close thus reducing competition and giving giants like Laidlaw acquisition opportunities. Laidlaw also won a court case and snagged waste disposal expert Tricil, formerly a joint venture split between Trimac Limited of Calgary and CIL Inc. of Toronto. This gives it a firm foothold in the hazardous and chemical waste disposal business.

UnderDeGroote's gifted leadership, Laidlaw has been Canada's premier growth company, with earnings per share increasing by 38 per cent compounded annually over the past ten years. "We are big now and cannot grow that quickly but I would say that 20 to 25 per cent annual compounded growth over the next ten years is not out of the question," says DeGroote.

Unfortunately, Laidlaw is one of those wonderful companies (like the Oshawa Group Limited or Canadian Tire Corporation) too good to miss out on but with two classes of stock, As with votes and Bs without. Votes are important when it comes to takeovers where a premium is paid for a control block of voting stock. But back in 1988, DeGroote and Canadian Pacific cut their own side deal and left the rest of the non-voting and minority voting shareholders out in the proverbial cold. I criticized it at the time, but it removed the issue of a takeover and which stock to invest in. Besides, Canadian Pacific is slowly accumulating both classes of stock in the open market by a few percentage points annually. Such nibbling away is like a sinking fund, providing some small but upward pressure on values.

Before Canadian Pacific made its bid, DeGroote announced he had been approached by a conglomerate, without naming it, in the hopes that a rival would come along and make an offer to all shareholders. It never materialized, mostly because of the sheer size of the takeover. But the announcement made headlines in the world's financial press and in the United Kingdom was noted by another remarkable *conglomerateur*, 44-year-old British hotshot, Michael Ashcroft, chairman of ADT Limited.

"I read about Laidlaw being for sale and we were in waste management, so I wanted to see if there was any mutuality," recalls Ashcroft. "I got to his offices and it was love at first sight because I saw my company's label 'ADT' stuck to the front door."

ADT is the world's biggest electronic surveillance company, with 90 per cent of its sales in the crime-ridden United States. There, paranoia means profits and ADT is twice the size of its biggest rival. Unlike others, ADT is debt-free. "It's counter-cyclical. Crime goes up during poor economic times," says Ashcroft. "So does the auction business. We own 5 per cent of art auctioneer Christie's and two car auction outfits, one in the U.K. and another with 21 of the 160 car auction sites in the U.S. We like the auction business. It is lucrative and has no inventory, no fixed assets, few receivables and is on land which is appreciating."

Canadian Pacific eventually snagged Laidlaw, but early in 1989 ADT sold to Laidlaw its 25 per cent stake in a U.S. waste outfit called Attwoods for US$125 million, then sold to Laidlaw 22 per cent of its stock for US$330 million. Then in July 1989, Laidlaw sold its Florida-based waste management operations to Attwoods plc of the United Kingdom in return for convertible preferred shares, bringing its interest to 34.2 per cent. About 70 per cent of Attwoods is in Florida and the rest in Britain and Germany. ADT's annual sales are around US$1.8 billion (bigger than Laidlaw's $1.1 billion) and Attwoods', only US$197 million.

ADT is a fascinating strategic play that each year installs in homes about 25,000 systems that include fire and heat sensors and an automatic dialling service to fire or police departments for a monthly fee. ADT also provides sophisticated monitoring systems for everything from the Canadian National Railways' 17,000-mile rail system (ironic considering Canadian Pacific's indirect interest) to the perimeters of military air bases around the world and all the top-secret activities inside Washington's Pentagon.

Now listed in London, Frankfurt, Toronto and NASDAQ too, ADT recently said it may bid for one of Britain's airports, soon to be privatized. As for Laidlaw, Ashcroft says there is a standstill agreement, and Ashcroft is on Laidlaw's board and DeGroote on ADT's. "We have no objection if Laidlaw wishes to increase its stake but it must have approval of ADT's board and Laidlaw has one of eight seats."

ADT, like Laidlaw, is in defensive, non-cyclical services. But to me, Laidlaw is a better bet, less confusing and better known to investors around the world because of its legendary track record. Ironically, their margins have been somewhat squeezed in early 1990 due to the relative prosperity and low unemployment in major cities where they operate. Such times mean labor is more scarce and hourly rates increase. "We hire a lot of part-time help, and lower unemployment has squeezed margins for us. Labor costs have risen because of the shortage by 20 per cent and labor is 40 per cent of costs," says DeGroote. "This is hard to pass onto customers right away under contracts."

Although hit with controversy over his sale in 1988, DeGroote's unblemished business record more than makes up for it. He has created one of Canada's greatest conglomerates and it will be his lasting legacy.

Caveats: DeGroote's departure would adversely affect both the stock price in the short term and may affect operations in the long term. But it's a large, well-managed firm, and will probably continue to perform well.

An investment of $10,000 in Laidlaw B in January 1980 was worth $361,698 by January 1990. With dividends reinvested, it totalled $371,479. Over the decade prices ranged from a high of $27 to a low of 54 cents, adjusting for splits.

(THE) LOEWEN GROUP INC.

Head Office: Burnaby, British Columbia
Incorporated: 1985
Ownership: Major shareholders Ray and Anne Loewen

Revenues in 1989: $73,906,000
Net Income: $7,201,000
Earnings per share: $0.75
Employees: 1,000
Year End: December 31

Ray Loewen has done a lot of things in his day. At 21 he was running his daddy's funeral home in Regina. He studied theology and bought a bigger funeral home in Fort Frances, Ontario. Then he built two funeral homes in British Columbia, ran for the B.C. legislature successfully, served one term as a Socred backbencher, then became involved in big-time real estate. Now, still on the sunny side of 50, Ray Loewen has created North America's second-largest funeral-home conglomerate, which simply does for funeral-home owners what you and I do before we need a funeral home's services: some estate planning. "That is why we will do very well. We provide estate planning, a corporate vehicle which can facilitate the orderly transition of ownership and management from one generation to another," says Ray Loewen.

The Loewen Group has grown from 14 homes in 1983 to 135 by 1990, 80 in Canada and 55 in the United States. It stepped up takeovers in 1990, buying the equivalent of two funeral homes per week at an average price of $1 million each. Loewen is like its rival, Arbor Capital Inc., and is cashing in on the ultimate counter-cyclical business. But the two firms are very different. Arbor wants to buy 100 more funeral homes in Canada during the 1990s, and Loewen wants to buy only south of the border. Loewen makes more money than Arbor doing so. Canada has 1,500 funeral homes in total, but there are 22,000 in the United States and a $4-billion-a-year market. Of the market potential, Loewen says: "About 17,000 are independently owned and most of the rest are multiple locations of one or two homes owned by an individual. The average age of a funeral director is 55 and the average cost is $1 million per home. So you have $22-billion worth of homes out there and half are going to change hands. That's $11 billion over ten years or $1.1 billion a year that's going to change hands. They want a way to do succession planning and ensure quality funeral service for the next generation and that is where we come in. It's an incredible opportunity."

Profits are handsome in the funeral business, running at an after-tax equivalent of nearly 10 per cent of revenues. Business never ebbs, particularly as the demographics of North America shift and the population ages rapidly. Revenues are not affected by economic downturns, low commodity prices or interest rates. People die in growing numbers (the death rate is expected to rise by 2 per cent per annum during the 1990s). And people have to be buried or, increasingly, cremated. The Loewen Group is starting to be compared to Michael DeGroote's successful Laidlaw Inc. as the growth play of the 1990s. Like Laidlaw, Loewen is in recession-proof sectors and may turn out to be one of Canada's greatest new high flyers. Only time will tell.

One thing is certain. Ray Loewen is one of those refreshing and likable prairie boys, a son of the Saskatchewan soil who always has time for family, neighbors and friends but who is, at the same time, tough-minded and seasoned by the adversity of a hostile climate and struggle for economic survival. Prairie folk are paradoxes: self-reliant and thoroughly co-operative. Loewen is a prairie metaphor. He is a casual, breezy entrepreneur who makes money by helping others solve their problems. "These funeral-home owners are professionals. They really care about the families they serve and are usually third- or fourth-generation businesses. They are concerned that the standard of professional care in their homes remains high. They care about the families they serve. My father regarded it very much as a ministry," recalls Loewen.

He also learned the funeral business the hard way. At 21, he was suddenly thrust into the family firm. "The first thing I had to do was fire my brothers," he recalls. "They didn't want to wash cars. They wanted a car and didn't want to help at the funeral home. They wouldn't go on removals with me. That was it. The next thing I learned was that you have to bring in more revenue than you pay out in expenses."

While most Canadians fail miserably making acquisitions in the United States, Loewen's formula is a real winner for a number of reasons. Takeover artists come unstuck through a combination of factors. They pay too much or they get too little. They often lose the people who made the acquired company so desirable. They lose the culture or cannot merge it with their own. They lose momentum, suppliers or customers. Loewen's acquisition strategy should avoid most of these pitfalls.

Most funeral-home owners are professionals who continue to run the operation and train successors after Loewen buys them out. Sometimes they stay on full-time, working seven-day weeks, or get paid on an hourly basis. No matter the arrangement, it is usual for the former proprietor to stay for some months or years. Loewen also provides alternative arrangements such as joint ventures and is growing in an interesting way.

Loewen provides a way to cushion the punitive succession duties the United States imposes on small businesses such as funeral homes. If the average price paid is $1 million, taxes could bite off more than half of that in many states. Loewen lets funeral home owners cash in their holdings before they have to and they can also participate in future profits. Owners swap their assets for cash plus stock in one of Loewen's regional entities run by a board of directors consisting mostly of ex-owners. This board, in turn, hunts for more acquisitions. After five years, they can cash in their stake, based on a formula for establishing value, thus providing an incentive to stay and help create a larger, regional chain for Loewen.

The proprietors continue to run their own operations on a full- or part-time basis, while Loewen taps their valuable contacts and business network. He also uses their market knowledge to gain an inside track on colleagues who are future prospects, industry intelligence that is invaluable in spotting good potential targets and avoiding bad ones. He also uses this fraternity of former owners to help convince potential sellers to join the Loewen Group rather than others. Loewen has also stocked its board with high-profile individuals from the funeral industry. It soft-sells itself as the gentle alternative from the north.

"We don't like [Robert] Campeau, though, for what he did [put America's two biggest retailers into Chapter 11 as a result of his high-flying antics]," says Loewen. "Americans don't like Campeau and we don't either because he gives Canadians like us who want to buy American assets a bad name."

Arbor is Loewen's chief competitor for homes in Canada and Service Corporation International, with 456 homes, is its biggest rival in the United States. Ray Loewen agrees that it makes sense that he take over one or both of these competitors, particularly Arbor, whose stock is trading at a significantly lower multiple to Loewen's share price. But it must be a friendly deal with Arbor's founder, Daniel Scanlan, who is at retirement age but still going strong. Perhaps his six children may want to sell control if a successor does not emerge.

The rivalry with Arbor is real and apparent at a meeting in Loewen's Burnaby office. Loewen lounges in a chair, kidding and jousting with his key executives. The atmosphere is collegial but competitive. He loves to needle. "Diane is writing a book on the 50 best companies to invest in, Bob," Loewen tells his right-hand man, Bob Lundgren, senior vice president. "And then she throws up a name like Arbor, which I can't understand. So why would you talk to Arbor? It is an interesting company, but interesting and best are two different things."

Service Corporation's stock has lagged, too, after it had some tough times as a result of its diversifications beyond cemeteries and funeral homes into caskets, monuments and other supply outfits. Unlike Arbor, it is more easily taken over because its founder-owner is down to 2 per cent shareholding and has been preoccupied with cutting losses by closing many of the facilities it bought. At $25 a share, Loewen has a market capitalization of $400 million. Service Corporation is at $600 million. "That would be interesting," says Loewen when asked to comment about a takeover.

When asked how big he wants his conglomerate to become he says, "In five years if we're not at least quadruple the size we are now, I'll be surprised. Why get so big? You only live once and you want to try to make a contribution. That's one reason we want to get big. The other one is, I suppose, the challenge of doing something. Doing as much as you can do."

Little wonder that acquisitions notably stepped up in 1990. "We said to ourselves a year ago [1989] we have to come up with a unique game plan for the U.S. So we decided that we were going to target the local consolidated companies and in almost every major centre there is a quality local, what we call local-consolidated company, a firm that is doing maybe 1,000 or 2,000 funerals a year out of five or eight doors," says Loewen. "Doors" are individual homes.

Increasing attention in the United States through purchases and as a result of analyst interest in Loewen since it was listed on NASDAQ in early 1990 promises higher stock multiples and more free money for even more U.S. takeovers. As long as acquisitions are financed mostly by equity and profits, and not by expensive bank loans, the Loewen Group should prosper. I wish them well.

Caveats: This business can weather recessions, but not overly aggressive takeovers. Although Loewen and his group have been conservative and have been winning by making small takeovers, a large buy-out of Arbor or SCI could prove troublesome.

An investment of $10,000 in Loewen in 1986 was worth $32,174 in January 1990. No dividends have been paid to date. Since 1986 prices ranged from a high of $18.63 to a low of $4.60, adjusting for splits.

MACKENZIE FINANCIAL CORPORATION

Head Office: Toronto, Ontario
Incorporated: 1971
Ownership: Widely held

Revenues in 1989: $105,000,000
Net Income: $23,000,000
Earnings per share $0.43
Employees: 300
Year End: March 31

Canadians pay punitive tax rates but also enjoy one of the world's most generous tax-shelter plans, the Registered Retirement Savings Plan. While our cousins south of the border can sock away only $2,000 per year toward individual retirement accounts, Canadians can currently set aside up to $7,500 annually ($15,500 by 1992 if a federal proposal is made law). Canada's population is also aging rapidly, and this will mean a jump in the savings rate. Older households have fewer expenses and more concerns that they have set aside sufficient savings for their retirement years. Such trends will have a profound effect on stock market investments in Canada during the 1990s as the amount of money put into RRSPs is expected to outstrip the total value of all Canadian stocks.

This book argues that investors should play the stock market selectively and create their own conglomerate or mini-mutual fund. In fact, most investors will opt for mutual funds and let the professionals manage their money for them. This is because they have neither the time, nor the interest, to make investment judgments. Still others were frightened by the publicity surrounding the October 1987 crash into believing that the market was for large, institutional investors like mutual fund houses. Even more will swing over to mutual funds with foreign holdings as a means of diversifying now that RRSP limits on foreign holdings will gradually increase to 20 per cent from 10 per cent by 1994.

That strategy makes sense simply in terms of hedging currency bets, as well as taking advantage of often better earnings offshore. Few brokers or their firms have the expertise to advise clients about direct investments, so more investors will turn toward mutual funds firms who have such expertise already in place. One major study in 1989 concluded that by the year 2000, Canadian mutual fund assets will multiply five-fold to $150 billion from the current $31 billion.

There is a way for those who invest directly in the market to capitalize on the others who do not: by purchasing stock in one of the four publicly listed mutual fund marketers. These companies earn profits from investment management fees charged to mutual fund unit holders. Fees are not tied to performance, as they are in some U.S. mutual funds, although a consistently poor showing will eventually decrease deposits by investors into mutual funds. Lower deposits mean lower fees and therefore lower mutual fund company profits. Simply put, the biggest share of this growing mutual fund pie will go to the most successful investment management team and the most successful mutual fund sales team. So far in Canada the best is Mackenzie Financial Corporation, whose stock has catapulted as the deposits have poured in. But even better than profits (its stock has catapulted, too) is the fact that it is a takeover target, a widely held company that any bank, insurance company, mutual fund or trust company would like to own.

Its stock has been expensive, however, because Mackenzie Financial Corporation through its Industrial group of funds has grown until 1990 by leaps and bounds. By 1990, it was managing $9 billion of other people's money, up from $6.6 billion in 1988. Like rival AGF Management Ltd. (another takeover target), it sells through brokers and now has an impressive customer base of 450,000 individuals owning pieces of Industrial Funds, as well as clients such as corporate, religious and non-profit association pension plans and wealthy estates. This is all the more impressive considering that Mackenzie went public in 1981 with only $6 million in revenue, which by 1988 had jumped to $86.49 million. Profits leaped from $1.8 million net to $16 million.

Masterminding this meteoric growth is Mackenzie chairman Alexander Christ and president James O'Donnell. "I think James O'Donnell is a super salesman and Alex Christ has called the market very, very correctly," says Albert Thompson, analyst with Prudential-Bache Securities Inc. He has recommended the stock for months. The only problem child is its U.S. subsidiary, which lost $5 million in 1989. But fee increases and the pass-through of new costs to fund holders more than made up for that.

Christ, like top performing portfolio managers Sir John Templeton and Peter Lynch, is American born and deeply religious. Born in 1937, he tithes, abstains from alcohol and lives modestly with his wife and eight children. Forerunner of Mackenzie financial was the Industrial Growth Management Ltd., a small company housed above a Harvey's hamburger restaurant in Toronto. Industrial Growth was the private holding company for Harvey founders, Richard Mauran and his family, now billionaires thanks to Christ's astute market calls. A series of acquisitions led to the formation of Mackenzie and Christ's ascension as its chairman.

"Mackenzie President James O'Donnell has used the best sales incentives in the business to get independent stockbrokers to sell Mackenzie funds. No one wines and dines the brokers like [Jimmy]," a competitor told the *Post* in 1990. "Entertaining the brokerage community is clearly an area Christ leaves to O'Donnell. Christ is the reclusive inside man who runs the four-man investment team, while O'Donnell is the adventurous outside man," wrote Susan Gittins in a *Post* article in April 1990. "It is O'Donnell who is behind Mackenzie's sponsorship of an Indy 500 racing car. It is O'Donnell who plays host to wild parties for Mackenzie's top products at the Indy or in exotic locales. And it is O'Donnell who covets the corporate jet." But the two form a winning team, Christ the strait-laced ex-U.S. marine and the flamboyant O'Donnell. The two, plus Mackenzie vice-chairman William Crerar, met at a firm which was predecessor of RBC Dominion Securities Inc. Christ then joined Prudential-Bache Securities Canada Ltd. as head of research before managing the Mauran family money. He's now reportedly worth $45 million, and in a speech to a Toronto group called the Downtown Christian Association, said prosperity follows Christian generosity. "Start giving away at least 10 per cent of your income, no matter what [it] is because this will ensure that your family will never want," he told the group. "That means you'll establish your downside and ensure that you will prosper. Then if you learn to give away 15 to 20 per cent and more, you'll really start to get rich."

Fuelling speculation as to a Mackenzie takeover bid in 1989 were insider trading reports that Mackenzie's Christ cashed in half of his stake for $19.3 million, leaving him as the largest single shareholder with only 6 per cent. Likewise, AGF is also another good growth company that is a takeover target. "Quite frankly, we're being solicited [for a takeover] all the time," says AGF chairman and founder, Warren Goldring, a personable financial analyst. He and his management group own 34 per cent of the stock.

(AGF's asset base is considerably smaller, some $2 billion invested in 22 AGF funds. This reaped revenues of $37 million in 1988 and $6.2 million in net profit. Like Mackenzie, AGF peddles its wares through the country's 9,000 registered representatives in brokerage firms. AGF has branched out by buying Chancellor Trust, a small trust company with $50 million in assets which contributes $1/2 million pre-tax to AGF's bottom line. That rapidly growing profit centre, combined with a diverse customer base of 160,000 clients, provides a solid business underpinning. AGF's stock prices have lagged behind Mackenzie's because corporate performance has lagged. It lost market share in 1987 and 1988 when service slipped because AGF did not have an in-house computerized account bureau. That translated into delays and frustrations, which annoyed broker-agents wishing instant information that was readily obtainable from Mackenzie and others, says Goldring. "But we have addressed that problem and have our own service now.")

Despite AGF's improvement, I think Mackenzie is a slightly better bet. About the only negative I can mention is Mackenzie's 21.7 per cent of a new merged brokerage firm Walwyn-Midland Inc., formerly Walwyn Stodgell Cochran Murray Limited and Midland Doherty Financial Corporation. The stake is described as passive, but may upset other brokerage firms through which Mackenzie sells its products. AGF and others are sure to publicize and capitalize on this close connection. Even so, Mackenzie's track record over the long term is hard to beat and I think the stock is too good to ignore.

Caveats: While the mutual fund pie grows faster than most sectors, the competition will increase both onshore and offshore. Buying shares in mutual fund houses is a bet that the RRSP phenomenon will continue to soar. It is also a bet on the ability of the fund to continue to post good returns in order to attract more business.

An investment of $10,000 in January 1980 was worth $273,438 in January 1990. With dividends reinvested, it totalled $280,625. Over the decade prices ranged from a high of $9.25 to a low of 28 cents, adjusting for splits.

MACLEAN HUNTER LIMITED

Head Office: Toronto, Ontario
Incorporated: 1891
Ownership: Major shareholder Maclean Hunter Holdings

Revenues in 1989: $1,426,200,000
Net Income $90,300,000
Earnings per share: $0.58
Employees: 12,731
Year End: December 31

Canada used to be a forest of television antennas reaching above roofs in order to capture the American airwaves. That gave birth to a unique Canadian "invention," cable television, and during the 1970s and 1980s companies with foresight bid for franchise areas and hit pay dirt. Now Canada is more wired than any other country on earth, with an average of 80 per cent of households hooked up to cable in most regions. The United States, by comparison, has a 55 per cent cable penetration. Although there are indications that the party may be over and near-windfall profits are coming to an end, these money machines have provided owners with enough surplus capital to buy other assets and to wire other parts of the world.

The cable business is counter-cyclical, faces no competitors and therefore earns monopoly profits. Future competition is unlikely despite threats from BCE Inc. that it will take on the cable companies with an alternative service. BCE's vaunted cable strategy, however, has more to do with its upcoming rivalry against Canada's biggest cable operator, Rogers Communications Inc., which intends to ask Ottawa for permission to compete against BCE for the lucrative long-distance telephone business. These matters may take years to resolve, because applications must be subjected to regulatory hearings before the Canadian Radio-Television and Telecommunications Commission. I'm not holding my breath.

Maclean Hunter Limited is much, much more than a cable company. It is one of Canada's oldest and greatest media conglomerates, offering investors regional and product diversity. Some 38 per cent of its bottom line is derived from cable, and the rest is more or less evenly divided among its three other businesses: forms and commercial printing; newspapers and periodicals; and broadcasting and communications services.

Col. John Maclean and Horace Hunter launched their first publication more than a century ago called *The Canadian Grocer & General Storekeeper*. Dozens more periodicals followed, and commercial printing was a natural vertical integration. In the 1970s, Maclean Hunter began diversifying in a big way, entering cable first during that decade, buying control of the Toronto Sun Publishing Corporation in 1982 and getting deeply into the television and radio businesses in 1989 with the purchase of Selkirk Communications Limited.

The Maclean family has long since sold out, but some 21 per cent of stock is held by the Hunter family (Don Hunter and his sister, Mary Margaret McCallum) through Hunco Limited. None of the family members are involved in day-to-day operations. The empire is ably run by two chartered accountants, Don Campbell and Ron Osborne, chairman and president respectively. Campbell is near retirement age, but Osborne is in his early 40s. Osborne is a language grad from Cambridge University who worked one summer in Canada in construction then decided to immigrate; he joined Toronto accounting giant Clarkson Gordon (now Ernst & Young), then in 1976 he opted for a stint in its Brazilian office. He was wooed away in 1981 by Maclean Hunter to become its vice president of finance. Quickly shooting up through the ranks, he gained the title of chief executive officer in 1984 and was president by 1986. Restless and hard-driving, he talks in bursts, like a machine-gun, and always hits the bull's eye. He puts in 11-hour days.

We meet on a Friday evening at 6 P.M., when phones are finally stilled, in a sitting room across from his Toronto office. His thick glasses aside, Osborne looks more like a footballer than an accountant. He is tall, stocky and loves to dance, rarely sitting one out at corporate or social functions. He and Campbell form a winning team, but it is ironic that two accountants manage Maclean Hunter's eclectic and creative army of 11,000 writers, editors, designers, photographers, advertising salespeople and broadcasters. On second thought, it's probably appropriate.

"With our cable interests, we want to do it well and dominate. We want a more balanced portfolio generally. We intend to add to business forms in Canada or to periodicals and consumer magazines. As for broadcasting, we're happy with the Selkirk purchase," he says. "We will build on all of them hopefully."

Osborne straddles a $1.3-billion-a-year empire, which is Canada's third-largest cable operator, its largest periodical publisher, with 90 business publications and dozens of consumer titles such as *Maclean's*, *Chatelaine* and *Flare*. Dozens more business periodicals are owned in the United States and United Kingdom, and everything from annual reports to magazines published by Maclean Hunter are produced in its commercial printing division. Maclean Hunter is also Canada's second-largest business forms printer. As for broadcasting, it owns 23 radio stations and three television stations – Calgary's CTV affiliate and CFCN and Hamilton's CHCH.

Through its ownership of Toronto Sun Publishing Corporation, Maclean Hunter is indirectly the country's third-largest daily newspaper chain, operating five large-circulation Canadian dailies, the Toronto, Ottawa, Edmonton and Calgary *Sun*s, as well as the *Financial Post*. It also owns 85 per cent of Bowes Publishers, with four small dailies, 12 weeklies in western Canada and a collection of magazines. The *Suns'* combined circulation is 1 million daily. *Sun* contributions have been down as a result of start-up costs at the *Financial Post* and *Ottawa Sun*, but both publications should eventually become winners.

As one of Canada's few widely held corporations, it armed itself in 1989 with a shareholder rights plan, which avoids the possibility of a creeping takeover by forcing large shareholders to bid for all the outstanding stock. It also merged voting with non-voting stock, another plus for shareholders. A takeover is probably out of the question, because a buyer has to be Canadian and there are too few big enough to buy it. But Maclean Hunter shareholders can expect more acquisitions.

I run down a list of potential targets with Osborne. What about business forms giant, Moore Corporation Limited, I ask. "It's a diversified company within a diversified industry. It would have to be a friendly takeover. We don't do unfriendlies." How about Southam Inc.? "We've made our bet with the *Toronto Sun* and we're very happy."

Maclean Hunter is bidding for virgin cable television franchises in Europe, an action that may reap benefits in the future. "U.K. cable is a bet. We have East Lancashire, East Anglia and we've applied for others. We were approached by Hungary and looked at Budapest, but must source all equipment outside. Then we have a currency risk. Too big a currency bet. It's enough of a gamble as it is."

Meanwhile, here at home, Bell Canada's threatened entry into the cable sweepstakes does not bother Osborne. But he is not ignoring it either. "Fibre optics to homes is years away. We're laying coaxial cable and Bell's laying copper. How would they go about it, assuming fibre optics were practical? Share one with us or lay two systems? Canada doesn't need another one. I think the analogy is with the Concorde. It's a great plane but at what cost?"

Television itself is in a state of flux, but cable's future seems certain despite the incursion of VCRs, home video rentals and satellite dishes. Videotron and Rogers have branched out into the movie rental business to hedge their bets, but Canadians continue to have a voracious appetite for the various media. The average Canadian every week watches 20 hours of television, listens to 18 hours of radio and reads magazines for 4.5 hours. "The U.S. networks have 60 per cent of the viewership, compared to 85 per cent a few years back, which isn't much [of a drop], given the proliferation of other programming. The same argument was made that radio was finished when television came along. But that's not the case," points out Osborne.

Maclean Hunter is also on the acquisition trail for trade magazines, data bases or electronic information operations, no matter where they are located. But Osborne feels that consumer magazines outside of Canada are off limits. "We would feel awkward buying a publication like *Maclean's* in Germany, for instance. And in the U.S. there are few consumer titles and the money required to buy one is so huge it would swamp everything else. *People* magazine has been valued at $1 billion. That's 50 per cent of Maclean Hunter's value."

Maclean Hunter stock has traditionally been pricey, but there is little doubt that this is the Mercedes of media stocks. On the other hand, some feel that its cable assets are still undervalued in terms of its stock price. If Rogers' price of $2,500 per subscriber paid by a U.S. purchaser in 1989 in the U.S. were applied, Maclean Hunter's U.S. cable operations alone would have a market value of $1 billion, far more than now awarded. A premium price for Maclean Hunter stock is warranted because of Maclean Hunter's risk-reducing diversification and its impeccable track record. Dividends are 40 per cent of earnings.

Caveat: Publishing and printing outfits track general economic conditions and linage falls if the economy slows. That's why 1990 won't be a banner year for earnings. Cable operations reduce such cycles in this case, but cable is mature in Canada and may face a challenge eventually from Bell. Technological breakthroughs in satellite dish technology could also hurt cable operations sometime in the distant future. The decision in May 1990 by Ottawa cable regulators to freeze profits made by cable companies for the next few years will limit profits, and therefore stock price increases, to cable outfits with diversified products, new franchises or unique opportunities for incremental growth.

An investment of $10,000 in January 1980 was worth $88,182 in January 1990. With dividends reinvested, it totalled $97,455. Over the decade prices ranged from a high of $14.88 to a low of $1.35, adjusting for splits.

MDS HEALTH GROUP LIMITED

Head Office: Etobicoke, Ontario
Incorporated: 1969
Ownership: Major shareholders MDS Deferred Profit Sharing Plan;
Ontario Municipal Employees Retirement Fund

Revenues in 1989: $224,557,000
Net Income: $10,890,000
Earnings per share: $1.25
Employees: 4,553
Year End: October 31

Ron Yamada remembers vividly what a famous surgeon told him and his team of IBM computer experts in the wee hours in 1969 while they worked on a computer project at Johns Hopkins medical centre. "The best surgeons leave the operating room and become administrators," lamented the doctor. At worst, Yamada thought, this was medicine's version of the Peter Principle. At best, it was a waste of talent. Yamada and the four others spotted a business opportunity and launched MDS Health Group Limited. "As IBM employees, we knew the value of being known by only three initials," quips Yamada, MDS senior vice president in charge of systems and corporate affairs.

MDS stands for Medical Data Sciences and is Canada's corporate doctor. It makes money by performing tasks for physicians that less skilled medical personnel can do. It also sells labor- and time-saving equipment and other types of services to 8,000 physicians across Canada and the northeast United States. Its 250 labs in 75 communities minister to the medical needs of 5 million patients a year, performing 24 million procedures. Six hundred thousand patients are seen in their homes or in long-term facilities by visiting nurses or x-ray technicians. Business is booming as the population ages and needs more medical attention.

MDS is a slick outfit. It has a fleet of 120 courier cars that pick up specimens from physicians' offices in remote areas, and it provides everything from computerized billing systems for use by doctors to hospital equipment and supplies. Through MDS's real estate arm, the company has helped 700 doctors develop and become owners of 700,000 square feet of medical office space, buildings that come complete with MDS lab facilities. MDS also provides 100 hospitals and 530 nursing homes with testing and management services and has spread its wings into biotechnology and medical research, landing a $17-million grant from Ontario in 1989.

With soaring medical costs a worry to politicians, MDS may cash in on the burgeoning move to privatize hospitals or hospital labs. "There are early indications that the public sector may be interested in transferring technology from public to private and three hospital labs are being managed by the private sector. In Hawkesbury, Ontario, near the Quebec border, American Medical International, Inc. of California in 1989 took over management of a hospital," says Yamada. "Usually payment is a fixed contract with fees up front plus a share in savings. There are 700 hospitals in Canada."

MDS is enormously successful, but there have been difficulties, particularly since medical ethics as represented in the Hippocratic Oath are sometimes on a collision course with the bottom line. MDS embraces two very different cultures – one medical and one financial – and has had to fashion what must be corporate Canada's oddest organizational structure. But it sure works.

"This is a professional partnership with physicians. We have a business head and a medical head who report to their peers in the form of a medical advisory board," explains Yamada. "And that advisory board is represented equally on the board of MDS with two directors, two management directors and five outsiders. We used to have fights like you wouldn't believe. Now we divide duties. What gauge needle you need to take blood samples is a medical decision. But what bank you use is a business decision."

Even so, there are potential clashes where a decision must be made that is both medical and business. "We can't afford to fight amongst ourselves and 15 years ago, for instance, we decided to standardize our chemical analyzers, which are instruments used to detect sugar diabetes, liver disorders, cholesterol, trigylcerides, etc. The medical advisory board evaluated all the instruments on the market and came up with a short-list of three acceptable ones. Then the business types chose from those on the basis of commercial considerations," explains Yamada.

If a clash occurs, the board deals with it. If the medical advisory board does not agree or is not satisfied, then every medical director is required to resign. In other words, the doctors get their way when push comes to shove.

MDS's headquarters are near Toronto's Lester B. Pearson International Airport in an atrium building littered with No Smoking signs. The day I interview its executives, employees are manning fitness booths to sign up colleagues for everything from charitable marathons to health outings. Morale is high from most accounts and its 1,700 employees, through a deferred profit-sharing scheme, own 27 per cent of MDS stock. Another 25 per cent is owned by OMERS, the Ontario Municipal Employees Retirement Fund. That means little is left and there's no chance for an unfriendly takeover. Unicorp Canada Corporation's predator George Mann tried in 1977, was given a board seat and realized that this was a unique organization, a partnership really, that by definition has to be controlled by employees, not bosses.

Even so, the company is still courted. "Large lab players in the U.S. talk to us but not many have the same interests," says Douglas Phillips, senior vice president of finance and administration. "We have great cash flow but are not an asset-based company. We do have undervalued assets; this building bought for $10 million, worth $20 million. Our stock price usually trades at a multiple of 16 to 17 times earnings. But in the U.S., one competitor traded at 60 times on takeover rumors and a pharmaceutical company eventually paid 22 times."

Multiples may lag because, like other Canadians, MDS has had some trouble digesting a series of U.S. acquisitions that hurt earnings in 1988. The U.S. businesses had to be reorganized, upgraded and relocated. But Yamada says problems are behind the company now, and MDS has been busy diversifying into related fields. It helped finance a management buy-out of the Canadian operations of Ingram & Bell, part of American Sterilizer and Canada's second-largest hospital supplier. MDS has 49 per cent with an option for the rest, owned by 20 key Ingram managers. MDS also owns manufacturers of medical products.

With labs and a medical products sales force, it was a natural for MDS to finance ideas and get into developing new technologies. MDS's subsidiary, Sciex Limited, joined with the University of Toronto to develop the "super sniffer" that was used in the Mississauga train derailment to chemically break down air samples in minutes in order to monitor air quality. Two more Sciex measuring devices, one to detect illicit narcotics, and another to measure toxins in water and fish, also show enormous promise. The Ontario Technology Fund granted MDS $17 million to miniaturize this latter device, which will open up a huge potential market for governments, industry and commercial fishermen. There are other small joint ventures with physicians, scientists and hospitals to develop various devices.

There's little doubt that MDS is well-positioned to cash in on Canada's changing demographics. The demand for medical services and supplies and the type of outpatient, home-care service that MDS is already set up for bodes well for the investors in this corporate doctor. With Canada's gold-plated medical system, there are never any bad debts, either.

Caveats: This stock has a small float, which always reduces investor liquidity. Concerns are that its U.S. operations underperform and that the company's aggressive entry into research and development may not yield pay dirt.

An investment of $10,000 in A shares in January 1980 was worth $59,241 in January 1990. With dividends reinvested, it totalled $61,519. Over the decade prices ranged from a high of $29.75 to a low of $1.93, adjusting for splits. (MDS stock split 2 for 1 in March 1990.)

NORANDA INC.

Head Office: Toronto, Ontario
Incorporated: 1988 (Ontario Amalgamation)
Ownership: Controlling shareholder Brascade Resources Inc.

Revenues in 1989: $9,158,000,000
Net Income: $442,000,000;
Earnings per share: $2.19
Employees: 59,000
Year End: December 31

Noranda is Canada's eighth-largest enterprise and employs 48,000 people – that's the population of Sarnia, Ontario. In 1990, revenues hit $11 billion, an amount six times larger than Prince Edward Island's gross domestic product. It is a resource monolith, controlled by the Peter Bronfman Brascan Ltd. empire along with Quebec's Caisse de dépôt et placements du Québec. After a series of head-spinning takeovers to reach this size, Noranda has become the country's premier resource-asset play. It now controls 10 per cent of Canada's forestry business, the country's single biggest export industry; is one of the ten largest mining companies in the world; controls three large oil companies; and owns manufacturer Canada Wire and Cable Limited as well as Polysar, the petrochemical giant pictured on the back of Canada's purple $10 bill.

Master of this universe is Alf Powis, a rumpled, chain-smoking executive who holds the Canadian record of 22 years as chief executive officer. Interestingly, the Gaelic name for the resource-rich northern portion of Wales is also "Powis." His high-rise office at Noranda reveals his longevity. It is filled with 1960s furniture and memorabilia dating back decades. The only modern fixture is his computer, which Powis pecks at painfully. "I'm a one-finger fellow," he confesses.

Few executives survive the rough-and-tumble world of big business as long as has Powis or his side-kick, the patrician Adam Zimmerman, chairman of Noranda's forestry division. But the two have transformed Noranda from a regionally based mining outfit with 5,000 workers to an energy, forestry and mining giant that should ring up $3 million per day in profit. Their staying power is all the more unusual considering they opposed Noranda's capture in 1981 by its current owners, the Toronto Bronfmans and the Caisse de dépôt. Now the two major shareholders control Brascan Ltd. with 46 per cent of Noranda.

Of Powis's staying power, Zimmerman remarks, "He's a medical miracle. Some kind of a superman. He takes worse care of himself than anybody I know and gets away with it. He smokes three packages of cigarettes a day, is not shy with martinis and yet he's always there when the bell rings."

Noranda's switch in emphasis from strictly manufacturing and mining to include oil, gas and forestry has been deliberate but speeded by unplanned opportunities. "I would have said we won't get much bigger in forest products, then we bought Normick Perron Inc. There's always Domtar (controlled by the Caisse de dépôt) but we're not acceptable buyers. We don't speak the right language," he says. Also in 1989, Noranda snapped up Falconbridge Limited with Swedish partners for $2.4 billion.

Noranda's diversification lops off peaks and valleys as research by mining analyst Terry Ortslan of Deacon Barclays de Zoete Wedd Limited in Montreal shows. He quantified the effect of 10 per cent changes in the prices of Noranda's important commodities and found interesting offsets, considering that energy, forestry and mining cycles often diverge. A 10 per cent change in oil prices, for instance, would affect earnings by $18 million one way or the other; 10 per cent change in fine paper prices, by $20 million; 10 per cent in zinc prices, $35 million; copper, $22 million; newsprint, $14 million; aluminium, $15 million; nickel, $19 million, to name a few. "It's not a buy until it hits the high teens for capital appreciation or long-term accumulation," he says.

Powis says such diversification has been a strategy since the beginning. "We have the same philosophy as we did in the sixties. All Noranda had was the Horne mine and smelter and some manufacturing. We knew by the mid-seventies the ore was gone, so we had to replace the mine or wind up the company so we set out on a deliberate course of growth. The Horne is essentially a copper mine and copper cycles are notoriously unstable so we diversified into other metals," he says.

Powis began his career as a financial analyst with Sun Life Assurance Company of Canada Limited in Montreal and was lured away in 1958 from his $300-a-month job in Montreal to earn $600 a month as the understudy to Noranda's treasurer. He found Toronto boring, populated by a WASPish old guard led by Argus Corporation's legendary Bud McDougald. "When I first came, there was an old boys' network. McDougald wanted to take over Noranda and we fought him off so he black-listed me from joining the Toronto Club for years. He eventually relented and I joined the club," says Powis.

Now a ranking member of Canada's establishment, Powis is also committed to heavy exploration. The result is that Noranda's metals and minerals exploration budget is the biggest in Canada – $73 million for grassroots or highly speculative exploration. Activities are restricted to North America and Australia but may return, as years before, to the Third World. Noranda's captive oil arm, Canadian Hunter Ltd., is run by talented geologists John Masters and Jim Gray in Calgary, who have discovered more natural gas than any other explorers. Gray says of Powis, "He backed us when no one else would. Hunter in 1989 had $100 million in revenues and we were given $250 million for drilling. Noranda's been a great parent."

When asked about Noranda's volatile stock as an investment, Powis's former persona of financial analyst rises to the fore. "No other company is as balanced between metals and forestry and energy as we are. You could say we get the worst of all cycles because all the businesses we're in are cyclical. If you buy Noranda, you are not buying a pure metals play and won't catch the great upside of metals cycles because we're mixed up with forestry products. But if, hopefully, cycles are all out of sync, you'll never get the worst of it either. This theory was tested in 1982 and everything sewered at once. It failed. But metals and forestry cycles are generally about 18 months apart. Forestry picked up early in 1986 and by mid-eighty-seven metals were good. Now forestry has been slipping since mid-eighty-eight and metals began to slip at the end of 1989."

For investors interested in Noranda, the secret is timing and to remember that Noranda is cyclical. Investors who bought its shares in late 1982 at $11 a share and sold in August 1987 at $38 would have been pleased. As for controlling shareholder Brascan, it is in there for the long haul, another comfort to investors who worry about Noranda's heavy debt load. Powis freely admits he wishes he'd won that battle back in 1981 to keep Noranda independent, but is philosophical. "I wish we hadn't been taken over but I cannot think of any set of rules to stop takeovers that wouldn't hurt the system in other ways. As things turned out, the Bronfmans and the Caisse put $500 million into Noranda's treasury back in 1981 before the last recession which, quite frankly, saved our ass."

Caveats: This is still a cyclical stock and long-term investors should not get involved unless prices are at, or near, the perceived bottom. It is affected by interest rates because it is highly leveraged and is also affected by a high Canadian dollar because most of its products fetch U.S. dollars. It is a member of the Bronfman empire, which I generally dislike, but because it has an important outside partner, the Caisse de dépôt, it is insulated from the confusing cut-and-paste restructurings which that group indulges in.

An investment of $10,000 in January 1980 was worth $10,778 in January 1990. With dividends reinvested, it totalled $14,276. Over the decade prices ranged from a high of $38 to a low of $11.38, adjusting for splits.

NORTHERN TELECOM LIMITED

Head Office: Mississauga, Ontario
Incorporated: 1914
Ownership: Controlling shareholder BCE.

Revenues in 1989: US$6,105,500,000
Net Income: US$376,500,000
Earnings per share: U.S.$1.47
Employees: 47,472
Year End: December 31

This is probably Canada's greatest corporation. Northern Telecom is one of Canada's few multinationals that is truly world-class. It has grown organically, through research and smart strategy, not by gobbling up smaller entities. Even better, Northern is a world-beater in a competitive marketplace where brains, as opposed to non-renewable resources, are the biggest asset. It has accomplished this by finding high technology niches, pursuing them with aggressiveness and spending millions of dollars on research. Northern Telecom is great because it makes its investors money but also because it proves that Canadians are just as capable as the Americans, Japanese or Europeans in brainy businesses that are highly competitive. And the icing on all this cake was spread in 1990 when Northern announced new technology that makes it uniquely positioned to profit from two worldwide trends, the dawning of the Information Age as well as the liberalization of trade.

Northern is one of the few Canadian players to have conquered the U.S. market. It is now America's second-largest central office phone equipment company and Western Europe's largest supplier of PBX systems, private networks used by corporations and governments. It dominates many Far Eastern markets and even sells to Japan and Taiwan. In fact, Northern dominates those two telecommunications niches around the world – digital switching sold as an industrial product to telephone companies and PBXs, or office systems sold as a consumer product to phone users.

With good positioning worldwide, it has the largest market share everywhere in both niches, and Northern Telecom will get a huge chunk of the burgeoning telecommunications pie. By the year 2000, the market for goods and services is expected to reach US$300 billion a year, up from US$75 billion in 1989.

"Northern Telecom looks like ninth out of ten among the ten world leaders in telecommunications. But the other competitors have other products. If you look just in terms of digital and PBX systems, which are the core of the telecom equipment market worldwide, they are number one in sales," says Northern fan Michel Guite, high-tech analyst with New York's Salomon Brothers.

Northern Telecom is really an American company with Canadian ownership. Most of its revenues, profits and even its chairman and chief executive officer are American. Little wonder that U.S. investors are returning to the stock and own about 25 per cent of the float after abandoning it in the early 1980s. Some left because of the recession; some left later because Northern got flabby and ran into some problems with its U.S. expansion. The company wrote down $200 million in 1988 and laid off about 2,500 employees, part of a global drive to prune administrative costs. The action paid off and recommendations by analysts started to clatter across wires in 1989, driving the stock up to goodly heights again. Guite says Northern Telecom is leaner and meaner than its rivals around the world. Even so, it spends an average of 11 per cent of its revenues on research, the highest of any private-sector firm in Canada.

It manufactures its products at 24 plants in Canada, 13 in the United States, 1 each in Ireland and France and 2 in Malaysia. Research is conducted through Bell-Northern Research Ltd., whose 6,500 workers operate out of labs in Canada, the United States and Britain. They concentrate on producing software for Northern Telecom products such as telephones and terminals, wire and cable, switching systems, transmission systems and operation and maintenance systems to manage networks. Northern Telecom owns 70 per cent of Bell-Northern and Northern's controlling shareholder, BCE Inc., owns the rest. Bell Canada owns 52 per cent of Northern Telecom.

Paul Stern became Northern's chairman and chief executive officer in April 1990, after having joined the board in 1988. His resumé is impressive. Before he joined Northern, he was president of U.S. high-tech giant, Burroughs Corporation, stickhandled its purchase in 1986 of the Sperry Corporation and created Unisys Corporation, where he was president until December 1987. He has held important positions with the who's who of high tech south of the border, including stints at Rockwell International Corporation, IBM Corporation, Braun AG, subsidiary of the Gillette Company and E.I. du Pont Corporation. He has a bachelor's degree in electronics engineering, a master's in science and a doctorate in physics.

"Paul Stern will guide us toward making money. In the first quarter earnings were up 50 per cent and debt to equity improved," points out Northern's executive vice-president John Roth, in charge of product line management. "Our strategy is to be first or second in all our products, we are not at the leading edge of technology, but at the leading edge in applying technology."

Typical of Northern's long-term view is its new $30-million Advanced Technology Lab in Ottawa where a new generation of semiconductor is being produced under germ-free conditions. "The plant is the ultimate in cleanliness and is designing the manufacture of the next generation of fibre optics," says Roth proudly.

Northern has mastered the art of marketing its products around the world and has pulled off a number of unique deals along the way. In 1988 it landed the first big contract in protectionist Japan by selling $100-million worth of equipment to Nippon Telegraph and Telephone Corporation. Ironically, it may find itself under increasing competition in its native Canada, where it enjoys a 70 per cent market share for central office switches and 40 per cent for PBX systems. However, its principal customer and research partner, Bell Canada, is virtually a captive customer. This home market has provided the springboard for Northern's spectacular export success.

"We just won a major portion of the cellular network in Mexico [in 1989]," says Roth. "We will be doing six of the eight regions. Cellular phones are important in developing countries because they can be deployed so quickly. You can put up a phone system in months . . . just by spotting radio antennas here and there. The biggest capital outlay is by the subscribers who put out the capital for portable units. It's a way for a country to get a system in quickly so that the infrastructure is there for business and commerce to proceed. We hope to be among the first wave into the Eastern Bloc and have made a deal in Hungary through our Austrian agent."

This success worldwide is all the more amazing considering it is up against giants such as IBM Corporation, with US$54 billion in sales, and American Telegraph & Telephone International Inc., with US$34 billion. The only way to compete is to focus on market niches, then come up with unmatchable technology through solid research. It has also got marketing or manufacturing operations located inside the markets it serves, including Europe, where it can bid for the lucrative Eastern Bloc or Soviet contracts that will be let during the 1990s as those countries replace their archaic phone systems in order to compete economically. Likewise, Northern is well placed to land contracts in the growing Far Eastern countries and to rebuild Mexico's deteriorated phone network, now that Canada and Mexico have signed a number of bilateral agreements to enhance two-way trade. Peace brings profits to companies like Northern Telecom, who simply serve the business world better.

Caveats: This company's stock has merely tended to track the Toronto Stock Exchange index in the past. This may change but has meant steady, although unspectacular, results.

An investment of $10,000 in January 1980 was worth $46,861 by January 1990. With dividends reinvested, it totalled $51,049. Over the decade prices ranged from high of $32.13 to a low of $4.96, adjusting for splits.

(THE) OSHAWA GROUP LIMITED

Head Office: Islington, Ontario
Incorporated: 1957
Ownership: Controlling shareholder the Wolfe family

Revenues in 1990: $4,948,200,000
Net Income: $69,600,000
Earnings per share: $2.11
Employees: 21,700
Year End: January 23

The Wolfe family immigrated from Lithuania and launched a retail business selling hay to the Canadian cavalry during the First World War. By the Second World War, they were nearly bust, bullied by the large food chains to whom they supplied fruit and vegetables. That is when Oshawa Group's late chairman, Ray Wolfe, found out about the IGA concept that began in the United States to enable small independents to compete against giants by combining forces to get the same volume discounts that chains were getting. Wolfe applied it here by offering his Oshawa Group as the central purchasing agency and it thrived. By the 1980s, Oshawa and its IGA customers were equivalent in size to Canada's fourth-largest food retailer.

Canada's retail food business is divided between independents (with 30 per cent) and six chains. Oshawa now owns and operates 100 Food City and IGA stores and also supplies everything from soup to nuts to another 800 IGA and independent grocers, as well as thousands of convenience stores. It also supplies its self-employed merchants with advice in such areas as engineering, real estate, public relations, advertising, insurance, accounting, recruitment and training.

Oshawa and its independents are well-positioned to beat rivals in the 1990s. This is why. The Maritime chain, Sobeys Inc., has considerably more debt and, without reinvestment, will find itself paying full income taxes. There may also be a capital gains problem for the family in 1993. Quebec's Provigo Inc. and Steinberg Inc. are both heavily in debt. Provigo underwent a management shake-up in 1989 after suffering poor returns from its sprawling, overextended empire. The Loblaw Companies Limited make considerably less money than Oshawa, and the German-owned A & P chain has debts racked up as a result of its rapid expansion through the purchase of most of the former Dominion Store chain. The story is the same out west, where Canada Safeway is king. That American-owned chain was loaded up with a huge debt load as a result of a leveraged buy-out of its assets by takeover specialists Kohlberg Kravis, Roberts & Co. of New York. The significance of all of this is that Oshawa, virtually debt-free, can afford to easily and determinedly undercut the others in order to grab market share in an otherwise shrinking market. That is a major advantage and the legacy of Ray Wolfe's conservative financing philosophy.

Oshawa fan Marty Kaufman, a retail analyst with Nesbitt Thomson Inc. in Montreal, says Wolfe, who died in January 1990, ran things with an iron fist, but left a strong management team in place. "Ray delegated things to Allister Graham [now president and chief executive officer] and Phil Connell in finance. One or two sons are in the business but no one knows if they are chips off the old block or not. But the business is too big for one person to run anyway. They will carry the ball. I'm not worried. No company in Canada has had the consistency in terms of increased profits each year and in less than six or seven years this stock will double."

Unfortunately, all of Oshawa's common stock, or voting shares, is owned by five separate sections of the Wolfe family and a new voting trust is "being worked on." I feel the creation of non-voting stock is deplorable, but Oshawa is too good an opportunity to dismiss. Besides, there is little likelihood that the Wolfes will be selling out in the near future, thus removing the disadvantage of owning non-voting stock.

Nine Wolfe family members are involved in the company's day-to-day operations, including Ray Wolfe's two children, two of his brothers, one niece, one nephew and three cousins. There are other heirs, more descendants of Ray's father, Maurice, and Max Wolfe, who had seven children between them. "Speculation is that there will emerge one leader of the family, as Ray was, or that the family will create a mini-board of directors," says Oshawa's chief financial officer Phil Connell.

Similarly, Graham does not foresee problems such as have plagued the Steinbergs, Canadian Tire's Billeses and others. "I have seen others get into difficulty, but I don't see that happening here."

Oshawa is an interesting play on a couple of less obvious levels – Canada's aging population, and the high cost of Toronto housing. First, its IGA network is mostly in rural, outlying areas that are fast becoming commuter suburbs as couples move further afield in order to afford to buy their own home. Like Standard Trustco, Oshawa is in a prime position to capitalize on this shift. But Oshawa also owns Food City in the urban areas, a chain of discount food stores catering to the underemployed, unemployed or bargain-conscious. This is a good defensive play because if times toughen, the grocery budget becomes more important and volumes shift to the Food City types of discounters. The same applies to Oshawa's successful Towers stores, a discount department store chain which, like Zellers, outsells the competition because of its everyday low prices strategy.

Oshawa is also an investment in the country's changing demographics because the company has positioned itself through acquisitions into a sizeable drugstore chain, renamed Pharma Plus Drugmarts with 107 stores in Ontario. It is considerably smaller than Imasco Ltd.'s Shoppers Drug Mart with its 52 per cent market share (Pharma Plus has 14 per cent). But Oshawa promises to be aggressive. It also owns Kent Drugs, half again the size of Pharma Plus, with another 48 stores in Ontario, Manitoba, New Brunswick, and Nova Scotia as well as pharmacies in Towers stores and supermarkets. Drug retailing now accounts for $400 million of Oshawa revenues, slightly behind the $500-million-plus Towers chain.

"In the future, food will continue to predominate and drugs are coming along well. But in our Towers division we have 52 stores in Ontario, Quebec, Prince Edward Island, Newfoundland and Nova Scotia and would like a little more for critical mass. It is tough to find new acquisitions," says Graham. "We will look for small acquisitions in the U.S. when the timing is right but now we are concentrating on increasing market share in each of our businesses."

All of which is sound, cautious strategy, watchwords for Oshawa's capable management team. There are few with track records as brilliant as this one, increasing earnings and sales for 13 years with the exception of a small slippage during one quarter. "We have good prospects and will remain conservatively financed," says Graham. "The mix will not change. The shareholders' equity is $550 million and debt $40 million. We are a growth company and on most buy lists, are clean, predictable and have good management. Better yet, we are in much better shape than our competitors."

Caveats: This is a recession-proof, defensive stock but the existence of Class A, or non-voting stock, could present problems. Bickering could lead to deteriorating operations or poor decisions. It could also result in the family, which owns only 10 per cent of the overall equity, cutting a side deal with a new controlling shareholder for a hefty profit, leaving public shareholders out in the cold. There is no coattail provision forcing a takeover bid to be extended to all shareholders. That may happen and would make a great deal of difference.

An investment of $10,000 in A shares in January 1980 was worth $155,281 in January 1990. With dividends reinvested, it totalled $165,476. Over the decade prices ranged from a high of $32.75 to a low of $1.79, adjusting for splits.

RENAISSANCE ENERGY LTD.

Head Office: Calgary, Alberta
Incorporated: 1982
Ownership: Widely held

Revenues in 1989: $130,632,000
Net Income: $17,915,000
Earnings per share: $0.61
Employees: 200
Year End: December 31

Canada's oil companies were slugged, during the 1980s, by the triple whammy of collapsed prices, a recession with high interest rates and punitive taxes imposed through the Liberals' ill-conceived National Energy Program. Investment darlings such as Dome Petroleum, Sulpetro and Turbo disappeared or were bailed out by banks. But in 1982, during this less-than-propitious time, a new oil patch star was born, Renaissance Energy Ltd.

A share of Renaissance bought back then for $3 would now be worth, after one split, more than $50. Its success has not been based on acquiring cheap assets from bankrupt oil companies, but on finding the stuff, thus making Canada more energy self-sufficient. Renaissance is Canada's most successful finder and its most aggressive one, drilling an average of 300 wells a year during the last few years of the 1980s. This represents more exploration wells than any other company in Canada, including gigantic Imperial Oil Limited.

Renaissance is also one of Canada's most land-rich oil companies, having leased for future exploration lands equivalent in size to Prince Edward Island. In terms of land holdings, Renaissance ranks second only to Canadian Pacific's PanCanadian Petroleum whose gigantic land spread came about from rights-of-way bequeathed to the railway decades ago.

180

But drilling and land don't mean anything unless finders get results. Renaissance has added to reserves every year while generating enough cash flow from past discoveries to more than finance its aggressive and unique exploration program. "Ours is a rifle, not a shotgun approach," explains its soft-spoken chairman and founder, Ron Greene. "We're growing through exploration not acquisition because finding and getting it onstream are lower than acquisition costs."

His "rifle approach" consists of hunting exclusively in the "Plains area" of Alberta, 55,000 square miles of farm and ranchlands, slightly larger than New Brunswick and Nova Scotia combined. It's also where Greene and his president and chief operations officer, Clayton Woitas, both grew up as farm boys. Both were born in 1948. Greene came up through the oil business as a landman, in the business end. Woitas was a petroleum engineer with Merland Exploration and left after it was bought by Turbo.

The Plains has proven to be one of the world's most prolific geological formations, yielding up massive discoveries, such as Turner Valley and Leduc, which ushered in decades of oil prosperity for Alberta. It is also where centuries' worth of oil-sands reserves await $50-a-barrel prices. And while other oil patchers used the cash flow from Plains discoveries to finance elephant-hunting exploration adventures around the world, Greene says there is still plenty of stuff there to find. And is proving it.

"The Plains Area is a flat and accessible area – a farming area. If you look at our activity level for the past three years, we have been the most active explorer in Canada and have concentrated in one area, giving us a higher degree of knowledge than our competition," says Greene.

Renaissance also operates on a high-leverage strategy, spurning the type of farm-in and farm-out partnerships that characterize the oil patch. "Of the 300 wells we drilled in 1989, our average working interest was 95 per cent. There is a higher risk, but a higher reward. But the biggest benefit is that you can work at your own speed, there are no time-consuming partner meetings and we can ignore critics," he says.

Most importantly, however, Renaissance has steadily accumulated its enviable land position. "There are 36 million acres in the Plains area. We might establish that one-quarter is proven up or condemned, which leaves 24 million and we own 1.2 million. In other words, we own 1/24th of the best oil and gas prospects in North America."

Renaissance benefited, along with others, in a mid-1980s Alberta land tenure policy that forced the major oil companies to turn over their leases. They had tied up lands and invited junior explorers to farm-in and do all the drilling. The majors, with their expensive bureaucracies, cannot easily make money drilling for, and finding, pools of oil with "only" 1.5 million to 4 million barrels that are produced from 75-barrel-a-day wells. But Renaissance and a whole generation of new finders can.

A steady stream of such smallish discoveries adds up to a great deal of success for Greene and his team. In 1983, Renaissance had reserves of only 75 billion cubic feet of gas and 1 million barrels of oil. Reserves by the end of fiscal year 1989 totalled 33 million barrels and 515 billion cubic feet and that year it sold a record 5 million barrels of oil and 35 billion cubic feet, resulting in record production volumes and a 25 per cent increase in reserves.

That has given Renaissance some $90 million in cash flow, more than enough to finance its aggressive drilling and land acquisition programs. This means it can generate enough funds internally to grow instead of raising funds through annual equity financings, which it did from 1983 to 1989, diluting Greene, Woitas and other members of management down to a mere 13 per cent of the stock. The rest of Renaissance is widely held, mostly by institutions. Theoretically, this makes Renaissance a takeover target. "I wouldn't like to see it [a takeover bid] happen. But that comes with running a public company. We've always taken the position that the best defence is a good share price," says Greene. There are no poison pills here and no plans for any.

With two young key executives at the helm who get along famously, according to most accounts, Renaissance should prosper, offering investors one of the most interesting growth plays in the oil business. After all, Renaissance prospered even during the bad old days of price collapses and investor disdain, and as expensive as its stock has been, the company has always commanded a premium because of its splendid track record. Even if the sheiks never again hold the world to ransom, Renaissance shareholders can look forward to growth. But if OPEC gets its act together this decade, as I think it will, Renaissance investors will be lighting Monte Cristos with $100 bills.

Caveats: Investors are betting on future oil and natural gas prices and continuation of the winning partnership between Greene and Woitas.

An investment of $10,000 in 1983 was worth $120,892 in January 1990. To date no dividends have been paid. Since 1983 prices ranged from a high of $25.75 to a low of $1.98, adjusting for splits.

RIO ALGOM LIMITED

Head Office: Toronto, Ontario
Incorporated: 1980 (Ontario Amalgamation)
Ownership: Controlling shareholder The RTZ Corporation PLC

Revenues in 1989: $1,711,910,000
Net Income: 104,602,000(B.E.)/$73,122,000(A.E.)
Earnings per share: $2.30(B.E.)/$1.58(A.E.)
Employees: 8,000
Year End: December 31

(B.E. - before extraordinary items; A.E. - after extraordinary items)

The world's largest mining company, RTZ Corporation PLC of Britain, owns 51.5 per cent of Rio Algom Limited, Canada's most cash-rich and debt-free mining company. With $500 million cash in the kitty, my guess is that unless Rio Algom spends its huge nest egg wisely and gets its stock trading at higher multiples, Rio Tinto will make a takeover bid to buy the 48.5 per cent of Rio Algom it does not already own. Consider the arithmetic: the public owns 21.19 million shares and at the average trading price of $20 a share, the cost of a takeover would be $423 million, less than the $500 million in the kitty. That means Rio Tinto could gain control of $2 billion worth of money-generating mining operations and pay for it with the $500 million cash in Rio Algom's treasury. Rio Tinto pulled a similar manoeuvre in Canada a few years ago when it privatized metal fabricator, Indal Ltd.

Rio Algom's vice-chairman and CEO Ray Ballmer is a friendly American engineer and says privatization is unlikely. He joined Rio in 1982 after years as a mining engineer with Amoco Minerals, part of the Amoco Corporation energy conglomerate. "I'm not aware of any desire to increase it. We believe RTZ would like to maintain that percentage," he says.

But I believe Rio Algom is a ranking member of what I call my "spoiler index," companies whose shareholders may one day be able to enjoy a large, swollen takeover bid by a parent company. Spoiler is a real estate term to describe someone with the last piece of property being assembled and who holds out for a premium price. Other spoiler plays in this book include Corby Distilleries, Campbell Soup, Coca-Cola Beverages and St. Lawrence Cement. The spoiler index is not to be confused with companies I have put on my takeover hit list such as CAE Industries, Renaissance Energy, Federal Industries, the Loewen Group, Mackenzie Financial and Finning.

Even if Rio Algom does not succumb to a takeout by its parent, it is still an interesting company. It is virtually recession-proof because of its diversification and bullet-proof balance sheet. It is also in a great position, going into another mining downturn, to cherry pick assets. With $2 billion in assets and $200 million in long-term debt, it could afford to make a major takeover itself in the future.

Rio was created through a series of mergers in 1960 and now operates mines exclusively in North America, where it produces uranium, potash, copper, molybdenum, metallurgical coal and tin. It distributes metals through a system of warehouses around the world through its Atlas Alloys division. Distribution contributes about 22 per cent of profits and made money throughout the recession in the early 1980s. Another 28 per cent of the bottom line is derived from Rio Algom's uranium mine in Elliot Lake, Ontario, which enjoys a sweetheart contract with Ontario Hydro that guarantees profits until 2020.

Rio has been making smallish takeovers with its nest egg and has been tire-kicking, or looking for takeovers. It is also conducting an aggressive exploration program by spending $8 million a year on grassroots drilling and prospecting. Rio's former chairman and CEO George Albino was rightly criticized for not cashing in on the Hemlo gold action in Ontario in the early 1980s. "It's fair to say that he let exploration activities run down. We had an opportunity to get involved in Hemlo but did not act fast enough. Now we are becoming aggressive and for the first time in my life I gave my exploration vice president all the money he asked for," says Ballmer.

Cash-rich Rio is poised to participate in joint ventures or pick up assets at distress prices. One such "distress" deal could be archrival

Denison Mines Limited, with its sickly coal, oil, potash and uranium operations. It is interesting to speculate whether the late Stephen Roman's successor, Helen Roman-Barber, will sell control on top of the assets she's been selling off. Roman once said, "Apart from my wife and kids, everything I own is for sale at the right price."

Ballmer hints there have been discussions with Denison and makes no bones about Rio's interest in Denison. "I think we might buy it [Denison] if the price were right. But sometimes people think a business is worth more than it is. We might also consider a joint venture with Rio Tinto Zinc if it was a large, desirable takeover. We have discussed 'what ifs' with them on occasion," says Ballmer.

Some say Rio is treated like a stepchild by Rio Tinto. Each does its own thing, which is good on the one hand but bad on the other. Some decry the fact that when Rio Tinto bought British Petroleum's minerals operations in the U.S. for $4 billion, it did not give Rio Algom a crack at any of those assets. Instead in 1986, Rio Algom ventured into the United States when it paid US$26 million for some old Kerr McGee uranium deposits in New Mexico and Wyoming that contain more ore than Elliot Lake, a possible hedge against protectionism if the free trade deal hadn't guaranteed the free, unfettered flow of Canadian uranium to U.S. utility customers. Even so, Ballmer says it's a good purchase and that Rio Algom is bullish on uranium despite current low prices due to an oversupply.

Interest in uranium is quite contrary, considering the conventional grim outlook for uranium. Uranium is around 20 per cent of Rio's sales but about 28 per cent of operating profits. This happy state of affairs is because Rio and Denison alike enjoy Ontario Hydro's generosity, which keeps their Elliot Lake mines viable. But the super-rich uranium mines in Saskatchewan, with the biggest and richest deposits in the world, will be impossible to compete against and will be supplying increasing amounts to Ontario Hydro. Because of this, both Rio and Denison in early 1990 announced large layoffs at Elliot Lake to take place over the next few years as production declines. Nevertheless, what remains will be profitable. The Hydro contract lasts until 2020 but by 1996 Rio's American, Japanese, British and European supply contracts will have expired. Even so, the cash-rich Rio just bought uranium properties in the United States and could easily afford to buy up to 20 per cent of the Saskatchewan Mining Development Corp. if it is privatized.

Through its 68.8 per cent holding in Lornex Mining Corporation of B.C., Rio Algom's earnings are indirectly linked to the copper cycle, which tracks industrial production. Every 10-cent change in copper prices adds or subtracts 25 cents from earnings per share. Copper has been hovering around $1.15 per pound. Lornex owns 45 per cent of Highland Valley Copper and 39 per cent of the Bullmoose metallurgical coal mine in B.C. The outlook for copper prices in the short to medium term is favorable, although in the long run it will be bleak if the anticipated switch to fibre optics replaces traditional copper wiring systems. Conversely, however, metallurgical coal prices are controlled by the Japanese, who have beaten down prices dramatically since the recession in 1982, but these prices are expected to only go up.

Rio and other Bullmoose owners, Teck Corporation, were luckier than Denison Mines, which has been saddled with arbitration for years after a dispute arose with its Japanese customers. The price collapse occurred in 1984 just ten months after Bullmoose made its first shipment. Contract prices were reduced by $10 per tonne for two years ending 1986 but at the same time, the Japanese agreed to buy more, virtually offsetting the impact of price reductions.

One year later, Rio Algom bought the Potash Company of America, Inc., with mines in New Brunswick and Saskatchewan. Although they have been in a slump, potash prices have now been strengthening, mostly due to concern that Soviet production may fall or remain flat because of the Soviets' current destabilized condition. The U.S.S.R. and Canada are the world's two significant potash producers. Tin may be another sleeper. Rio bought a bankrupt Maritimes tin mine when the cartel controlling production fell apart and the world price collapsed.

Rio also holds small interests in two Vancouver-listed junior explorers called Pan Orvana Resources Inc. and Continental Gold Corp. and may make bids for the portion of stock Rio doesn't already own. And there are other small plays that may find themselves part of the Rio family of companies. But whatever happens, Rio is an anomaly within the high-flying and crapshooting mining community. It is a dividend-paying critter whose watchwords are fiscal conservatism and caution.

Caveats: Rio is somewhat counter-cyclical for a mining company due to its uranium contracts with Ontario Hydro. But closures at Elliot Lake may mean a wind-down from that lucrative profit centre.

An investment of $10,000 in January 1980 was worth $21,211 in January 1990. With dividends reinvested, it totalled $26,930. Over the decade prices ranged from a high of $28 to a low of $8.92, adjusting for splits.

(THE) ROYAL BANK OF CANADA

Head Office: Montreal, Quebec
Incorporated: 1871
Ownership: Widely held

Interest Income in 1989: $3,624,680,000
Net Income: $529,073,000
Earnings per share: $3.29
Employees: 46,000
Year End: October 31

The Toronto headquarters of the Royal Bank of Canada is the most beautiful building in the skyline. It glitters because its window-walls are literally laced with gold. The Bank's Montreal headquarters are housed in the equally dominant Place Ville Marie, the cross-shaped skyscraper. Like its two prestigious headquarters, the Royal Bank of Canada is well-situated in a business sense, too. It is the country's biggest and perhaps best all-around banking franchise. In an age where globalization of money markets means financial institutions must be monolithic to win big, the Royal fills the bill.

It is Canada's largest chartered bank by most measures, its largest brokerage firm, its biggest purveyor of RRSPs and bank mutual funds, its biggest swap artist, its most successful entry in the U.S. banking market, the world's third-largest foreign exchange bank and North America's largest branch banking system. In 1989 *Euromoney* magazine pegged the Royal as the world's third-largest foreign exchange bank. As such, the Royal skims commissions off trading transactions involving Canadian dollars around the world. Although such fees are mere slivers, the pennies add up, making the Royal a unique play on Canada's future trading success.

Its chairman, Allan Taylor, is a friendly and enthusiastic booster of his bank's benefits. We meet in the bank's hexagonal blue and gold foyer, which forms a hub from which offices and boardrooms shoot off like spokes. The interview is conducted in a beautifully appointed blue and gold boardroom, and Taylor chats fluently about his bank's successes and prospects. A Royal Bank "lifer," he has the well-scrubbed looks of a benevolent patriarch. He began his work life as a Royal Bank teller in his native Saskatchewan and is very proud of his bank's accomplishments. For good reason.

"We are the pre-eminent banking franchise in Canada and perhaps North America," he crows. "We have 25 per cent market share in everything in Canada in banking. We have 25 per cent of deposits' business in total against all other banks. But since there are other deposit-taking institutions like credit unions and trust companies, we have 13 per cent of all deposits in Canada.

"We have a very sizeable share of corporate business and the largest share of U.S. business by a Canadian bank, or 30 per cent of the Canadian market share. Overall in Canada, we'd like to have 23 per cent of corporate banking, total business, not loans. There's not a lot of joy in loans, but I mean treasury products, swaps, options. We're the leaders in new instruments, swaps, foreign exchange and money instruments, T-bills. This is the strength of our bank."

The Royal is Canada's only truly national bank, with large market shares in all regions, an important factor in evaluating a bank's financial strength. Such regional diversity cushioned the blow of collapsed oil prices, then real estate, in Alberta where the Royal held 37 per cent of energy loans. "We are truly nationwide, which is a strength. In banking, diversity is a big part of risk management. We were hit more heavily than any other bank by the collapse of oil and real estate prices in Alberta," says Taylor. "In Ontario and Quebec we're putting most of our resources into growth because we have a low-20s market share and want to hit at least 25 per cent."

Although swaps and other fancy financial dealings are more profitable on a per-transaction basis, the bank's extensive system of 1,560 branches (the biggest in North America) provides it with another hidden profit centre, automatic teller machines. Between the Royal's branches and hundreds more machines in airports and shopping malls, the Royal now gets the lion's share of ATM business, in effect poaching customers from competitors. The Royal's 3,000 ATM machines can be used by anyone's customer through the co-operative Interac system. With twice as many machines as the next biggest competitor, the Royal is able to skim 75 cents per transaction off other banking customers with virtually no additional cost involved. It is like being in the lucrative long-distance telephone business.

The Royal is also the biggest bank in the Bahamas. Until 1945, the bank's notes were used as Bahamanian currency. Its operation down there, with 18 branches, is small potatoes and that is just as well. The Royal faces tough new competition from the newly formed Bank of the Bahamas, half owned by the government and half by Toronto real estate developer Gerhard Moog. The two acquired the Bank of Montreal's ailing local bank chain and plan to expand rapidly to capture market share.

But the biggest blue sky for the Royal is its continuing dominance of the Registered Retirement Savings Plans business. It is expected that by 1992 the annual contribution an individual can make to an RRSP will more than double to $15,500. RRSPs are big business in Canada, with more than $100 billion socked away by wealthy, tax-weary Canadians. However, some feel, as I do, that the revenue-starved federal government may delay the escalation of this tax-shelter scheme (the most generous among industrialized countries). But even at current levels of up to $7,500 annually per person, RRSP business will continue to be an important profit centre for the Royal and its securities operations, led by broker RBC Dominion Securities Inc. The Royal has also sold $1.5-billion worth of Roy Funds mutual funds.

The Royal got into the brokerage business in 1987 with its purchase of Dominion Securities after Ottawa allowed banks into that sector for the first time. Unfortunately, two stock market crashes followed and have reduced most brokerage firm earnings, and volumes, to rubble. The exception is RBC Dominion, which has managed to outperform the pack, posting a 1989 profit of $32 million, or an 18 per cent return.

Another opportunity for the Royal Bank is the eventual unravelling of the U.S. ban against bank-broker cross-ownership, enshrined in the Glass Steagall Act, says Taylor. However, the bank is not interested in buying any of the troubled "thrifts" (U.S. savings and loans) which are expected to cost US$300 billion to bail out over the next decade. Taylor feels there were "a bunch of frauds" among the thrifts. Even the six best ones don't have healthy earnings. "There's not much joy there," he says.

Taylor says his bank would like to buy a U.S. bank that can be expanded into a "super-regional," across a four- or five-state area. Branch banking has been illegal across state lines since President Andrew Jackson's day, but super-regionals are springing up with selective permission granted by state legislators to allow operations beyond borders. And Canadian banks, unlike American counterparts, are experienced in running large-scale, international, multibranch operations. Taylor, like others, sees this as a great opportunity if the price is right.

There is little doubt in my mind that Canadian banks like the Royal and T-D will continue to enjoy competitive advantages in the United States. Tougher regulations in Canada that forced our banks to set aside at least 50 per cent of reserves for questionable Third World loans have created an industry with strong balance sheets and an ability to borrow money more cheaply than American rivals. Canada's banks, particularly the Royal, should benefit from legislative changes to the banking business in the U.S., and careful expansion will provide important benefits to its shareholders in future.

Caveats: Continued high inflation and interest rates hurt bank stocks traditionally. Another looming problem could be protectionism in the United States, a reaction against Robert Campeau's fiasco and foreign ownership in general. But a lowering Canadian dollar *vis à vis* the U.S. dollar, deutsche mark and pound sterling will boost trade and the Royal's exchange business.

An investment of $10,000 in January 1980 was worth $23,599 in January 1990. With dividends reinvested, it totalled $32,689. Over the decade prices ranged from a high of $51.38 to a low of $18, adjusting for splits. (The Royal's common split 2 for 1 in early 1990.)

ST. LAWRENCE CEMENT INC.

Head Office: Mount Royal, Quebec
Incorporated: 1951
Ownership: Major shareholder Hofi North America Inc.

Revenues in 1989: $727,225,000
Net Income: $72,057,000
Earnings per share: $1.78
Employees: 3,300
Year End: December 31

Concrete is the lifeblood of an industrialized economy, and cement is the heart. That is why cement has been a duty-free commodity for decades and, like the mining and oil businesses, has globally rationalized its production locations. That rationalization has resulted in the domination of the business worldwide by a handful of European giants who own 80 per cent of Canada's cement business and 60 per cent of America's. One of the strongest entries is Canada's pre-eminent cement company, St. Lawrence Cement Inc., controlled by Switzerland's Holderbank NV. It is a cyclical stock, but St. Lawrence promises to cash in on the growing environmental movement and on the easing of international Cold War tensions. As peace breaks out, the United States will trim defence expenditures and will be able to rebuild its tattered and decayed infrastructure. That means new concrete bridges and highways.

Holderbank is controlled by Switzerland's powerful Thomas Schmidheiny family and, through a number of separate entities such as St. Lawrence, has 3.3 per cent of the world market. But it enjoys 15 per cent market share in all the countries in which it operates. Holderbank owns 60 per cent of St. Lawrence's A stock at one vote apiece and all of its B stock at three votes each, or 78 per cent of all votes. Slightly larger in Canada is France's Lafarge Canada Inc. Those two and all others in Canada meet the country's needs and are able to export about 30 per cent of production to the United States.

St. Lawrence's headquarters is in a low-rise building across the street from a school and library in upmarket Mount Royal. It is by far the most profitable of all of Holderbank's cement companies. Holderbank owns two more cement outfits in North America. St. Lawrence operates in eastern Canada, the Maritimes and in 14 U.S. states (in the eastern half of the country). Its sister cement outfit, Dundee in Michigan, sells into the U.S. midwest, and in 1989 financially troubled Ideal Basic was bought out of near-bankruptcy to serve the west coast.

Early in 1990, the Swiss rolled all three into a New York Stock Exchange-listed company called Holnam Inc. (Holderbank-America). Holam owns 100 per cent of Dundee and Ideal and holds Holderbank's 60 per cent of St. Lawrence's A stock. Some $40-million worth of stock was sold to the public. This unorthodox move into public markets by Holderbank is why most observers feel it is unlikely Holderbank will privatize St. Lawrence. "There are no plans to privatize," says St. Lawrence's chief financial officer Guy Turgeon.

For investors, the problem is that the cement business is cyclical. "Residential is 32 per cent of the market; public works, 25 per cent; industrial, 26 per cent; and commercial, 17 per cent," says Turgeon. "We follow the general curve of the construction industry and lag six months behind the general economy."

The recession in the early 1980s devastated the bottom line, but things are different now since St. Lawrence trimmed debt from its balance sheet. "In 1982, we had $172 million of debt on $250 million in sales. Now we have $164 million debt on sales of $700 million or 30 per cent debt-to-equity," says Turgeon. "We are less cyclical for different reasons. The industry is more solid and we could run through three to four years of lower volumes without any real volatility. We are more solid."

There are also reasons to believe that cement prices may escalate due to the easing of Cold War tensions and disappearance of the Iron Curtain. The Eastern Bloc infrastructure needs a massive overhaul, as does the United States', and facilities may not keep up with demand.

St. Lawrence, with its state-of-the-art facilities, is in a great position to cash in, particularly in the United States, unless protectionist measures against Mexican and Spanish outfits also end up resulting in duties against Canadian cement. But that is unlikely. The creation of Holam and the sale of stock to American investors was designed, in part, to avert that possibility.

St. Lawrence, like other foreign-controlled companies, benefits from being linked to a worldwide giant. Dividends are always more generous and St. Lawrence tries to hand out on average 35 per cent of its earnings each year. This makes it an institutional favorite. Another benefit from its connection to Holderbank is in the area of research and technology. Believe it or not, there are one dozen different types of cement, as well as additives that allow it to be poured in Arctic temperatures or to dry quickly. "In the U.S., some competitors' plants are falling apart, whereas Canadian plants are well-maintained and have better technology," says Turgeon. "There are hardly any cement imports into Canada and some 30 per cent of our production goes into the U.S. And 'Buy America' policies don't hurt public works contracts, either."

Most ironically, however, St. Lawrence and other cement makers may cash in on the green movement, even though for years activitists have routinely battled their smokestack-scarred plants and huge quarry operations. These facilities, suggests Turgeon, may solve the land-fill problems that will plague North America in the 1990s. Land-fill sites are few and because of politics, new ones will be impossible to get approved, so that companies with existing, approved waste-management sites such as Canada's Laidlaw Inc. or Waste Management Inc. in the United States are favorite investments.

"As we run out of well-located reserves, our quarries are good holes for land-fill purposes and would make excellent dumping sites," he says. "We also have kilns which get up to 1800 degrees Celsius which can be fuelled by burning waste and which can destroy toxic substances, such as PCBs. We will be test burning PCBs in Canada. They are destroyed at 1500 degrees for two seconds. Our 300-foot kilns reach 1800 degrees for six seconds."

Turgeon says cement kilns can also destroy refuse, such as solvents, garbage bags or paper cups, in no time, and at the same time save the cost of fuel. "A cement plant in Ohio is burning solvents. In Quebec, the ministry of the environment is going to let us test burn solvents, used oils, green garbage bags and PCBs. I think our future is garbage," he says. "We could replace coal by burning 25 per cent of the garbage and get rid of another 50 per cent by burying it in our quarries." An intriguing thought, and a logical one. But it will take some time to pull off.

Caveats: St. Lawrence is cyclical and thinly traded so investors must hang in for the long haul.

An investment of $10,000 in January 1980 was worth $53,462 in January 1990. With dividends reinvested, it totalled $63,138. Over the decade prices ranged from a high of $22.25 to a low of $1.63, adjusting for splits.

SCOTT'S HOSPITALITY INC.

Head Office: Toronto, Ontario
Incorporated: 1968
Ownership: Controlling shareholders Fairwater Capital Corp;
Langer Company Ltd.

Revenues in 1989: $1,120,912,000
Net Income: $52,385,000
Earnings per share: $0.88
Employees: 24,400
Year End: April 30

Until the summer of 1989, the head office of Scott's Hospitality used to reside at the Chestnut Street Holiday Inn behind Toronto's avant-garde City Hall. But it moved over to a glitzy tower in the nearby Eaton Centre when it sold that hotel, and 38 others, for a $225-million profit.

That is just one of the many "portfolio" investments this management company has made that have turned into pure gold. Managed by a capable but decentralized team, led by chief financial officer and senior vice-president Bruce Dodds, Scott's is a first-class, billion-dollar baby with four profitable businesses. His predecessor, Ken Lyons left the firm in the spring of 1990, but it remains in good shape. It owns Black's Photography, the Canadian franchise for Kentucky Fried Chicken, the Holiday Inn franchise in the United Kingdom and North America's third-largest school bus company with a fleet of 4,000 vehicles. It also owns a trucking company and a warehouse business, but it parted with Commonwealth Holiday Inns and its 39 hotels around the world, which were acquired in the early 1980s and turned around into profitability.

"We sold it because it was an underperforming return on assets, capital intensive, too much supply and not enough demand for moderately priced hotels," explains Lyons. "We bought it ten years before that. It was in difficulty and we pruned the 60-hotel chain to 38 hotels. It cost us $60 million in 1979 and we sold it for $285 million in May 1989. We decided that our long-term thrust was to be the number one brand name in the world. We kept the U.K. hotels. It took five months to get our price. BASS PLC [the British brewery] bought it."

Like Cara Operations, Scott's is one of Canada's most successful companies with booming growth, good prospects and virtually no debt. It is considered a good defensive stock during a recession because earnings are divided, geographically as well as sectorally, into: hotel, photography, bus transport and food services. Assets and revenues are half in Canada and the rest are divided more or less equally between the United States and the United Kingdom.

Even though a British multinational struck the deal to buy Scott's hotels, it did not part with its U.K. Holiday Inn chain in a country where American-style hotels outside London are rare. It has 11 full-service hotels and plans to build a separate chain of some dozen no-frills hotels. "We feel that between 1992 and the chunnel [tunnel under the English channel] action, we can exploit the U.K. market. We are also looking in France for acquisitions around the channel," says Dodds.

When Scott's made the sale, it declared a $3-per-share dividend, but is still flush with cash and a $300-million credit line for other acquisitions. "All our businesses are well-positioned in very strong industries. But we are looking for acquisitions in the food services and specialty food retailing areas. We have done $200-million worth in the last three years. We also bought Charterways, with 250 buses," says Lyons.

Scott's also bought Manchu Wok, a Chinese fast-food chain with 150 stores in mall food courts, and Second Cup stores. Both are the type of specialty food retailer that Scott's still seeks. "We don't like concepts that rely on price. They are not enduring. Anyone can copy a price with a stroke of a pen. We are always looking at ten things at any given time. Hostile takeovers are not our game. You go in and beat up management and they won't operate as well as if it's friendly."

Scott's also grows organically and is experimenting with a Black's pilot store in a Minneapolis shopping mall. "In photography, we have saturated the Canadian market and our big decision is whether the

Quebec market is right for us with its cultural differences. Other than that, we are looking at certain U.S. regions," he says.

"We are primarily into North American brand names in the consumer or business services with a brand-oriented product with repeat business," says Lyons. "We bought Black's in 1985 with 100 stores and now it has 225 stores. We tend to buy stand-alone businesses and let them operate in a decentralized fashion. We manage the money and don't need synergies."

Its school bus business is spread throughout a dozen or so states and Ontario, and the company is always on the hunt for acquisitions. As for its chicken franchise, Scott's renegotiated a new licence agreement until 2003 with Kentucky Fried's parent, Pepsico. It operates 185 outlets in Canada and all are profitable, but margins may be squeezed unless the marketing board questions raised under free trade can be addressed. Right now, U.S. chicken is 40 per cent cheaper and Scott's and others have been lobbying for a two-tier pricing system, one for processors like themselves and another for consumers buying fresh chicken.

A fifth business that Scott's intends to enter by building and buying is the public warehousing business, which it expects will prosper under free trade. Its first facility will be a 750,000-square-foot warehouse outside Toronto that will handle distribution, invoicing and inventory recording for U.S. manufacturers who want to test the waters in Canada but don't want to build or lease their own premises.

The strategies now being carried through are very much the work of Scott's brilliant founder and former chairman, George Ryerson Gardiner. Now in his late 60s, Gardiner obtained a Harvard MBA during the Second World War, then founded the Gardiner Group Stockbrokers Inc. on Bay Street. He ran Scott's almost like a portfolio investment after he inherited his father's troubled restaurant chain. He is no longer a director of the firm, which is now run by his son, Michael Ryerson Gardiner, who now runs the family's affairs, for himself and two sisters. He is chairman of various private holding companies, the family stock brokerage firm and Scott's. The family owns Ryerson Oil and Gas Ltd., a portion of Fleck Manufacturing Inc., a portion of GSW Inc. and of Rossland Corporation.

Michael Gardiner learned from a master. Besides, the company has been professionally managed for years. When asked why investors should consider this stock, Lyons said, "This company has an excellent management team, is decentralized but well-focused through strategic plans and is proactive rather than reactive. And the type of consumer services it is in are going to constitute the growth areas of the future."

Caveat: There's speculation that Kentucky Fried Chicken is losing market share amid consumers' concerns about fried foods and other chicken outlets. The succession question continues to nag even though the company has been professionally managed for years. Scott's has subordinated stock without votes and no coattail provisions protecting minority shareholders. This means the family can cut a side deal – including a merger with Cara Operations for instance – which could leave other shareholders out in the cold. Scott's may be considered pricey, but like Cara I consider it a Cadillac amongst a lot of clunkers.

An investment of $10,000 in January 1980 was worth $57,000 in January 1990. With dividends reinvested, it totalled $62,120. Over the decade prices ranged from a high of $20.75 to a low of $1.67, adjusting for splits.

(THE) SEAGRAM COMPANY LTD.

Head Office: Montreal, Quebec
Incorporated: 1928
Ownership: Major shareholder Bronfman family trusts

Revenues in 1989: US$5,055,671,000
Net Income: US$389,460,000
Earnings per share: US$1.18
Employees: 16,200
Year End: January 31

The world's longest undefended border has made smuggling one of North America's biggest businesses. It also gave birth, in the Roaring Twenties, to Canada's most brilliant industrial strategy resulting, albeit accidentally, in the creation of two world-class Canadian corporations. The strategic edge was the fact that Canada never made the manufacture of liquor illegal during U.S. Prohibition, with the result that most of the Canadian-made liquor ended up south of the border in the hands of bootleggers. Not surprisingly, once Prohibition ended, the world's biggest and best distillers were up and running in Canada, owned by the country's two pre-eminent booze baronies, the Hatches of Ontario and the Bronfmans of Montreal. The Canadian Royal Commission into bootlegging in 1927 asked Harry Hatch whether he realized that the U.S. Volstead Act prevented him from exporting liquor there. "It does not prevent us from exporting at all," he chuckled. "It prevents somebody there from importing. There is a distinction."

Harry Hatch was eventually fined by Ottawa and the Hatches were indicted by the United States but were never extradited. They went on to form Hiram Walker Resources, which was eventually taken over in 1986 by Britain's Allied-Lyons plc. Meanwhile, Samuel

Bronfman and his brothers stayed out of trouble and went on to create the Seagram Company, which Sam's children now control. It is now the world's largest distillery.

Seagram has 15 per cent of the entire United States market for distilled spirits, 37 per cent for wine coolers and 18 per cent of Canada's distilled spirits market. Seagram makes the leading brand in each of the three most expensive categories, Chivas Regal Scotch, Martell cognac and Mumms champagne. Other brands include Myers's Rum, Seagram's V.O., Seagram's 7 Crown, Crown Royal, Captain Morgan Rum, The Glenlivet Scotch and a clutch of wines. It also owns retail operations in Britain and Germany to peddle its wares and is well-positioned for when the tariff walls come down in Europe in 1992. It also has made huge acquisitions in the non-alcoholic beverage industry, most importantly buying Florida's Tropicana orange juice giant, number one in non-frozen orange juice with a 50 per cent market share in the eastern seaboard markets. It has 27 per cent of the entire U.S. orange juice market, ahead of Coca-Cola Inc.'s Minute Maid with 25 per cent.

But the liquor giant has its problems. As Corby Distilleries Limited has found, the health and fitness concerns felt by baby boomers is ravaging revenues for the industry as a whole. U.S. liquor consumption has declined from 190 million cases in 1980 to 155 million in 1988. Seagram's best-selling 7 Crown fell from nearly 7 million cases in 1980 to less than 5 million by 1988. V.O. fell from slightly more than 4 million cases to little more than 2 million in the same period of time. Meanwhile, upscale brands like Chivas, Myers's and Martell have increased from 2.5 million cases to nearly 3.5 million during the same time. Adding to the woes is proposed legislation prohibiting liquor sales in many parts of the United States and the effect of grim health warnings that were added to all liquor labels in the fall of 1989.

Although it all seems dismal, both Corby and Seagram are good bets in fact. Corby's saving grace is that it has made some astute takeovers of rivals and has stuck to upmarket brands that are defying the trend to lower liquor consumption. Seagram's saving grace, on the other hand, is its diversification in the liquor business, notably its purchase in 1981 of 20 per cent of America's ninth-largest corporation, chemical giant E.I. du Pont de Nemours & Company. Seagram now owns 23.3 per cent, more stock than the du Pont family owns. There is a standstill agreement, but Seagram may act as a white knight and acquire more stock if another bidder or large shareholder comes along. The du Pont investment was made after a high-profile takeover battle over Conoco Inc. pitted Seagram, flush with $2.3 billion in cash from selling another oil company, against du Pont and Mobil Corporation. Seagram settled when du Pont offered 20 per cent of its stock to Seagram in return for Seagram's Conoco stock.

Du Pont is spectacularly successful. With US$34 billion in revenues, its sales are equivalent in size to half the revenues collected by the Canadian federal government. Since acquiring its stake, Seagram's profits have nearly tripled and the 23.3 per cent of du Pont's profits added to Seagram's bottom line is equivalent to 80 per cent of its profits each year. This makes Seagram's profit figures somewhat misleading, considering du Pont's dividends are considerably less (typically 30 to 40 per cent) of the accounted-for profit. Still, those dividends are an important profit stream for the company and, more importantly, those du Pont shares are an important underpinning to Seagram stock. They represent a huge unrealized capital gain because they are carried on Seagram's books at a cost of $3.9 billion or $52.75 a share while the market value nearly doubled by 1990.

Besides, there are signs that Seagram's operations are also improving. In 1989 for the first time dollar revenues from liquor sales actually increased by 18 per cent, a good sign that its strategy of switching to high-quality liquor and away from its traditional but decreasingly popular whisky brands, is working. Also working is its investment in non-alcoholic beverage companies like Tropicana and a handful of smaller ones, which now account for about 20 per cent of operating revenues. Of course, Seagram is taking on a giant by battling Coca-Cola's Minute Maid for the orange juice market, and its pre-eminence in the wine and spirits coolers business is a hollow victory; the beverage proved to be a fad, and the market has been shrinking by 30 per cent per year after a peak in 1988.

The cooler market was fun while it lasted and Seagram's current president and heir apparent is credited with that success. Edgar Bronfman, Jr., is a young, 35-year-old whiz kid who never went to university but left home to get into the film business. His claim to fame there was a box-office non-event with Jack Nicholson called *The Border* which nonetheless achieved some critical plaudits if not profits. But by most accounts, he is proving to be a chip off the old block, Edgar Sr., who is still chief executive officer and chairman but is more interested in his duties as head of the World Jewish Congress.

Seagram's founder, Samuel Bronfman, died in the 1970s and left four children, Edgar Sr., Charles, Phyllis Lambert and the late Minda. Phyllis, who tangled greatly with her father all her life, is an architect who lives in a converted paint factory in Montreal. Feisty and totally unorthodox, she owns about 2 per cent of Seagram stock. Minda left three children, and her estate still owns roughly 5 per cent of the stock. Her widower, Baron Alain de Gunzburg, still sits on the Seagram board.

Edgar Sr. and Charles own 17 per cent of the stock apiece and are an odd couple. Edgar is flamboyant and a naturalized U.S. citizen who has had four marriages, five children and lived a jet-set existence all his life. Charles is a shy and retiring philanthropist, best-known in his native Canada as the owner of the Montreal Expos baseball team. He runs his affairs from a splendidly renovated 19th-century complex in downtown Montreal, where he gives away millions each year to his causes, as do a number of Bronfman family charitable trusts. Charles's two children are considerably younger than Edgar Jr., but he was reportedly miffed at Edgar Sr.'s selection of his second-eldest as the heir apparent. Charles is the co-chairman of Seagram and his business duties include looking after the du Pont investment.

"After they bought du Pont, Charles [Bronfman] and some of his execs went down to Delaware for a one-week chemistry course," Lorne Webster, a close Montreal friend of Charles's and fellow Expos shareholder, once told me. "Can you imagine that? The company makes $3 billion a month."

The Seagram stock is the subject of a family voting trust controlled by the brothers until the year 2009. But many of the grandchildren are uninterested or uninvolved in the family business, even though they indirectly own it. That is where CEMP Investments Ltd. has come into play, a family holding company set up by the late Samuel (the acronym is derived from the initials of his children's given names). Sam's four children have resulted in ten grandchildren, and CEMP's trustees have been divesting, selling control of hockey equipment manufacturer, Warrington, and also development giant, Cadillac Fairview Corporation Limited. This yielded some $2 billion in 1988 in capital gains for the grandchildren, who are now rich in their own right. "You see, everybody thinks that a Bronfman is rich, but these kids don't have any money and that's why the divestitures. The control block [for Seagram] is tied up and dividends flow to their parents or in trust. The kids wanted out," explains a source close to the family.

Those transactions saved the Bronfman family from the fate of other dynasties who have found the need to sell control blocks because some heirs were not interested in participating in operations and were unable to live on smallish dividends. However, it remains to be seen if Edgar Jr. can match the successes of his father, uncle and grandfather. More importantly, if he cannot, it remains to be seen if the family would admit that and find someone more appropriate.

Caveats: The jury's still out as to whether young Edgar Jr. will do a good job running Seagram. Du Pont earnings will continue to outperform the economy generally and the outlook is good. But Seagram's beverage operations face increasing competition and a shrinking marketplace. It must overcome this by astute acquisitions, and these are always risky.

An investment of $10,000 in January 1980 was worth $66,711 in January 1990. With dividends reinvested, it totalled $73,033. Over the decade prices ranged from a high of $109.50 to a low of $13.33, adjusting for splits.

STANDARD TRUSTCO LIMITED

Head Office: Toronto, Ontario
Incorporated: 1971
Ownership: Controlling shareholder Concorde Finance Corp.

Interest Income in 1989: $40,871,000
Net Income: $16,152,000
Earnings per share: $2.15
Employees: N/A
Year End: December 31

A bungalow in Toronto now fetches as much as family farms, and a parking space in the downtown core earns more than the hourly minimum wage. The meteoric rise in land prices in overheated southern Ontario has driven home-owners to small towns within commuting distance of Toronto. This flight to less expensive land has proven to be a boon not only to small-town marketers such as Gendis (with its small-town department stores) or Oshawa (with its rural IGA franchises) but also to Standard Trustco Limited, a gem of a financial institution with the best track record of any trust company in the land.

Standard Trustco is a no-frills purveyor of financial products operating mostly in small-town Ontario. Its downtown Toronto office belies its rural roots and *raison d'être*. The only symbol is the pastoral painting by Canadian artist William Kurelek that hangs in Standard's tiny foyer. And it is those rural roots that led flamboyant mining magnate, the late Stephen Roman, to launch Standard Trustco. Best known for his Denison Mines and Roman Corporation Limited empire, Roman's first love was farming and over the years he became upset with the way that big Canadian banks treated farmers. So in 1973 he launched Standard Trustco, now, ironically, the jewel in the Roman empire crown, which includes sometimes troubled uranium, coal, potash, packaging and oil and gas assets.

Today, Standard has 36 deposit-taking branches across the country, with the lion's share in prosperous southern Ontario. Besides cashing in on the flight from high-priced Toronto, Standard has been cashing in on the flight of money from stock markets since October 1987's crash. Investors have switched from stocks to guaranteed investment certificates, mutual funds or savings accounts. Of course other financial institutions have benefited from the same phenomenon, but Standard has done so more than others. That is because it also benefits from the changing demographics of southern Ontario. As the well-heeled population ages, residents of the city are taking advantage of their huge gains in real estate, buying a home in a rural area for considerably less, then putting the difference in safe, high-yield investment instruments. Standard caters to the over-50s, and a 1990 marketing campaign to gain deposits underscored this: the trust company offered a Royal Doulton china figurine to anyone opening up a new account.

"We don't nickel and dime our customers with service charges," says Standard's president, Brian O'Malley. "The over-50s is the fastest growing market in Canada. Inflation rocked the concept of loyalty. We do not offer personal loans, secured loans or foreign exchange services. We offer savings services simply. Daily and monthly interest savings accounts at rates one-quarter of a percentage point higher than banks. GICs and RRIFs are Standard's market focus."

More importantly, Standard's growth in deposits outstrips the industry's because its unique business strategy allows it to pay more for deposits than most others do. Like other financial intermediaries, Standard's bottom line is the result of the spread between what it pays on deposits and what it lends money out at. It can pay more interest because of its unique positioning. A rival doing the same is a company called Municipal Financial Corporation, another successful little trust outfit located in Barrie, Ontario.

Standard collects deposits in small towns where it pays small-town wages and small-town rents, allowing it to offer the slightly higher interest rates. Then it lends to big-city slickers at slightly more favorable rates than are current, dealing mostly in construction mortgages. Standard cherry picks this market because it can undercut banks and trust companies paying big-city wages and big-city rents. Cherry picking makes for more profits but also eliminates risk.

Standard's investment philosophy is as conservative as its customers' is. It spreads risk by lending across Canada, even though deposits come from go-go Ontario, but does not get caught up in high-flying price hikes. It lends money through offices in Halifax, Montreal, Toronto, Kitchener, Winnipeg, Calgary and Vancouver. "Those branches provide the same deposit-taking activities but are primarily there to service the gathering of funds outside the city and its investment in urban centres," says O'Malley. "We are careful. We did not have too much invested in Toronto because we get nervous about high prices. Vancouver too."

Standard's vice president of investments, Scottish-born Bill Paton, explains the mandate. "We provide construction financing if the project is pre-sold. We will lend on a takeout [remortgaging to take out higher values] on a graded formula. We are not in luxury condos, and our biggest market is construction loans and commercial/retail. We like shopping centres and office buildings because you are lending on cash flows, not emotion. We look at the buildings' leases."

This tight-fistedness insulated Standard from the disaster that nearly befell banks 100 times larger after the collapse of oil and property prices. Standard wrote off the equivalent of 1 per cent of its Alberta exposure, proof positive that small and stingy is indeed beautiful.

"We provide a consistently good return, pay out good dividends of 40 to 50 per cent of the previous year's earnings every year. And we have ample opportunity to develop our niche markets over the next five to ten years. Our rural franchise is showing more life and we have the ability to develop further there," says O'Malley. Another plus is the fact that 75 per cent of its workers own stock, which adds to motivation and cost-cutting.

Their expansion is cautious, as is everything else about this trust company. Its operating costs are the lowest in the financial services area and it grows organically, opening branches in good years when the return on equity will not be adversely affected. In 1988, seven new branches were christened, but only one new one was opened in 1989.

That cautiousness, coupled with the fact that Standard may be a potential takeover target, is why it has been the darling of analysts for quite some time. Roman Corporation owns 45 per cent of its stock, gained in a tacky manoeuvre in 1988 just after Roman's death. The speculation was that it would be sold, and the stock heated up from $16 to $20.50 in expectation of a bid. Then it was bought from financially troubled sister company, Denison Mines (37 per cent owned by Roman Corp.) for $22.95 a share, considerably higher than the average trading price had been for months, but the amount paid was not sufficiently higher than the prior month's price of $20.50 per share. The significance was that Roman Corp. did not legally have to make a follow-up bid to all shareholders, automatically triggered in Ontario if a bid to one shareholder is 15 per cent higher than the average trading 20 days prior to the bid. Minority shareholders instead were left out in the cold and the stock fell back in price.

A takeover could still happen in the future as Roman's successor, Helen Roman-Barber, tries to sort out the troubled empire by jettisoning assets or hanging in for the longer term. Besides, there are other significant shareholders, notably the Manufacturers Life Insurance Company (now Manulife Financial) and the CBC Pension Fund with 10 per cent each. "We view the ownership of shares by major outside shareholders as positive since it inhibits depreciation of the company's assets by management or a controlling shareholder," says Prudential-Bache Securities analyst Albert Thompson, who recommends accumulation for long-term capital appreciation and income growth. Hear, hear.

Caveats: This stock is interest-rate sensitive and will drop as rates rise. But it's a good long-term hold with the best history of profits among trust companies in the country.

An investment of $10,000 in 1982 was worth $34,107 in January 1990. With dividends reinvested, it totalled $39,619. Since 1982 prices ranged from a high of $24.75 to a low of $4.75, adjusting for splits.

(THE) THOMSON CORPORATION

Head Office: Toronto, Ontario
Incorporated: 1982
Ownership: Controlling shareholder K.R. Thomson

Revenues in 1989: US$4,726,000,000
Net Income: US$436,000,000
Earnings per share: US$0.80
Employees: 40,000
Year End: December 31

Canadians own more information assets per capita than any other nationality in the world, and our foremost entry is the Thomson Corporation, started by high-school drop-out Roy Thomson. A Toronto barber's son, Thomson spent the initial part of the Depression peddling clumsy, crackling wirelesses in rural Ontario. In 1931 he switched to the transmission end of the radio business and bought his first radio station in North Bay at the age of 37. A frenetic series of takeovers followed, founding a family fortune and also gaining it fame when Roy was granted Britain's last hereditary peerage. Lord Thomson of Fleet's humble roots in the radio business made it all the more fitting that his children in 1979 bequeathed $4.5 million toward construction of Toronto's stunning Thomson Hall, which boasts the best acoustics in the world.

Now, just a few blocks from that concert hall, Roy's son, Lord "Ken" Thomson of Fleet, commands a media empire that is second to none in Canada. The family-controlled Thomson Corporation is an amalgam of the former Thomson Newspapers Limited and International Thomson Organisation Limited, which merged in 1989 to create a media monolith that rings up profits of US$2.5 million every single working day, or US$631 million annually. Among the world's biggest information conglomerates, Thomson Corporation now ranks fourth with US$4.7 billion in revenues, after West Germany's Bertelsmann, Capital Cities/ABC and Time-Warner Inc.

Without a doubt, the Thomson Corporation is a superb conglomerate with excellent assets and good managers – Michael Brown and financial guru Nigel Harrison, two Britons who operate from Thomson's Park Avenue offices in New York City. Another plus is the fact that investors can be certain that they are getting into partnership with a very classy controlling shareholder. Lord Thomson does not own companies with subordinated voting stock and insisted in 1989 that the merger go forward only if it were blessed by a majority of the minority shareholders of both Thomson companies.

After the merger, Michael Brown became Thomson Group president (a promotion from president of just International Thomson). A British chartered accountant, he's the reincarnation of the old man, living on airplanes and maintaining Roy Thomson's frantic pace of takeovers and expansionary projects. He came by his high energy level and acquisitiveness honestly, by serving for several years as Roy's understudy as the two unsuccessfully attempted to turn Britain's venerable *Times* and *Sunday Times* into profitable ventures. They eventually sold out to Rupert Murdoch, who made a go of it, thanks to union-busting legislative assistance from Prime Minister Margaret Thatcher. Brown recalls his apprenticeship.

"Roy was a sucker for deals and he would talk to anyone about anything and then get us involved," recalls Brown. "I remember once he left for Lebanon because there was a television station for sale. We told him just to look at the station and not look at anything else. He said okay and came back with the station. But it took two weeks more before we finally prodded him into admitting that he had bought something else. An orange grove."

Naturally, the Lebanese orange grove did not go into the public company, but the anecdote illustrates why the Thomson empire has been so eclectic in the past. Brown has changed all that, and for the past several years he has been steadily shedding non-publishing assets. North Sea oil interests and some 40 unrelated operations were sold for $700 million during 1988 to pave the way for the 1989 merger. The only extraneous business left is Thomson's travel operations, but Brown says these are not for sale because they are increasing in profits and importance. Thomson owns Britain's largest charter airline; it has a fleet of 43 planes and 550 travel agencies.

Although a lucrative sideline, travel is not as profitable as Thomson's information and publishing and newspaper divisions. Travel posted profits of only US$60 million in 1988 out of US$2 billion in revenues, while the other two divisions rang up US$571 million in profits out of revenues of US$2.76 billion. Besides being a drag, the travel business is risky. If the pound falls against the Canadian dollar, earnings are lower. If the pound falls against the currencies of countries that are popular vacation destinations, travel volume will fall. Besides, Thomson's travel business is only as good as is Britain's economy and its future is in a state of flux as European Confederation looms in 1992.

Travel aside, Thomson is still a sound investment. It owns 40 dailies and 12 weeklies in Canada; 103 dailies and 75 weeklies in the United States; and 120 newspapers in Britain and Europe. Besides that, it owns some 25,000 individual products ranging from magazines to newsletters, from software packages to reference books. When I visited Thomson's New York office, Brown took me on a quick tour past bookshelves lined with Thomson publications on everything from crafts to auto repair; there were handbooks and reference periodicals such as *Jane's* shipping guide and *American Banker-Bond Buyer*. "If it's not boring enough or authoritative enough, we're not interested," he joked. "We don't want to be in television, films or trade books. These are off limits to us. We're looking for very solid franchises that are going on forever. Consumer magazines and trade books [non-educational or non-reference books] are sold through gimmicks and froth. We like essential or serious educational, reference books."

As for Thomson newspapers, I can attest to their profitability, having worked for the now-defunct *Brampton Daily Times*. At least in respect of this small paper, it was both miserly and non-controversial. I can remember at least once being pulled off an assignment involving a testy strike because the news offended one of the chain's biggest advertisers. As for stinginess, I remember we used our own cars to get to assignments, but we were paid mileage rates according to the number of cylinders we had in our cars. Four-cylinder rates were considerably lower than eight-cylinder ones. Not surprisingly, I quit after little more than one year. While many Thomson papers are very good, in some cases lousy journalism makes for enhanced profits.

And the money mounts. Once a month, Brown treks up to Toronto to visit with Thomson and mild-mannered John Tory, deputy chairman of the Thomson Corporation. Tory is also president of Woodbridge Company Limited, the family's private company, which owns the Thomson control block. There, in the muted, art-filled surroundings of Thomson headquarters overlooking Toronto's city hall, the three discuss strategy and results regarding their media holdings. That's all been good news.

The bad news has been the family's foray into Hudson's Bay Company, Simpsons Ltd. and Zellers Inc. bought in 1979. Plagued with poor locations and a shrinking base of loyal customers as younger generations prefer specialty stores, the retail side has preoccupied Tory and Thomson alike. Not coincidentally, the next Lord Thomson, David, is mostly involved in that side of the family portfolio as president of profitable Zellers Inc. in Montreal. Overcoming those problems takes the type of patience only a Thomson can afford. As for the average investor, my advice is stick with Thomson Corporation and leave The Bay for another day.

Caveats: Thomson's fortunes are linked to those of the British pound and British economy. Sluggish or no growth there hurts publication and newspaper linage and the travel business. The Common Market realignment in 1992 should be beneficial to Britain's economy but a Labor or left-wing government would not necessarily be.

An investment of $10,000 in Thomson Newspapers (Thomson International and Thomson Newspapers merged in 1989) in January 1980 was worth $61,697 in January 1990. With dividends reinvested, it was worth $68,268. Over the decade the two predecessors (Thomson Newspapers and Thomson International) if merged would have traded as high as $20.13 and as low as $2.18, adjusting for splits.

(THE) TORONTO-DOMINION BANK

Head Office: Toronto, Ontario
Incorporated: 1955
Ownership: Widely held

Interest Income in 1989: $1,940,446,000
Net Income: $694,657,000
Earnings per share: $0.71
Employees: 22,000
Year End: October 31

The T-D is the Mercedes of moneyhandlers, with a great capital position, no Third World exposure and hidden values in real estate that could be worth $2 billion, says Hugh Brown with Toronto broker Burns Fry Limited, considered the doyen of banking analysts. The T-D's valuable property portfolio is ironic considering T-D has the fewest branch outlets, but chairman Richard "Dick" Thomson has led his gifted management team into large-scale real estate development in a big way, making his bank a unique real estate and banking play for its shareholders.

Following the T-D's success in this endeavor, most of his banking rivals followed suit, building their own towers rather than leasing them from builders. But none have as splendid a portfolio. The T-D owns half of the Toronto-Dominion Centre – five black towers in downtown Toronto; 20 per cent of the Eaton Centre (a bigger tourist attraction than Niagara Falls); and 20 per cent each of Vancouver's Pacific Centre and Calgary Centre. Book value, or cost, for all of this is a meagre $229 million. Some say it's worth $1 billion, or $3 for each of its 350 million outstanding shares. Others, even more.

Tall, ramrod-straight Dick Thomson says he doesn't get concerned about the bank's real estate values because they fluctuate. Besides, the buildings aren't for sale. The eldest son of Harry Thomson, who became vice chairman of rival Canadian Imperial Bank of Commerce, Thomson is a lifer at the T-D, having joined it right after university even though he had earned an engineering degree, then a Harvard MBA. "I chose the T-D because it was open to change."

Thomson runs Canada's most entrepreneurial bank. He encourages executives to buy stock, with the result that he and his president, Robin Korthals, along with others, have become multimillionaires. Thomson's own stake is worth about $3 million, shares that he bought, not shares that were given to him. He has also gathered around him a relatively young team and created a climate for new ideas. Top dogs include Thomson, Korthals and third-ranked Ernest Mercier, who were all born in 1933. Thomson became Canada's youngest banking chairman in 1979 when he was only 46 years of age.

Since they're hardly ready for retirement, some still wonder what the trio can do for an encore. Of course, more of the same would do quite nicely. The Toronto-Dominion is fifth in size in Canada but is the second most profitable bank, racking up an impressive record of growth in assets, profits, dividends and stock prices. Its return on capital has averaged 21.92 per cent per annum dating back to 1985, compared to the industry average of 14.63 per cent. Not surprisingly, it is only one of two banks in North America that enjoys a Triple A credit rating. Morgan Guaranty Trust Co. of New York is the other.

The secret?

"Think change," Thomson replies. "We try to be entrepreneurial, to hire carefully and give opportunities. We recruit from within," he says. "We can't insure that same performance in the future. But we will try to by nurturing our people and hiring high-quality people. We encourage everyone to think change. Everyone has his own personal way of looking at problems. Some analyze them to death and never make a decision. Contrarians like to get all the evidence on the table. But often the most difficult part is getting evidence and defining the problem. Some of our best decisions have been not to enter a market. They have saved us millions.

"Another belief is that you don't get too far in the world following the herd. If you simply do what others do, then you become a commodity and cost is everything," he adds. Leaning against the wind has been what Thomson's bank has been all about. First, its lucrative entry into real estate has shored up its stock price for years. Then in 1987 when banks rushed in to snap up the country's brokerage firms after rules changed, the T-D broke ranks by opting for organic growth and founding a discount broker, the T-D Greenline Investor Services Inc., and an underwriting arm, the Toronto-Dominion Securities Corp. "We will make more than $100 million in profit from that and underwriting," says Thomson, triple what the Royal Bank's RBC Dominion Securities, the country's largest, makes. "People have more confidence and like to serve themselves."

The Lesser Developed Country (LDC) debt crisis was handled in a unique way when the T-D set aside reserves more rapidly than most, then sold virtually all remaining loans at dramatic discounts to others willing to take the risk that restructurings and repayments will occur. "The LDCs business was wrong and I cannot say anything good about that. We haven't tallied up costs, because you must also tot up profits and net it out. There is no question it cost us several hundred million dollars and it had to do with the way the world worked out. It was oil inflation then deflation in early 1980s. Capital was exported out of the Third World because of lost confidence and the political system fell apart. There have been books written on why Latin America simply hasn't worked."

In future, the T-D is going to pressure Ottawa to change rules so that it can get into the insurance and auto-leasing business. The bank also wants ownership restrictions imposed on new trust companies so that individuals cannot control them. But opposition is fierce and several draft proposals have fallen by the wayside in Ottawa.

As for future business strategies, Thomson says his bank is not goint to get sidetracked. "We are not interested in U.S. acquisitions or acquisitions here. We want to be Canada's best retail banker. From far away, fields sometimes look greener but maybe they aren't. We feel we have a good market here in Canada. Even though Canada is overbanked and overbranched, the same is true elsewhere and we are gaining market share slowly through service, the right products, the right image and the right people," he says.

Caveats: Bank stocks are cyclical. Prices fall during higher interest rate periods and increase with rate declines. Longer term holds are advisable. Risks include revisions to rules governing financial institutions in both Canada and the United States, which may lead some banks to make unwise acquisitions or to open up the T-D and others to more competition in the lucrative corporation lending side from trust or insurance outfits. The T-D is not acquisition minded, preferring to grow organically instead.

An investment of $10,000 in January 1980 was worth $51,518 in January 1990. With dividends reinvested, it totalled $61,608. Over the decade prices ranged from a high of $23.13 to a low of $3.84, adjusting for splits.

TORSTAR CORPORATION

Head Office: Toronto, Ontario
Incorporated: 1958
Ownership: Controlling shareholder the Atkinson Family

Revenues in 1989: $983,000,000
Net Income: $95,200,000
Earnings per share: $2.38
Employees: 4,600
Year End: December 31

Liberal also-ran Jim Coutts has always enjoyed special access to the corner suite on the sixth floor of One Yonge Street in Toronto. That is the roomy office of Canada's foremost publisher, Beland Honderich, a Mennonite who has built Canada's largest and most profitable daily newspaper, the *Toronto Star*.

Torstar was issued 22.4 per cent of Southam's common stock and Southam, 30 per cent of Torstar's non-voting stock. The two also signed a standstill agreement for ten years, a deal that was fiercely fought by Montreal investment counsellor Stephen Jarislowsky on behalf of a large group of Southam shareholders on the grounds that it removed Southam from play as a potential takeover candidate and therefore damaged stock prices. Federal government officials agreed some months later and cut the standstill agreement in half. It expired on June 30, 1990, but before that ended Southam put in place a poison-pill arrangement.

Now David Jolley and David Galloway, run Torstar with two divisions, the *Toronto Star* and romance publisher Harlequin Enterprises Ltd. Honderich is chairman of the board and the two Davids alternate the title of publisher and chief executive officer. Both are former management consultants and are capable executives. "The

Toronto Star is about the size of the *Boston Globe*, about 12th in North America. We sell 200 million papers a year and 200 million books through Harlequin a year," says Jolley, the *Star*'s soft-spoken, chain-smoking publisher in 1989. In 1989, the paper made a whopping profit of $92 million.

Does Torstar want to buy control of Southam? "I can't answer that," he says. "At the time of the swap, our stock was in the $30s and theirs in the $10s. Now they are roughly equal. We gained what we paid for it. It's been a great investment."

Jolley keeps his cards close to his vest in his fifth-floor office, located behind an unmarked door. Visitors getting off the elevator there are greeted with a photograph of "Holy Joe" Atkinson, a philanthropic and left-leaning tycoon whose daughter and grand-daughter still control Torstar. Since 1968, 18.2 per cent of Torstar's voting shares are held by Holy Joe's daughter, Ruth Atkinson-Hindmarsh and her 19 heirs, another 30.6 per cent is controlled by Holy Joe's only son's child, Catherine (Betsy) Atkinson-Crang; Honderich, Burnett Thall and the estate of William Campbell have another 14 per cent each. The rest is owned by Harry A. Hindmarsh. "The Atkinsons always vote unanimously," says Jolley. "Joe [Atkinson] Jr. left his estate to both his daughter and his second wife, who had been his secretary, Elaine. What a way to punish your kid and your wife. Betsy's the major shareholder and Elaine is the minority."

Torstar's Harlequin Romances operates in 100 countries and prints its paperbacks in 19 languages. The *Toronto Star* occupies the dominant place in the country's market, with 52 per cent of the advertising linage in Toronto. Southam, on the other hand, is more diversified as owner of the Montreal *Gazette*, the Ottawa *Citizen*, *Edmonton Journal*, *Calgary Herald*, *Vancouver Sun*, Hamilton *Spectator*, dozens more magazines and newspapers and Coles Book Store chain. Southam is also cash rich, swollen with the $600-million from the sale to Maclean Hunter and others of its control block of Selkirk Communications with numerous radio and television outlets.

Consensus among astute media analysts has been that investors buy Torstar stock, rather than Southam, if prices are low enough. Torstar stock with its Southam stake has been cheaper to buy, based on a multiple of earnings in both, compared to Southam stock with its Torstar stake. This is due to the fact that Southam has been the perceived takeover candidate, while the most likely company to be taken over is Torstar, possibly by Southam.

That is why Torstar is a good succession play. A complicated voting trust with 96 per cent of voting shareholders has kept peace within the Atkinson camp, but Honderich has managed it. His partial retirement and eventual departure may mean control of the company is up for grabs. "In the 1950s, Harry [Hindmarsh] died looking for a family successor. There were divisions in voting and fights and Bee [Beland Honderich] emerged as the chairman and Mrs. Atkinson-Hindmarsh supported him. We are one generation behind the Southams [with more than 100 heirs] and they keep reminding us of that."

Even if multiplication divides that family as it has so many others, the list of potential acquisitors is exceedingly short because no more than 25 per cent of any Canadian newspaper can be foreign-owned. Those already in the business who could pull it off are Desmarais's Power Financial, Conrad Black's Hollinger Ltd., Maclean Hunter Limited and the Thomson Corporation. However, Thomson and Maclean Hunter already compete against Southam and would not be allowed to acquire, then fold, the newspapers. But the Southam poison pill, and Southam board seats held by Torstar nominees, ensure that sneak attacks by Desmarais and/or Black are not in the cards. "Southam is simply not for sale at this time," Black once told me after he sold his 5 per cent Southam stake in 1989.

Torstar is a more likely takeover candidate for a number of reasons. Only one family member, Mrs. Atkinson-Hindmarsh's grandson Peter Armstrong, is involved in its management. He is an assistant financial editor, whereas at Southam, John Fisher, Hugh Hallward and Harvey Southam are family members actively involved in its operations. In the past, families like the Atkinsons who mostly clip coupons often lose interest in ownership, since they're able to earn more money by putting their holdings into a bank. In the past, the Billes family of Canadian Tire Corporation fame and the McLeans who own Canada Packers Inc. have tried to sell out their control. More importantly, Torstar's earnings must be leavened with new acquisitions because its newspaper and romance publisher are mature businesses. However, raising capital has been frustrated. Its attempt to sell Harlequin has failed due, ironically, to the type of protectionist policy the Star has editorially supported, a policy that prohibits more than 49 per cent foreign ownership of any Canadian publishing outfit. Similarly, raising funds by selling more equity will dilute the Atkinsons' power because rules forbid the sale of non-voting stock in future.

"My view is that the *Star* is the better bet. We view both those businesses as mature, but I assume Toronto will continue to be prosperous because of its dynamic economy," says Jolley. "We got out of the catalogue business in the U.S. because of competition. But we are keen to acquire something in the publishing field. We feel cable assets are too expensive, but we are interested in broadcast. We are looking at public companies in the U.S., trade mags and so on. We have virtually no debt and could pay up to $500 million without straining."

Torstar nearly sold half of Harlequin to German interests in 1989 but the potential partner withdrew in the end. "It is difficult to sell it all, but it is a great cash cow," says Jolley. "The newspaper is a mature situation for a couple of reasons. The amount of competition is on the rise, from weeklies to broadcast magazines and specialty ad sheets such as the *Auto Trader*."

Torstar's best defence has been offence and it has been busily snapping up competitors, small weeklies across Southern Ontario, through its wholly owned Metroland printing and publishing arm. Torstar does not break down its profits, but Metroland is believed to contribute $20 million annually to profits through "cash cows" such as the *Mississauga News*, a thrice-weekly monopoly. "Metroland is growing like Topsy and most newspapers would envy the operating profits of the *Mississauga News*," Jolley says.

Unfortunately, there's nothing left in Canada unless Torstar makes a grab for Southam which it cannot do until it sells Harlequin for a big dollar. "To date, we've said no to getting into unrelated businesses, but not with a lot of careful consideration. Given the high price of media properties, I'm not sure we shouldn't consider it. We bought *Auto Trader* across the country with a Montreal partner but the future's not certain. We have our eyes and ears looking in Europe for properties, too."

Jolley says Torstar is not interested in buying into the volatile forestry business or commercial printing. It passed on buying Selkirk from Southam for $600 million because "we were not prepared to pay the large price that Ron Osborne [Maclean Hunter president] paid. We also were not let on the board of WIC Ltd. a few years back."

Caveats: Torstar has only non-voting stock available but a coattail provision provides partial protection to investors in the event of a takeover premium offered to voting shareholders. Advertising linage has been down in lockstep with Canada's general economic malaise and this may provide a buying opportunity for Torstar as newspaper profits will shrink and prices pull back in 1990. There is concern that Harlequin may suffer from increasing competition and hopes are it can be sold. The *Star* has no place to expand in Canada.

An investment of $10,000 in B shares in January 1980 was worth $46,333 in January 1990. With dividends reinvested, it totalled $51,920. Over the decade prices ranged from a high of $37.88 to a low of $3.63, adjusting for splits.

TRIDEL ENTERPRISES INC.

Head Office: Downsview, Ontario
Incorporated: 1981
Ownership: Controlling shareholder Tridel Financial Corp.

Revenues in 1989: $694,000,000
Net Income: $45,000,000(B.E.)/$81,000,000(A.E.)
Earnings per share: $3.66(B.E.)/$6.56(A.E.)
Employees: 27,000
Year End: December 31

(B.E. - before extraordinary items; A.E. - after extraordinary items)

When rock group Pink Floyd toured North America, their entourage included 12 semi-tractor trailers full of sound equipment and scaffolding. At every show in a different city, dozens of stage hands erected the stage and skeleton framework for the huge amplifiers using miles of aluminium beams. A similar army of workmen sets up banks of 30,000 seats for spectators attending Molson's Indy Grand Prix through Toronto's streets every summer. Tridel Enterprises rents such gigantic Tinker-Toy sets around the world as a sideline through its successful division called Aluma Systems Corp. It also rents out a unique construction technology used worldwide and Aluma's sales have swollen from $35 million in 1984 to around $330 million by 1990. Estimates are that revenues will hit $1 billion by 1996, but before then Aluma will be a separate public entity.

Tridel stands for "Three Del Zottos" – Angelo, Elvio and Leo Del Zotto. They share 87.7 per cent of the company with long-time family partner and accountant Harvey Fruitman. Few Canadian investors have ever heard of Tridel, particularly outside Toronto where it is known for its well-built, upscale condominium developments.

The publicity-shy Del Zottos offered up for an interview two of their top officers in the splendid surroundings of a Tridel building. It is like all Tridel buildings, a luscious high-rise with marble-lined lounges, an indoor-outdoor pool and spa facility surrounded by huge boulders, full-sized trees and sculpture. Executive vice president and chief financial officer Austin Page attends and so does Tridel legal counsel Martin I. Applebaum, riding shotgun. Since a series of revelations in the Ontario legislature, the Del Zottos have ducked interviews and so have their execs. Their family holding company, Tridel Corporation, was implicated in allegations that one Ontario Liberal took a bribe and another routed charitable funds into political warchests. The hearings were to drag on well into 1991 but were ended by court edict. "The public company is not involved. Tridel Corp. is paying the legal fees," Applebaum says firmly.

Tridel stock lags other real estate companies. This bugs Austin Page and for good reason. "Take a company like Bramalea Limited, which trades at an earnings multiple of seven times, while we trade at only four times earnings. We have 50 per cent of the condo market in Toronto and we'll do better than Bramalea when times get tough," says Page.

One of the reasons for Tridel's lagging performance is, frankly, the rotten headlines. But to believers, this merely provides a buying opportunity. Tridel is a conservatively financed company, with upside potential in Aluma. But prices haven't been disastrous. Since the 1986 issue price of $12.50, they have hit $18, not high enough considering the generous dividend policy, which has averaged a 17-per cent yield.

Of course, earnings may be adversely affected by the soft housing prices in Toronto where Tridel sells condos exclusively. While Toronto remains the most buoyant of Canada's regions, by late 1989 the banks stopped lending any money to new condo projects unless buildings were 100 per cent pre-sold with healthy down payments in hand. If this marks a stoppage in construction, Tridel's bottom line may shrink a year or so down the road – but not calamitously.

Tridel has never overstated revenues by prematurely adding condo sales as revenue to its financial statements; it waits until the building is finished, the deals closed and buyers, or their tenants, moved in. As for partially completed projects, Tridel is somewhat insulated because its marketing arm spurned the type of low down payment and multiple purchase techniques that other developers used to encourage speculators who may never close.

Besides, when things slow down, Tridel won't be laden with an expensive land bank that must be carried at high interest rates for years. It also can afford to rent units that have not sold and wait until the market returns. It can also turn more to public works projects and concentrate on building affordable housing units for governments and third parties on a turn-key basis. Tridel also builds houses in joint ventures with experienced home builders. "We may pay more for sites but do our business by option," says Page. "And we don't exercise the option until we get the land zoned."

The downturn is long overdue and will provide acquisition opportunities, of sites or projects or even development companies. Tridel is flush with $145 million from institutions in late 1989, using Aluma as security, while many over-extended developers will go to the wall. Tridel can benefit in the medium to long term when things turn around again, as they inevitably do.

Even so, there will be tough times. About 55 per cent of Tridel's revenues and 65 per cent of profits are derived from residential construction. Aluma Systems Corp., its construction technology outfit, contributes 45 per cent to revenues and 35 per cent to profits. Overall sales are 63 per cent in Canada and 37 per cent in the United States.

The Del Zotto story is a remarkable one. Their father was a stone mason from northern Italy who came to Canada in 1934 to work in Sudbury's nickel mines. But he hated the cold and moved to Toronto. There he built a house and lived in it until he had enough capital to build two more. Now his three sons run a multinational manufacturing and development conglomerate. Day-to-day operations are left to professional managers, but the eldest son, Angelo, is the driving force and deal-maker as the firm's chairman and chief executive officer. "Angelo is a graduate of the scaffold – the mason's, not the hangman's," jokes Applebaum. Angelo has never been interviewed but associates say he is a quick study, mercurial and philanthropic. Second oldest is Elvio Del Zotto, whose law firm does much of the company's legal work but whose passion is politics. He heads the Ontario Liberal Party. Youngest son is Leo, in charge of the firm's design and marketing operations. He is considered a gifted salesman. "They believe in hiring good people and listening to their advice," says Page. Tridel also has some strong outside directors, including Elvio's friend and neighbor, Conrad Black.

Because of perceived conflicts in a family-controlled public company, the board's auditing committee is chaired by outside director, Gordon Cowperthwaite, an auditor by trade who is also a director of blue-ribbon mutual fund outfits like Investors Group and Sceptre Investment Counsel Limited. That committee must approve all non-arm's-length transactions, such as the fees charged by the brothers' family firm to manage buildings for condo owners until buildings are fully occupied, as well as sales commissions and legal services by Elvio's law firm. "The 5 per cent management fee is low in the industry and that company essentially breaks even. Marketing fees are 1 per cent, normally they are 2 or 2.5 per cent," says Page.

Although the go-go condo days may be over in Toronto for some time, the sizzle in this steak is Aluma Systems, Tridel's potential billion-dollar baby. It all began in the late 1960s as a joint venture project with Alcan Aluminum Limited in Montreal when it was looking for new applications for its metal. By the early 1970s, Tridel bought Alcan out and came up with, essentially, a Meccano set consisting of aluminum-extruded forms to facilitate the quick pouring of concrete. The system saves time, and therefore millions, because the forms need not be dismantled and rebuilt from one floor to the next. "This grew out of the desire by the brothers to achieve high productivity in high-rise building construction," says Page. "This system reduces the 'pour cycle' from ten days to three days, halving the labor content at the same time. There are huge savings."

Now Aluma sells its systems, rock-concert scaffoldings and some 5,000 products at 80 distribution yards in North America. It also runs its "Aluma bank," which allows a developer to "deposit" his forms in Halifax "without storage cost or insurance" and withdraw the same system anywhere in North America closest to his next job. While that form is "on deposit," Aluma can rent it out to someone else. Aluma also provides incredible back-up service; customers send blueprints into Aluma's 110 applications engineers, who set up CADCAM programs in order to teach customers how to make the best use of the Aluma system. Not surprisingly, Aluma is Alcan's largest extrusion customer in Canada.

Aluma is also a counter-cyclical company, too, because its systems can be used on public works projects, usually undertaken during tough times to kick-start the economy. Because of its potential use in repairing and building highways, bridges, dams, tunnels and subways, it may be uniquely positioned to benefit from the lessening of Cold War tensions. If peace has indeed broken out, a great deal of the $1 trillion out of the world's $13-trillion economy spent on armaments may be diverted to repairing or replacing infrastructure in the United States, Eastern Bloc and Third World.

Page exudes enthusiasm about the company that's been his employer since 1984. "There is only one reason to invest in this company. It knows how to make money better than most. It is exceptional. The stock has continued to go up (not enough) since the controversy, but the multiple is low. The market doesn't understand Aluma, our revenue-producing asset on wheels. This is not a development company caught with a see-through building in Dallas or empty condos. This is a manufacturing giant which also happens to build 1,500 to 2,500 units a year more efficiently and beautifully than anyone else in Canada. Perhaps North America."

Caveats: This stock is thinly traded so does not react as it normally should. But the introduction of the GST in 1991 will harm condo sales, making for lower profits that year and possibly the next. The firm is not overextended in land sites. The market may not appreciate Aluma until it is spun off separately.

An investment of $10,000 in Tridel in 1986 was worth $13,900 in January 1990. With dividends reinvested, it totalled $16,860. Since 1986 prices ranged from a high of $20.50 to a low of $5.75, adjusting for splits.

TRIZEC CORPORATION LTD.

Head Office: Calgary, Alberta
Incorporated: 1960
Ownership: Controlling shareholder Carena Development Inc.

Revenues in 1989: $1,190,800,000
Net Income: $112,200,000
Earnings per share: $0.50
Employees: 10,000
Year End: October 31

Corporate Canada is a family affair and investors can clean up by riding the coattails of the country's most successful families. Their biggest fortunes by far were amassed in real estate, most notably the billions made by the Reichmanns and by Peter and Edward Bronfman. The two families share control of Trizec Corporation Ltd., a Calgary-based enterprise, which has become Canada's pre-eminent real estate company and North America's largest public developer. Trizec is a way for the public to participate in an important asset play, a great company with a track record and superb prospects, all the more remarkable considering it was rescued in 1978 from the jaws of bankruptcy. Trizec's turnaround, along with Canada's unique economic circumstances, conspired to propel the real estate index between 1978 and 1988 on the Toronto Stock Exchange higher and faster than all the others.

Canada's developers are among the world's biggest, an important factor in an industry that makes money by borrowing it at the lowest possible rates of interest. A mix between financiers and manufacturers, developers have made a killing because that business remains one of the few untaxed enterprises in an overtaxed world. Developers here can avoid capital gains taxes by never selling. So they don't, unlike the owner of an oil field, mine or car factory.

The game has been to buy, hold, remortgage at an inflated value and take out the difference to buy some more. That, combined with misguided government policies and barriers to entry imposed by our large banks who favor large developers and large projects, has created a hothouse effect. In Canada, the big get bigger.

Trizec is the safest way to cash in on real estate. It is uniquely capable of capitalizing on opportunities and is highly diversified, with assets split evenly between the United States and Canada, as well as among various regions in order to reduce risk. It is heavily committed, however, in southern Ontario and southern California, two North American regions that have been immune to normal cycles. In California, geographic and environmental constraints have limited the availability of developable land. In Ontario, rent controls, anti-development local politics and regulatory red tape created shortages of supply, and demand leaped due to immigration, foreign investment and the migration of Canadians to jobs there. This supply-demand crunch will continue into the next decade, making Toronto and Los Angeles's Orange County housing costs the highest in North America.

Concerns about earthquakes in California are misplaced. Trizec builds housing to sell and its subsidiary passes that risk on to new home-owners once homes are completed. But it also builds retail and office space to rent. These are all insured and the cost is passed along to tenants. "The San Francisco quake caused a mere $500,000 in damage, including damage to a San Mateo shopping mall near the catastrophe's epicentre," says Trizec chairman Harold Milavsky.

Although those two regions are important, they do not dominate. The beauty of Trizec's portfolio is that it is spread across the continent and consists of 300 rental properties with 110 million square feet of office and retail space, equivalent in size to 3,666 football fields. Assets total $10 billion, up from $900 million in 1977, and plans are aggressive. "We will be adding 23 million square feet of space of first-class development in the next five years in major office and retail," says Trizec's president, Kevin Benson, a ginger-haired, freckled chartered accountant from South Africa who looms in the interview like a football linebacker.

Benson shares the role of chief executive officer with Milavsky, Trizec's well-liked and well-connected chairman. Milavsky, an urbane executive born in Alberta, sits on many prestigious boards in

Canada and handles strategy and external relationships. Benson is a number-cruncher with good people skills who looks after day-to-day operations. The two occupy neighboring offices in Trizec's Scotia Tower in downtown Calgary, nestled amid towers built by oil fortunes. In fact, Trizec is the only large head office operation in Calgary that is not in the oil business; it's an unusual locale for North America's biggest real estate giant, who might be expected to be found in Toronto or New York. But Calgary is where Milavsky, who sits on a number of oil company boards that are not part of the Peter Bronfman group of companies, prefers to live. Besides, with such far-flung interests, Trizec could arguably be located anywhere in North America.

Besides being among the brightest real estate minds anywhere, Milavsky and his team have a track record and professionalism that place them a cut above some of the other Toronto execs who run companies affiliated with Bronfman's gigantic Edper-Hees-Carena-Brascan monolith. Like their Bronfman counterparts, they accept stock options in lieu of high salaries, a good incentive that benefits shareholders. But their ambition has not led them, as it has others, to squabble publicly and spend shareholder money on court battles, as was the case in the 1989 battle over Enfield Corporation. And Milavsky's Trizec has not indulged in the type of byzantine restructurings popular with this group, a corporate version of cut-and-paste, which mostly leaves minority shareholders and tax officials in the dark.

The difference may be because the Reichmanns own just as much stock as the Bronfman group, or 37 per cent each. And the three reclusive Reichmann brothers have always bent over backwards in the interest of minority shareholders, thus distinguishing themselves honorably as partners. The Reichmanns also exercise control if they own control, whereas the Bronfman bunch tend to try and gain managerial control without owning at least 51 per cent of the stock. Despite these differences, Trizec trades at a discount. I think not. Trizec is a compelling, blue-chip way to participate profitably in the real estate business.

"We have had the benefit of having had the Reichmanns on the board who are knowledgeable people in our business," says Milavsky. "This helps with decision making. It is always good to have a rich poppa, in terms of selling new shares to raise money. And we have two rich poppas."

Another thorny issue is the fact that Trizec could be in conflict with some of the other Reichmann or Bronfman real estate holdings. The Reichmanns own Olympia & York Developments Limited with a rumored $20 billion in assets and have control of Campeau Corporation, which tottered on the brink of bankruptcy after buying America's two largest retail chains, many of whom are Trizec tenants. Then there's Carena Developments Limited, which technically owns the 74 per cent combined Reichmann and Bronfman holdings. It owns chunks of house-builder Coscan Development Corporation, Consolidated Carma and shares with BCE Inc. its troubled BCE Development Corporation real estate giant, and formerly Oxford Developments and Daon Development Corporation.

Milavsky says there are no conflicts. "There are no specific rules. But there are no transactions we've done with any of the Hees-Edper group as tenants. We've done some mortgage financing with London Life. These are all public companies and we play by public company rules. It's not an issue," says Milavsky. "We compete [for sites and projects] against the Reichmanns and Bramalea."

Milavsky and Benson sit atop an empire that includes Canadian landmarks such as Montreal's Place Ville Marie, Toronto's Atrium on Bay, Yorkdale and Scarborough Town Centre complexes and Calgary's new Banker's Hall. Trizec also owns eight hotels; 70 per cent of Bramalea Limited, a major housing contractor in Ontario and California with a $5-billion office-and-retail portfolio (it also owns 24 per cent of J.D.S. Investments Ltd.); 100 per cent of nursing home chain Central Park Lodge with 42 sites and 6,372 clients per year; 100 per cent of the Hahn Company, the fifth-largest shopping centre developer in the United States with 50 large retail centres; and 23 per cent of the Rouse Company, the largest publicly owned U.S. developer, with US$1.85 billion in assets, which includes 75 retail centres, 13 downtown developments, 107 office projects, warehouses, industrial properties and land.

Of course, so many tentacles mean that investors have many choices to make. Do they invest in Trizec, or its parent company Carena, Bramalea, Rouse or J.D.S.?

"Trizec is the finest public real estate company in North America, in terms of accounting, management, future growth, size, stewardship and its ability to raise money cheaply, which is very important," says Canada's doyen of real estate analysts, Frank Mayer, with Toronto brokerage firm Brown Baldwin Nisker (now known as BBN) James Capel Inc. "But if you like Trizec, you like Carena. For every share of Carena, you get three-quarters of a Trizec share. Buy whichever one is cheaper."

I disagree and feel that Trizec's the best bet. It's an actual operating entity, not some convenient holding company that speculates on turnarounds as Carena does. Trizec is also a management company, too, with an unblemished track record, unlike the others, of 13 years of increases in earnings, assets and dividends. This is a gigantic asset play and a fundamentally sound company that is conservatively managed, with only $1.1 billion carried on its books. It also uses "reserve accounting." "The classic example was in San Diego, when Trizec took a $14-million writedown because there was a chance city council wouldn't approve a project. It got approval but the writedown wasn't reversed. This means writedowns don't come out of left field and it also depresses stock prices, allowing insiders and the public to get in there," explains Mayer.

The bottom line is, there should be a goodly amount of real estate in most portfolios. The best investment most of us have ever made is buying a home of our own, so why not do more of the same? Buying Trizec for a long-term investment is the way to do that and leave the risk of timing, pricing, financing and renting to professionals.

Caveats: The main concern about this or any company that is part of the Bronfman empire is that it becomes a pawn in some reshuffling of assets. The chances of this happening are slim, but head for the hills if one is announced. A bad sign would be the departure of Milavsky. Another bearish sign is declining retail sales. Trizec depends upon prosperous store tenants for a good deal of its revenue. Another problem area is its exposure to California, where another major earthquake or two could wreak damage to property and stock prices.

An investment of $10,000 in B shares in January 1980 was worth $80,833 in January 1990. With dividends reinvested, it totalled $86,878. Over the decade prices ranged from a high of $32 to a low of $8.75, adjusting for splits.

UNICAN SECURITY SYSTEMS LTD.

Head Office: Montreal, Quebec
Incorporated: 1964
Ownership: Controlling shareholder A.M. Fish

Revenues in 1989: $125,927,000
Net Income: $4,585,000
Earnings per share: $0.62
Employees: 1,800
Year End: June 30

Aaron Fish may be Canada's most fascinating, if least known, president and chief executive officer. Among other accomplishments, he unwittingly taught the Watergate burglars how to break and enter and is the only chief executive officer in Canada invited to President George Bush's inaugural. He is also the only one with access to the head of the FBI and who can crack a safe in minutes and pick a lock in seconds. When only 16, he invented the world's first push-button lock and now, nearly 58 years of age, he has travelled the world as a guest of governments because of his special security expertise. Aaron Fish is all of this and more, a locksmith by trade, a tycoon in practice and a thoroughly charming individual.

His company, Unican Security Systems Ltd., is low-tech at its best. Anytime you buy a key, have one copied, use a magnetic access card to get into your office building, or use a push-button lock, chances are it was made by Unican. With $126 million a year in sales and 1,500 employees, his company is pre-eminent in three specialized areas and intends to stay there through new products and customer service. And just consider the potential. Fish says key blanks make Unican ten cents each, but "North Americans lose 4.5 keys a year per person on average," crows Fish and his shareholders laugh all the way to the bank. Fish owns 18 per cent of the stock.

Unican is thoroughly recession-proof and counter-cyclical. Bad times mean more crime and security is Unican's stock-in-trade. Every day, in its Montreal and North Carolina plants, Unican cranks out 1.5 million key blanks or 400 million a year, more than any other manufacturer in the world. There are 4,500 different types of keys extant in North America and Unican has the moulds to make most of them. Labor is about 30 per cent of cost and Unican has cut its raw materials expense by rolling its own metal sheets to make blanks from. Another overhead is tooling costs, which run about $10,000 per key type. "We spent $45 million in three years but I don't like debt. We are going to pay off $10 million in bank loans in 1990," says Fish.

Unican also makes more zinc furniture handles than anybody else – 265,000 handles daily. It also makes the machines that cut keys in stores. Unican branched out into these lucrative sidelines because the products are made with the same machinery used to make thousands of push-button locks every year.

Fish's head office is in a no-frills industrial building near Montreal's Blue Bonnet Race Track. He returned to his native Montreal in 1987 after five years in Rocky Mount, North Carolina. He had bought a competitor there in 1982 but once it was running smoothly, he and his family moved back home and to better schools for his youngsters. He cycles from his home to work when weather permits.

Fish comes from a family of entrepreneurs. He and his cousin, Ab Fish, were Grade 11 drop-outs who grew up in the rough-and-tumble St. Urbain section of Duddy Kravitz fame. Both created empires and Ab founded and built Bi-Way, now part of Dylex Ltd. Ab is a vice president with Eaton's of Canada Limited.

Virtually everything about Aaron Fish and his company is unorthodox. He's an enthusiastic, down-to-earth fellow who spurns the posturing so many other builders indulge in. No fancy clubs or name-dropping. Aaron Fish is one of Canada's most ingenious and deserving success stories. His unusual manner and management style are partly why none of his operations are unionized. "I used to give a Christmas bonus and annual raises in January. Now I stagger raises five times a year instead of once a year. Psychologically this is better. Before if a worker knew he was going to get a rise of $20 a week, he would spend it ahead of time and buy $2,000 worth of furniture or whatever. By April, he was broke and bothered again. Now they get raises all the time."

Fish also entered the publishing world, another clever departure from the norm. He was approached in 1986 by the publisher of the only locksmith trade magazine in North America to buy it, and he did. He paid $2 million for *Locksmith Ledger*, published in Chicago and with a circulation of 23,000. Besides the periodical, *Ledger* also publishes spiral-bound handbooks such as the bestseller *The Picking Book* (How to Pick a Lock by Aaron Fish) which retails for $60 each. It's an inspired strategy, because Unican sells to the trade, or locksmiths, as opposed to the public, and his publishing venture keeps his company's name before that important public. The *Ledger* also created and manages a guild for locksmiths, employs five full-time smiths to train them at seminars and sponsors free trade shows where speakers deal with professional development topics such as how to blow newly designed safes, break into the newest models of cars or pick the latest locks. When asked if he uses his magazine to push his products and bans competitors as advertisers, Aaron says characteristically, "The first guy who buys the space, gets it. I told my publisher that we must never show arrogance."

Caveat: Fish must delegate and streamline the management of his firm or he will burn out. Performance may suffer while new young lions are put in charge, but it is the key to even greater growth in the future. Although it's not a one-man band, Unican has been steered by the visionary and charismatic Fish, and his sudden departure would hurt the bottom line. With 70 per cent of sales in the United States, the company is exposed to some currency risks.

An investment of $10,000 in January 1980 was worth $143,750 by January 1990. With dividends reinvested, it totalled $149,138. Over the decade prices ranged from a high of $11.50 to a low of 32 cents, adjusting for splits.

WIC WESTERN INTERNATIONAL COMMUNICATIONS LTD.

Head Office: Vancouver, British Columbia
Incorporated: 1981
Ownership: Controlling shareholder Western Broadcasting Company

Revenues in 1989: $150,000,000
Net Income: $17,235,000(B.E.)/$7,700,000(A.E.);
Earnings per share: $2.50(B.E.)/$1.12(A.E.)
Employees: 750
Year End: August 31

(B.E. - before extraordinary items; A.E. - after extraordinary items)

Television parody SCTV with its famous Doug and Bob McKenzie skits still ranks as the most successful Canadian production ever to hit the American airwaves. It was ethnic WASP, working class WASPdom at its inarticulate best, something that Texans, hillbillies and Newfies alike could relate to. It catapulted SCTV to top ratings and creators Dave Thomas and Rick Moranis into international stardom. But the Doug and Bob characters were a last-minute revision designed to pay lip-service to nervous CBC executives who buy programs based on passports. Initially, the CBC rejected the Canadian-produced, Canadian-casted, Canadian-financed show on the grounds that it was not Canadian enough.

Doug and Bob were named after the show's producer and executive producer, who both worked for the show's godfather, Edmonton entrepreneur Dr. Charles Allard. Millions had been invested in taping 52 shows and Holtby successfully flogged the series to NBC. Then he approached the CBC but they rejected it because it was not Canadian enough. "I told Dave Thomas and Rick Moranis what CBC said and they got irate because they are Canadians and it was an all-Canadian show. They said, 'What the hell do they want? Us sitting in front of a Canadian flag or a map of Canada acting like a bunch of hosers?' I said,

'I don't care but we have no budget and we've got to do something cheap to get the CBC sale.' So Moranis and Thomas put the weather map behind them, put on some toques, got a six-pack of beer from the dressing room and did a number of skits ad lib. There was not one line written and we just filmed one after another. But it became the most significant thing that they did. We left it in for NBC, too, and they loved it," he says.

Now Holtby is in charge of $50-million worth of Canadian television production as president and CEO of media conglomerate WIC Western International Communications Ltd. in Vancouver. Although another SCTV may not come along for a while, Holtby has an even bigger impact on Canadian broadcasting now that WIC has become Canada's second-largest private broadcaster after Baton Broadcasting Inc. of Toronto. WIC broke out of its strictly regional profile when it bellied up to pay $217.50 million to Maclean Hunter Limited for Selkirk Communications Limited's broadcast assets. WIC, under Holtby's capable custodianship, promises to become one of Canada's sexiest media conglomerates in the 1990s.

WIC owns five television stations in B.C. and Alberta and nine radio stations in large cities spread across Canada as far east as Toronto. Most importantly, however, WIC's franchises occupy first or second slot in their respective markets, thus enabling them to command top advertising dollars. Its CTV station, BCTV, outperforms the CTV network generally, which has been losing market share. BCTV's newscasts have more viewers than any other newscast in the country, thus yielding premium advertising dollars for commercials.

Broadcasting is a tough business, but WIC is uniquely and well positioned. Roughly half of Canada's radio licences are losing propositions, but WIC's strong entries are all profitable. Big-city positioning makes a broadcaster immune from recessions or economic downturns that can destroy small-city radio or television. "We went through a downtrend in Alberta after the great boom of the 1970s. Major advertisers want to keep the brand awareness up so when times turn tough an advertiser will still buy Vancouver or Toronto but will cut back the smaller markets," Holtby says.

Big-city broadcasting is counter-cyclical while publishing is not. During bad times, more advertising dollars switch to television or radio because people stay home, do not go out to movies or to dinner. They listen to radio or turn on the tube. "In the dirty thirties, the movie business did very well. We had an Ontario pay television company and all of a sudden we saw tremendous sales in Oakville and Oshawa because there were auto plant layoffs there. These guys came home and didn't want to watch soap operas so they subscribed to pay while they were laid off," he says.

The broadcast business, like cable, pipelines or telephones, is strictly regulated. The Canadian Radio-Television and Telecommunications Commission grants monopolies and tells broadcasters how much Canadian content they must have, when, where and at what cost. They are on a very short leash and bottom-line considerations are only part of the commission's job. It also tries to meet social and political objectives, notably spreading the socio-economic benefits to all regions. That is where WIC has a special edge. There's little doubt in the minds of most commission-watchers that WIC is a darling of the regulators, who see it as western Canada's countervailing media conglomerate. In fact, when Maclean Hunter sought permission to spin off many of the Selkirk assets in 1989, commissioners would have liked WIC to buy more than it did, including Hamilton's CHCH-TV, which had been pre-sold to the Blackburn media group of London, Ontario. WIC passed, but future acquisitions for WIC will be a a piece of cake, a hidden asset to a broadcaster in this country that is impossible to quantify in bottom-line benefits.

"I think the fact we're in western Canada will put us in good stead for additional acquisitions, and I know that the CRTC is looking to it to be a major broadcaster in Canada, or one of the majors. One of the commissioners said that he can see the industry being dominated by more groups so they want a western group. The stations we bought from Maclean Hunter had all been owned by Selkirk, which was based in Toronto. So we repatriated those. They like that. They are looking for balance," he says.

WIC has another hidden asset, its 51 per cent in Canadian Satellite Communications Inc., or Cancom. It is Canada's largest user of the government's telecommunications satellites, buying then re-selling time from government-owned Telesat Canada. Created in 1981, it was licensed to provide television and radio services to remote communities, but, more importantly, it is also licensed to serve businesses.

Telesat's privatization should benefit. Cancom buys from and also competes against Telesat and was forced in 1989 to take it to task before the commission. That December, Telesat was punished when the commission cut rates by 7.2 per cent and denied a 5 per cent rate increase request.

"Cancom is going to be a very big company and growth is going to be on the business services side. Canadian Tire has a little dish on each store [in] about 380 locations. When you buy something at Tire and they look at your account and inventory code, it is automatically updated and the inventory of that store is updated," he says.

Holtby is a chartered accountant who plied his trade with Edmonton entrepreneur Dr. Charles Allard, who made a fortune in real estate and television. Now he works for entrepreneur Frank Griffiths, founder of WIC, who controls 85 per cent of the votes. Griffiths remains chairman and his son vice chairman, but operations are left to Holtby. The family has no intention of selling out, says Holtby, a young executive born in 1946. "I think they hired me more for age than anything else."

Griffiths bought his first radio station in New Westminster, outside Vancouver, but it became the leader in ratings in the lower mainland, then grew from that. The only other significant shareholder is Rogers Communications Inc. with 9.9 per cent. Torstar Corporation owned a whack of stock years ago but Griffiths refused to give it any board seats, fearing a takeover. Torstar got the hint and cashed out.

Caveats: This is a closely controlled company that may have succession problems in the future, even though trouble is not on the immediate horizon. It also sells subordinated stock, something that should never have been allowed, but there is an untested coattail provision forcing a bid to all shareholders. Its concentration in western Canada makes it vulnerable should a downturn in energy, forestry and mining prices re-occur.

An investment of $10,000 in B stock in 1983 was worth $20,000 in January 1990. With dividends reinvested, it totalled $23,292. Since 1983 prices ranged from a high of $17.13 to a low of $5.75, adjusting for splits.

THE BEST OF THE BEST

While the 50 companies you have just read about are all excellent bets at various times, some are better now than others. Given the deteriorated economic and market conditions in Canada, here are some counter-cyclical, recession-proof candidates which I especially like, in alphabetical order:

Canadian Tire Corporation, Limited
Cara Operations Limited
Coca-Cola Beverages
Corporate Foods Limited
Deprenyl Research Ltd.
Greyhound Lines of Canada Ltd.
Imasco Limited
Imperial Oil Limited
Laidlaw Inc.
(The) Loewen Group Inc.
(The) Seagram Company Ltd.
(The) Toronto-Dominion Bank
WIC Western International Communications Ltd.

INDEX